Tribal Life in Northeast India:

Ethno-cultural Practices and Reproductive Health Issues

Tribal Life in Northeast India:

Ethno-cultural Practices and Reproductive Health Issues

Editors

Kh. Narendra Singh

Sarit K Chaudhuri

Indira Gandhi Rashtriya Manav Sangrahalaya
(National Museum of Mankind Bhopal)

GYAN

First Published, 2017

Published by

Gyan Publishing House
5, Ansari Road
Daryaganj, New Delhi-110002
Phone: 9811692060
E-mail: books@gyanbooks.com

Printed at: G. Print Process, Delhi.

and

Indira Gandhi Rashtriya Manav Sangrahalaya
Shamla Hills, Bhopal
Phones: 0755-2661290, 2661319
Fax: 91-755-2661458

Cataloging in Publication Data—DK
Courtesy: D.K. Agencies (P) Ltd. <docinfo@dkagencies.com>

Indian Anthropology Congress (2016 : Department of Anthropology, Assam University)
Tribal life in Northeast India : ethno-cultural practices and reproductive health issues : Indian Anthropology Congress: 2016, Diphu, Assam / editors, Sarit K Chaudhuri, Kh. Narendra Singh.
pages cm
Organised by Department of Anthropology, Assam University, Diphu Campus, Diphu in association with Indira Gandhi Rashtriya Manav Sangrahalaya, Bhopal during February 21-23, 2016.
Includes bibliographical references.
ISBN 9788121213752

1. Tribes—Health and hygiene—India, Northeastern—Congresses. 2. Reproductive health services—India, Northeastern—Congresses. 3. Tribes—Medical care—India, Northeastern—Congresses. 4. Traditional medicine—India, Northeastern—Congresses. 5. India, Northeastern—Social life and customs—Congresses. I. Chaudhuri, S. K. (Sarit Kumar), editor. II. Singh, Narendra (Associate professor), editor. III. Assam University (Silchar, India). Diphu Campus. Department of Anthropology, organizer. IV. Indirā Gāndhī Rāshṭrīya Mānava Saṅgrahālaya, organizer. V. Title.

LCC DS485.N67I53 2016 | DDC 305.8009541 23

Contents

PART - II
REPRODUCTIVE HEALTH BEHAVIOUR

PART - III
ETHNO MEDICINE AND HEALTH CARE PRACTICES

List of Tables

Acknowledgements

We received enormous help from individuals and Institutions in preparation of this book. First of all, we are grateful to the Indian National Confederation and Academy of Anthropologists (INCAA), especially, Professor A.K. Danda and Professor K.K. Basa for giving the opportunity to organise the Indian Anthropology Congress: 2016 at the Department of Anthropology, Assam University Diphu Campus.

The present volume actually created a space largely for the emerging scholars who really deserves attention so that their contribution get circulated to the wider domain of anthropology and in the process we believe that Anthropology Congress under the leadership of INCAA will attract more younger anthropologists of our country in future.

We gratefully acknowledge the support provided by the authorities of Assam University, Silchar and Diphu Campus, specially, Vice Chancellor, Pro Vice Chancellor, faculty, staff and members of the organising committee. Our special thanks to the faculty members and staffs of Anthropology Department of Assam University for their cooperation and help in successful organization of the seminar. We sincerely extend our gratefulness to Indira Gandhi Rashtriya Manav Sangrahalaya (IGRMS), Bhopal; as a prime collaborator for this INCAA. We also gratefully acknowledge Indian Council of Social Science Research, New Delhi; Indian Council of Medical Research, New Delhi, Indian Council of Historical Research, New Delhi and Assam University, Silchar for their financial assistance for organizing Indian Anthropology Congress: 2016.Sri Arun Kiro, Sri Tapas Biswas and Sri Sudhir Srivastava of IGRMS, deserves special thanks for their tireless involvement in organisational matters of the seminar.

Last but not the least we are very much thankful to all the contributors for their cooperation and support leading to the completion of this volume. Hope this book will add value to address variegated issues which has great contemporary relevance to the tribal/ indigenous people of Northeast India. We like to place in records our sincere thanks to the members of Gyan Publishing house for taking utmost care for publication of this book.

List of Contributors

Afsana Shabnam, Department of Anthropology, Dibrugarh University, Dibrugarh, Assam, India. 786004, e-mail: afihazel1816@gmail.com

Ajit K Tamuli, Associate Professor, Department of Life Science and Bioinformatics, Assam University- Diphu Campus, Diphu, Karbi Anglong, Assam-782462, Email: ritamoni96@gmail.com.

Ak. Bojen Meetei, Assistant Professor, P.G. Department of Anthropology, D. M. College of Science, Imphal, Email: bojenmeeteiak@ gmail.com

Anand Sharma, Department of Anthropology, Dibrugarh University, Dibrugarh 786004, Assam, Email:anand.as854@gmail.com

Arundhati Devi Maibam, Asst. Professor P.G. Department of Anthropology, D.M. College of Science, Imphal, Manipur, Email: arundhati.maibam@ yahoo.com

Baphinda S. Thangkhiw, Ph.D Scholar, Department of Anthropology, North Eastern Hill University, Shillong- 793002, Email: bafincarius@ gmail.com

Barnali Das, Department of Anthropology, Gauhati University, Guwahati -781014, Assam.

Bikimoni Gogoi, Department of Anthropology, Dibrugarh University, Dibrugarh 786004, Assam, Email: bikimonigogoi7@gmail.com

Biplob Bhuyan, Department of Anthropology, Dibrugarh University, Dibrugarh 786004, Assam, Email: biplobhuyan1@gmail.com

Deepanjana Dutta Das, Associate Professor, Department of Anthropology, Dibrugarh University, Dibrugarh-786004, Assam.

Dibyajyoti Das, Research Scholar, Department of Anthropology, University of Delhi, Delhi-100 007, Email: ddibya.2013@gmail.com

Jyoti Hazarika, Department of Anthropology, Dibrugarh University, Dibrugarh-786004, Assam. Email: jyotihazarika1989@gmail.com

Jyotismrita Phukan, Research Scholar, Department of Anthropology, Gauhati University, Guwahati -781014, Assam, Email: jyotismrita.p@gmail.com

Kh. Narendra Singh, Associate Professor, Department of Anthropology, Assam University: Diphu Campus, Diphu-782 462, email: kh.singh@rediffmail.com

M. Monoranjan Singh, Assistant Professor, P.G. Department of Anthropology, D. M. College of Science, Imphal, E mail: bojenmeeteiak@gmail.com

M. Shyamchand Meitei, Asst. Professor, P.G. Department of Anthropology, D.M. College of Science, Imphal, Manipur, Email: arundhati.maibam@ yahoo.com

Melody Seb Rengma, Research Scholar, Department of Anthropology, Dibrugarh University, Dibrugarh-786004, Assam, Email: melodyrengma@gmail.com

Rakhi Rani Das, Assistant Professor, Department of Anthropology, Email: Margherita College, Assam, Email: rakhirani_das@yahoo.in

Ratna Tayeng, Asst. Professor, Department of Anthropology, Apex Professional University, Gumin Nagar, Pasighat (Arunachal Pradesh), Email: ratnatayeng991@gmail.com

Ritamoni Konch, Research Scholar, Department of Life Science and Bioinformatics, Assam University- Diphu Campus, Diphu, Karbi Anglong, Assam-782462, Email: ritamoni96@gmail.com

Robindra Teron, Assistant Professor, Department of Life Science and Bioinformatics, Assam University- Diphu Campus, Diphu, Karbi Anglong, Assam-782462. Email: ritamoni96@gmail.com

Sarthak Sengupta, Professor, Department of Anthropology, Dibrugarh University, Dibrugarh-786004, Email: jyotihazarika1989@gmail.com

Satyawati Mili, Department of Anthropology, Dibrugarh University, Dibrugarh 786004, Assam, Email: satyawati.mili10@gmail.com

Somnath Sonowal, Department of Anthropology, Dibrugarh University, Dibrugarh, Assam, India. 786004, Email: somsz1314@gmail.com

Tame Ramya, Assistant Professor, Department of Anthropology, School of Human and Environmental Sciences, Saint Claret College, Ziro –

791 120, Lower Subansiri District, Arunachal Pradesh, India, E-Mail: taramya@live.com

Tanuj Tayeng, Research Scholar, Department of Sociology, Tezpur University, Assam

Thiyam Rabikanta Singh, Assistant Professor in Anthropology, D.M. College of Science, Imphal, Email: trabikanta@yahoo.com

Introduction

The present edited volume brings to light an overview of the studies carried out by scholars from specialised disciplines of anthropology with an emphasis on the themes such as culture and society, reproductive health behaviour, ethno-medicine and healthcare practices among the tribal communities of northeast India.

The volume contains twenty articles contributed by the participants at the Indian Anthropology Congress: 2016 under the auspices of Indian National Confederation and Academy and Anthropologists, organised by the Department of Anthropology, Assam University, Diphu Campus, Diphu, in association with Indira Gandhi Rashtriya Manav Sangrahalaya, Bhopal, during February 21–23, 2016. The volume has been classified into the following broad three sections. **Section- 1: Culture and Society, Section-2: Reproductive Health Behaviour, and Section - 3: Ethno-medicine and Healthcare Practices.**

These articles are based on anthropological studies conducted on different tribes living in northeastern region of India. The authors provide descriptions of the findings from their intensive fieldwork carried out during the recent days.

In Section **Culture and Society** there are **eight** articles.

Th. Rabikanta Singh discusses the diverse ethnic movements in Manipur. These ethnic movements in the present context are dominantly steering to establish favourable socio-political supremacies as well as in engineering strategies for ethnic survival.

Ratna Tayeng, in his paper "Living on the edge": An Anthropological Study on the Mishing of Arunachal-Assam Borders, indicated how the Assam-Arunachal Pradesh border comes into being and how borderlanders and their respective governments construct, negotiate and experienced this reality and how people, who live along and are divided by state borders, have adjusted to the borderland situation and the strategies they adopted in their socio-cultural life.Tame Ramya's paper, entitled 'Knowing the

Less-Known: An Ethnographic Exploration of the Bangru Community in Arunachal Pradesh', discusses the various facets of traditional Bangru society that provides them a better place in terms of their access to various basic facilities which they deserve in a state like Arunachal Pradesh.

Land alienation among the tribal people is a very acute problem in India. Tanuj Tayeng has discussed on the causes and impact of land alienation on the live and livelihood among the Mising tribe living in the Dhemaji district in Assam.

In their paper, 'The marriage system and religious beliefs and practices among the Ponthais of Changlang District, Arunachal Pradesh', Bikimoni Gogoi and Satyawati Mili found that the marriages among the Ponthais are monogamous and polygamy is strictly prohibited. Cross-cousin marriage is a favoured form of marital alliance, but parallel cousin marriage is strictly prohibited. Their religion is marked by adoption of a new system of worship and prayer called *Rangfraism*.

Biplob Bhuyan and Anand Sharma in their paper examined the death rituals among the Sonowal Kacharis of Kapahuwa village of Tengakhat, Dibrugarh District, Assam. They also pointed out the rituals related to normal death, suicide, infant death and the death of pregnant women.

Dibyajyoti Das has examined the impact of economy and tourism on the oral tradition of the Konyak Nagas of Longwa village of Mon district in Nagaland. The Konyak Nagas, always known for their violent practice of head hunting and tattooed face also referred to as 'Tattooed Nagas', are known for their rich oral tradition. The findings revealed that there is an impact of economy and tourism on the oral tradition of the Konyaks' of Longwa, Nagaland.

Jyotismrita Phukan has presented the ethnographic outline of the Tawang Monpa, a subgroup of the Monpa tribe inhabiting in the Tawang district of Arunachal Pradesh. The findings also revealed that the growth of tourism has immensely helped the Monpa tribe to emerge as a friendly community to the outsiders.

In Section **Reproductive Health Behaviour** there are **seven articles**

Afsana Shabnam and Somnath Sonowal in their paper "Social Problems and Stigmas Related to Women Mental Illness: Patient Admitted at Assam Medical College and Hospital, Dibrugarh, Assam" focused on the social problems and stigma related with mental illness among the patients admitted at the Psychiatry Department of Assam Medical College and Hospital, Dibrugarh, Assam.

In her paper, "HIV/AIDS in Meghalaya: Issues and Challenges", Baphinda S. Thangkhiw has critically examined the issues and challenges faced by people living with HIV/AIDS (PLHIV) in Meghalaya. The findings of the study have revealed various implications on individuals infected and affected with HIV/AIDS and how they cope with the disease.

Paper on "Functional Abilities of the Ageing Tiwas of Morigaon District, Assam" by Barnali Das, has elucidated the functional ability of the ageing Tiwa population living in Morigaon district of Assam.

In their paper, 'Access to Reproductive Healthcare Services and Effect of Some Bio-Social Covariates on Prenatal Wastages and Infant Mortality among the Rengma Naga Women of Karbi Anglong, Assam', Melody Seb Rengma and S. Sengupta have highlighted the ways of treatment, and explained about medicinal plants used by the healer.

An attempt has been made to focus on the reproductive healthcare practices prevalent among the Idu Mishmis of Lower Dibang Valley District of Arunachal Pradesh by Rakhi Rani Das and Deepanjana Dutta Das. Their findings have revealed that the Idu Mishmi did not go for immunisation against Tetanus Toxoid during their pregnancy period and many deliveries took place under unhygienic conditions in absence of any trained medical personnel.

In their paper, entitled 'Reproductive factors and risk of cervical cancer in Manipur: A case-control study', Arundhati Devi Maibam and M. Shyamchand Meitei have concluded that cervical cancer is the second leading site of cancer among Manipuri women. They have mentioned 64 incident cases of histologically confirmed cervical cancer and 256 neighbourhood controls with intact uterus and matched by age were included in the study.

The paper on 'Maternal Overweight and Obesity during Pregnancy and Birth Outcomes: An Overview' by Ak. Bojen Meetei and M. Monoranjan Singh, provides an overview of the complications associated with maternal overweight and obesity including diabetes, pre-eclampsia, miscarriages, congenital anomalies and birth defects. They have highlighted the updated information on the increasing trend of overweight and obesity among women of childbearing age and prevention studies aimed at adolescents and women prior to pregnancy.

In Section **Ethno medicine and Healthcare practices** there are **five** articles. Ritamoni Konch, Robindra Teron and Ajit K Tamuli in their paper discussed about the ethnomedicinal practices of the Sonowal Kacharis of Lakhimpur district, Assam with reference to childcare. A detailed discussion on ethnomedicines and traditional knowledge of the Sonowal Kacharis was made in their paper.

In study carried out among the Mishings living in Majuli, of Jorhat district of Assam, Somnath Sonowal and Afsana Shabnam have described the traditional system of treatment and the use of medicinal plants collected from the nearby forest areas by the Mishings.

Kh. Narendra Singh, in his paper '**Ethno-medicine and Traditional healthcare practices among the Karbis of Assam**', has illustrated the traditional healing practices in the primary healthcare among the Karbis. He has also emphasised the need for an effective implementation of health programme through effective communication among health providers, health seekers, and traditional healers.

Indigenous ethno-medicinal system is widely practised in a variety of problems associated with pre- and post-natal periods among the Kaibartas of Assam. Jyoti Hazarika and S. Sengupta, in their paper, have also emphasised that even though the accessibility of the modern medicine for various type of diseases is not totally out of their reach.

In chapter Traditional health care practices in Nongpok Sekmai, Manipur authors describes the health care systems of this potters community. Authors studied causes of illnes and their remedies and natural anf folk medicine system popularize among the community.

In order to provide total culture, health and development issues of indigenous communities of northeast India, comprehensive research studies need to be carried out by the native anthropologists in the region.

We are glad to present this special volume to the readers of Anthropology and Social Sciences.

PART - I

CULTURE AND SOCIETY

Chapter - 1

Multi-ethnic Movements in the Cultural Pluralism of *Manipur*

—*Thiyam Rabikanta Singh*

Introduction

The elements of diversity in the form of cultural pluralism exist even in homogenous societies with minimum variability and inter-group conflicts could not be ruled out in absolute terms (Sharma, 1996:2). In a multi-ethnic area, there may be conflicts in terms of alienation, immigration, expatriation and dilemma in the quest of identity. Ethnic movements may appear to unite, merge or split ethnic group(s) as well to draw special attention for the ignored ones to persist cultural personality. The ethnic movements for such determinations may choose violent or non-violent paths. Again, the most curious feature of such ethnic mobilisations is the plasticity of identities in whose name such mobilisations are done, with such identities constantly invented and reinvented. The phenomena of invention and reinvention of identities take important part of the movements. The present paper focuses on the studies of the situational and relational contexts of multi-tribal conglomeration in Manipur related to the effects of partition, division and reunification in shaping the ethnic-group identities and ethnic boundaries. There is still the view of similarities amidst differences, whereas others can see differences amidst similarities. So, the present paper attempts to unfold some aspects of socio-political elements to highlight the ethnicity and identity related movements among the peoples of this north-eastern state of India.

Methodology

The present cross-cultural study, with empirical data to discuss diverse ethnic movements in the region, has adopted in-depth interviews and observation methods. The primary data are complimented with secondary data.

People Under Study

Manipur, a north-eastern border-state of India, with its physiographic personality of hill and valley barriers, embodies an ethnic mosaic. Ethnically, there are thirty-four Scheduled Tribes (ST) along with some tribes demanding for their inclusion in the list of STs, seven Scheduled Castes (SC), the Meiteis, and the Pangal (Manipuri Muslim). The Meiteis, the Pangals and the SCs comprising Dhupi/Dhobi, Lois, Muchi/Ravidas, Namsudra, Patni, Sutradhar and Yaithibi occupy the plain region along with some tribal pockets. Of the SCs, the Lois and the Yaithibi belong to the Meitei community. As per Census 2011, the total population of Manipur is 2,570,390 in the sex ratio of 992. Of this, the population of SCs and STs is 97,042 (3.8 per cent) and 9,02,740 (35.1 per cent), respectively. The Pangals constitute about nine per cent of the state population. The tribes of this state inhabit particularly in the hilly regions. Thus, physiographic division of the state correlates to its indigenes as *Tami* (people of valley) and *Chingmi* (people of hill). In Manipur, the Meiteis are Tamis, whereas the tribes are Chingmis. The hilly areas of the state are the abode of the tribes. Under section 2 (j) of Manipur Land Revenue and Land Reforms Act 1960, the state declared a number of villages and areas in the hill tracts of the five hill districts (including some villages of Jiribam) as Hill Areas and scheduled as the areas of the tribes exclusively. The scheduled tribes of this geographical territory include 1. Aimol, 2. Anal, 3. Angami, 4. Chiru, 5. Chothe, 6. Gangte, 7. Hmar, 8. Kabui, Inpui, Rongmei, 9. Kacha Naga, Liangmei, Zeme, 10. Koirao, Thangal, 11. Koireng, 12. Kom, 13. Lamkang , 14. Mao, 15. Maram, 16. Maring, 17. Any Mizo (Lushai) tribes, 18. Monsang, 19. Moyon, 20. Paite, 21. Purum, 22. Ralte, 23. Sema, 24. Simte, 25. Sahlte (Sukte), 26. Tangkhul, 27. Thadou, 28. Vaiphei, 29. Zou, 30. Poumai Naga, 31. Tarao, 32. Kharam, 33. Any Kuki tribes, and 34. Mate. Of these, the Marams are the exclusive particularly Vulnerable Tribal Groups which were earlier Primitive Tribal Group (PTG) in Manipur.

Linguistically, all the tribal groups belong to Tibeto-Burman language family. Grierson divided them into two groups – Naga group and Kuki-Chin group. Linguistic classification, based on the works of Grierson (2000: 375, 510-511), Shakespear(1912: 149, 189), Das (1985: 5,6,19), and Rabikanta and Arundhati (2013: 97), also categorise them on this line. According to Grierson (*op. cit.* 510), the term Kuki denotes various tribes which have successively been driven from the Lushai and Chin Hills into the surrounding country to the north and west. He wanted to use the term Chin and Kuki synonymously and divided it into four groups. A uniqueness of the Kuki groups is that they can communicate among themselves. However, the Naga tribes are not intelligent of other's dialect. Even in certain tribes, there are intra-tribal dialects which are totally different and not communicable. For instance, dialect of a Tangkhul village is not known by a Tangkhul of another village. So, a common Tangkhul dialect has been developed and is being used as the *lingua franca* of the people.

Upsurge in Violent Ethnic Movements

The multivariate ethnic groups of Manipur resist against the existing Indian nation for the preference of their subjective nation-state. They raise violent movements to culminate coincidence in the existing ethnic nation and state boundaries, and to develop a rigid boundary. According to the data updated on December 6, 2015, uploaded by South Asia Terrorism Portal, within the territorial bound of Manipur having an area of 22,347 square kilometres (8,628 sq miles) only, there are six proscribed terrorist/ extremist groups, six active terrorist/insurgent groups, twenty-four inactive terrorist/insurgent groups and six in peace talks/ceasefire (groups/ conglomerates). But, there are still other factions or groups of insurgents, which are not mentioned in the report. For instance, the list does not include NSCN-R, NNC, etc.

Manipur has a long record of insurgency and inter-ethnic violence. The first armed opposition group in Manipur, the United National Liberation Front (UNLF), was founded in 1964 to gain its independence from India, which had merged Manipur in 1949 and to form Manipur as a new sovereign country. So, even though Manipur became a separate state of the Indian Union on 21st January 1972 from erstwhile Union Territory, the insurgency movement continued. The armed conflict movement of the Meiteis was the consequence of Manipur's joining into India unwillingly (Kamal, 2014: 2). The Meiteis feel about Manipur having 'territorial contamination of the blood', the metaphorical infusion of biological descent into spatial location drawing sincere loyalty and love to their 'native land' (Grosby, 2005:48-50). So, the uneven look of mainland India ignited the spark of insurgency to separatism, is the view of Meitei laymen. In 1980, the Nagas founded the National Socialist Council of Nagaland (NSCN) to form a greater Nagaland or Nagalim, by encompassing parts of Manipur, Nagaland, the North Cachar Hills (Assam) and later in 1988 NSCN was separated into two groups, namely NSCN(IM) and NSCN(K). To counter the situation, on 8th September 1980, Manipur was declared an area of disturbance, when the Indian government imposed the Armed Forces (Special Powers) Act, 1958 in the region. The Act currently remains in force. Skirmishes between the Naga and the Kuki took place during the period of 1990s. The Kuki insurgent groups were created in order to protect their interests from alleged Naga violations; but, afterwards, they wanted a separate state for the Kukis to be carved out from the present state of Manipur. The Kuki National Organisation (KNO) began to fight for a Zale'n-gam, that is, Kukiland. Other ethnic groups, such as the Paite, the Vaiphei, the Hmars and the Pangals, followed suit establishing militant groups. An incident of conflict in 1993 between the Meiteis and the Pangals had costed many lives of the latter. Militant Islamic outfits such as People's United Liberation Front (PULF) were formed to counter the challenge of Meitei insurgents. Another insurgent group, called the Hindu, was established in 2000s to protect the Bangla refugees from Bangladesh, but in a short period, it became defunct. In this way, many violent ethnic movements are taking place in this small state and the nature of the Meitei, Naga and Kuki insurgents is secessionit while that of the Pangals is protectionist.

Struggle For Ethnic Survival

The Meiteis, the dominant Tamis, think of Manipur as a nation wherein the 'spirit' of their trans-generations has filled up the spatial setting with patriotic love. It was a Princely State ruled by the Meiteis. Their integrative nature caused the formation of the Pangal ethnic group whose ancestors were allowed to settle in the land by giving Meitei wives. The Meiteis with the help of the Pangal and the Chingmis had protected the land from various historic invasions. But, at present, due to their main ancestral habitat areas at the central valley and the validity of Sixth Schedule in the hilly areas, they are confined in the valley exclusively. The valley, thus, is inhabited by the Meiteis, the Pangals, and various tribes plus influx population of non-Manipuris. Prior to its merger to India, Manipur had become a state and nearly had the Inner Line Permit (ILP) system. However, in 1951, it was lifted by the then Chief Commissioner Himmat Singh and allowed unregulated entry of immigrants (Chen, 2015). Mr Yaima, President of UPF, a social organisation, analysing as per 2001 census, mentioned that the Meiteis exceed the non-locals by just 44,000; but due to alarming increase, the population of the non-locals was not given in the 2011 census. Thus, the autochthones are entrapped in their homeland. After a mass movement related to implement the ILP system, on 31st August, 2015, the Government of Manipur passed three Bills–1. The Manipur Shops and Establishments (Second Amendment) Bill 2015 to amend further the Manipur Shops and Establishment Act, 1972 (Manipur Act No. 4 of 1973); 2. The Protection of Manipur People Bill, 2015; and 3. The Manipur Land Revenue and Land Reforms (Seventh Amendment) Bill 2015. But, the Bills for the safeguards of the indigenous people of the state were highly protested by the Chingmis, particularly the Kukis, and on 11th May, 2016, the President of India withheld his assent from these Bills. Again, a group of the Meiteis, including the Bamons (Brahmins), under the banner of 'Scheduled Tribe Demand Committee of Manipur' (STDCM), which was established in December 2012, demands for the inclusion of the people in the list of Scheduled Tribes of India. Mentioning various government records that described the Meitei as a tribe such as *Census of India 1931*, *Imperial Gazetteer of India Provisional Series-Eastern Bengal and Assam* and *Gazetteer of Bengal and North-East India 1909*, *Gazetteer of Manipur* by Capt. E.W. Dun (1886), etc., the committee demands for the recognition of the people as a ST. Again, referring the report of Socio-Economic and Caste Census (SECC) in the *Hindustan Times* on January 5, 2015 that Manipur's urban population comprising mainly the Meiteis (less than 10 per cent of the total population) tops the urban poor in India, STDCM also expresses the threat of ethnic survival within the limited area which was being engulfed by outsiders. Thus, the autochthones who belong to Other Backward Classes (OBC) and who are at the juncture of the General Category and ST, are at the verge of extinction in their soil. If the Meiteis are recognised as ST, they can improve their economy or at least survive as their land would be protected under Scheduled VI. So, it is an ethnic movement to *tribalisation* from an earlier state kingdom to a marginalised status for their existence as per the environmental creation of the Indian Constitution. However, the Government of Manipur and another section of the Meiteis are not in a position to support the demand for the shyness of degeneration. Meanwhile, some intellectuals, instead of demanding for the recognition to *tribal* status, want to regain the *status quo* of the land before the merger agreement in 1949.

Though the term 'tribe' is described by many contemporary writers as a discriminatory one, many ethnic groups in India demand to be ST. In addition, at present, all the *Anusuchit Janajatis* (ST) are not the tribes in the true anthropological sense of tribes. Nadeem Hasnain (1992: 264), after analysing various social scientists, remarked that the scheduled tribes do not at all fulfil the criteria of a tribe as conceived by the anthropologists for theoretical purpose and there is no clear cut ideal type formation of Indian tribe. In the present study, the Meiteis, who own a traditional territory with the emigrants having loyalty to it as their home and who are coerced by a common language and group endogamy besides tolerating the shyness and isolation from the mainland Indians, are one of those ethnic groups eyeing for tribal status. They look for the constitutionally created isolation like 'Scheduled Area' as a major means of ethnic survival and demand to be a ST. In some areas of the country, "to be ST" is also taken as a solution of economic degradation and insurgent issues. For instance, six peoples in Assam are demanding for ST status. It is one of the consequences of talks between Government of India and a proscribed group called United Liberation Front of Assam (ULFA), led by chairman Arabinda Rajkhowa. Thus, the Centre is planning to notify NEW DELHI: In a move that will turn Assam into a tribal-majority state, the Centre is planning to notify six communities in the state as Scheduled Tribes. "As per a key demand of Ulfa's pro-talks faction, with which tripartite negotiations were held here last week, six Assamese tribes—Koch-Rajbongshis, tea tribes, Tai Ahoms, Morans, Motoks and Chutiyas-are being actively considered for ST status. The home ministry is in touch with the tribal affairs ministry to see the proposal through," a senior home ministry official told TOI on Monday, six OBC communities of Assam-Chutiyas, Koch-Rajbongshi, Tai Ahom, Tea tribes, Morans, Motoks as scheduled tribes (*Times of India* daily, 2015, 19 May). In other words, *tribalisation* in India carries a significant meaning whether it may be expressed in pessimist or optimist view.

Naga and Kuki Polarity

The tribes or the hill peoples of Manipur are embraced under two main generic names, that is, Naga and Kuki. British writers used these two terms to cover all the hill peoples of this region. However, after independence from the British rule, and when the Indian Government began to mobilise integration and economic development, the Kukis began to disintegrate reducing the generic name 'Kuki' to a loose connotation in the ethno-political scenario of the region. About the same time, some tribes began to integrate under the umbrella term 'Naga' demanding autonomy or independence. The small tribal groups living in the low hills bordering the central valley also began to proceed towards intergroup integration under the tribal leaders with the aim of bringing unity and forming a wider ethno-political block. Thus, an organisation called Komrem was formed in 1949 for the tribes such as the Kom, the Koireng, the Chiru, the Aimol, the Purum, the Kharam, etc., which are affiliated to Old Kuki Language Sub-Group. The organisation has a favourable basis of socio-cultural nearness. But, it could not become powerful enough to achieve tribal aspiration, and later on, became disintegrated on superficial group of unjust acronym and more clearly on leadership issue. After a long ineffective period of time, many of the member tribes came out of Komrem and formed a new organisation, called "Rem Union", excluding the Kom in 1989, under the leadership of a Chiru personality. The Koms also formed a union of their own. Thus, the Komrem was disintegrated; but, the Rem Union also became dysfunction in 1993.

Earlier, there was an inter-tribal group, called Khul Union, organised by the Anal in association with various tribal villages. The Lamkang, Chothe, Aimol, Kom, Koireng, Chiru, Purum and Kharam were member tribes of the Union.

Another change was that the tribes such as the Gangte, Paite, Zou, Simte, Hmar, Thadou, Vaiphei wanted to unite leaving behind the lesser tribes as Aimol, Chiru, Chothe, Koireng, etc. They formed an organisation in 1961 under the banner of United Zomi Organisation (UZO). This alienation has effects to the oscillation of some tribes towards Naga pole. On the other hand, with the advent of Christianity about which the Tangkhuls played a major role in bringing the expansion of political integration movement, some of the old Kuki tribes had shown socio-political inclination towards the Naga pole. The Anal, the Moyon and the Monsang who claim themselves belonging to Pakan group, along with the Lamkang, the Chothe, the Chiru and the Kom, have tried to align themselves within the Naga ethnic framework (Das, 2001: 1-16). Thus, associations were formed under the ethnic-umbrella of Naga, for instance, Chothe Naga Baptist Association (estd. on 13th March 1987), Monsang Naga Students Union (estd. 1957), Moyon Naga Council (estd. 1937), etc. But, at present, some of these lesser tribes prefer to live independent of any affiliation. Embracing all their villages, such tribes form their own organisations, for instance, Aimol Tribe Union (estd. 1991), Koren Youth Organisation (estd. 1962), Kharam Tribe Union (1972), Chirrup Tribal Union, etc. Thus, there are three socio-political forces among the old Kuki tribes–Naga, Kuki-Chin and independent tribal identity. However, the Naga insurgents are compelling more in homogenisation of cultural personalities under the Naga ethno-nationalisation. For such an authorityship, the Aimol Tribe Union Manipur (ATUM) condemned the incidence of brutal killing of Walunglua alias Manglun Aimol of Ngairong village and attacking the house of the former village chief with grenades by NSCN(IM) and some pro-Naga Aimol in the morning of August 22, 2015 for the deceased's involvement in self-determined identity of the tribe. These movements mark a new ethnic identity formation in plurality of cultures under the Naga fold or identity shift to redefine ethnic boundary.

Misinterpretation of Tribal Identity

Another mention worth point regarding the ethnic boundary is that some tribes do not want to identify themselves separately. The Raltes, a scheduled tribe of the state, say that they are not a tribe but a clan of the Mizo to avoid ethnic separatism (Singh, 2012: 1-11). But, Shekspear (*op. cit.* 140) described the Raltes as one of the clans influenced by Lushai (Mizo) though they were linguistically connected with the Thadou. The Purums also declared that the word 'purum' is a toponym and not an ethnonym and preferred reunion under the tribe name 'Chothe'. Nevertheless, another group of people who have closer affinity to the Kom claims that they are the real Purum. The former Purum (affiliated to Chothe) settle in Chandel district, whereas the latter Purum (having close affinity to Kom) settle in Senapati district.

Again, after a movement, Kacha Naga, as entered in the list of ST of Manipur, has been replaced by three names as Kacha Naga, Liangmei, and Zeme. Likewise, the ST list has rectified the name "Kabui" as Kabui, Inpui, Rongmei in the list of STs.

Confused Identity

Yuet Cheung (1993: 1216) defines ethnic identification as "the psychological attachment to an ethnic group or heritage" and thus centres the construct in the domain of self-perception. However, a certain section, comprising some of its people in an ethnic group, may have elements of out-group feeling with the other sections of the same ethnic group. Besides, the other members also note differences in this section. In the context of Manipur, such a confusion of identity crisis also occurs and a case study is produced here. At present, the Mongmis, having a population around 1000 souls, belong to the Maring tribe of Manipur. But, to the other Marings, they are better known toponymically after their three villages–Saibol, Narum and Yongkhul in Chandel district, Manipur. At present, they settle in fourteen villages, while the core Marings inhabit in about thirty villages of the same district. Five villages are located near Pallel town and the remaining villages are situated in Indo-Myanmar border. Even though they are affiliated and benefitted the status of scheduled tribe under the Maring ethnicity, their worldview sees ethnic differences from the Marings. They cannot communicate with the core Marings and depend on Manipuri, the state language, to communicate with the latter. The Mongmis have different linguistic identity from that of the Marings. Besides, Mongmi dialect and the dialect of the Kuki and the southern Tangkhuls settling at the villages such Nambasi, Meiring, Kasung, etc., are inter-communicable. So, linguistically, Mongmi dialect has closer affiliation to this section of the Tangkhuls. Their oral tradition also traced that a group of the Mongmis had assimilated to the Tangkhuls of this area. Here, it may also be noted that both the Tangkhuls and the Marings also possess Kuki elements as they belong linguistically to Naga-Kuki sub-group. Thus, it may otherwise be interpreted that they conform to the Kuki elements among the Marings and the Tangkhuls.

Again, there are certain differences between the Mongmis and the main Marings in material aspects of culture. Dress and ornaments are a marker of the differences. Traditionally, they do not stain their teeth whereas the core Marings stain their teeth in black colour. In their patrilineal societies, there are seven clans of the Mongmis, whereas the main Marings has four clans. The clans of the former are Nangsa, Maku, Marim, Thoupom, Narang, Thoumon, and another extinct one which could not succeed to emerge from the legendary cave whereas the clans of the latter people are Dangsawa, Makunga, Tontanga, and Charanga. Again, in their traditionalism, house entering ritual is distinctly performed by walking on sparkling embers to exorcise malevolent spirits. On the basis of such unique commonness, they begin to think of their self-determination as a separate ethnic identity. The 'descent rule', identified by Fearson and Latin (2000: 13), which is the most recent attempt to clarify the role of descent in the definition of an ethnic group, has also its support. As they pointed out that in deciding a person's ethnicity, we do not need to know anything about his or her cultural habits, mother tongue, religion or beliefs of any sort. Rather, we simply need to know about parentage. All that is necessary to be counted as a member of an ethnic group is liable to have accepted the claim to be immediately descended from other members of the group. Attributes associated with, or believed to be associated with descent, are conservative and constrained to change. Thus, they can also claim their independent identity despite the question of considering the socio-economic and religious aspects of the group.

At present, though their culture is somewhat diluted due to their inferior status of being minority as well as the adoption of Christianity, the marginalised Mongmis want to revive their originality along with Diaspora in Tangkhul villages. Their socio-political movement has been started long back in 1970 when they formed their group name as Khusaina– a nomenclature having the combination of Khulimol (Yongkhul), Saibol and Narum villages. Later, in 1980s, they reformed their group under the title–Saibu Organisation, as derived from their village name mentioned by the British writer R. Brown (1975: 43). Around 2009, they again changed its name as Mongmi Union. Mongmi is the mythical place where they settled first in this world after their exodus from the nether world through a cave. And thus, they preferred to be self-identified as the Mongmi *en route* their ethno-genesis. Nonetheless, they still confuse about their ethnicity. Because, they are under the ethnic affiliation of the Marings to whom they cannot communicate, while a section of them was assimilated to the southern Tangkhuls. The mainstream of both the Tangkhuls and the Marings have strong feelings of belongingness to the Naga fold. On the other hand, their main village names still bear the word Kuki as Narum Kuki village, Saibol Kuki village and Yongkhul Kuki village. It was recorded as if they belong to Old Kuki group to whom the southern Tangkhuls and the Mongmis find certain coincidence in dialect and cultural elements. Besides, the Kuki insurgents demanding their ethnic nationalism called Zale'n-gam include the Mongmis under 'any Kuki category' of the scheduled tribes in Manipur. Then, what is the ethnic status of this minority group who lost their ethnic name and actual affinity? Though they have the characteristics of an ethnic group, which is a group of human beings whose members are thought by themselves or others, to have a common origin and to share important segments of a common culture and who, in addition, participate in shared activities in which the common origin and culture are significant ingredients (Yinger, 1997: 3), they neither raise their voice against the dominant Marings to be self-determined nor erase the lexicon 'Kuki' from their village name. Despite remaining in confused-ethnicity, they are organising conferences and seminars as part of their movement under the self-coined Mongmi ethnic group towards the ethnic consciousness and cultural identity reformation.

A Tussle to Self Determined Identity Formation

Another ethnic movement of identity issue is the striving of some tribes to be recognised as scheduled tribes. In their 'identity work', they also attempt to gain from others' confirmation as to their self-identity. In addition, such groups, for instance, the Khoibus, question the *status quo* of their hidden identity under suppression. They attempt to perceive themselves as different and demand separatism from the larger Maring tribe. In the meanwhile, the Marings disapprove and threaten the Khoibu/ Uipo for their subjective demand.

The Khoibus, having a population of 1675 (847 males and 828 females) distributed in 276 households as reported in October, 2002 (Tontang and Sharma, 2004: 26), are the people who, at present, are affiliated as one of the sub-cultures of the Maring tribe. They are found inhabiting mainly in Chandel, Senapati and Ukhrul districts of Manipur. Their settlement villages are Khoibu Khullen, Biyang,Yamolching, Thalem, Karyam, Ringdam, Nungourok, Khangshim, Salemram. Even though they are popularly known as Khoibu, they call themselves Uipo. In historic times, they were the suppliers of beehives and honey to the Meitei kings and their neighbours. Khoibu (*khoi* means 'bee', *bu* corrupted from *pu* means 'master') means 'master of bees' and it was the epithet of the Uipo. Later, their group name was identified in the epithetic manner. The Marings and the Khoibus were believed to be the offshoot of the Pawi of Falam who had their hair-knot at the forehead (Kamkhenthang *et al.,* 2002: 3). The Khoibus had good relations with the Meitei king and they were nicknamed as *Nongpok Thongngakpa,* meaning 'the protector of the eastern gate' against foreign aggression from the Burmese. In the fifteenth century, the Meitei king Kiyamba also erected a stone inscription at Khoibu Khullen village describing them to be the protector of the eastern gate as well as protecting them from neighbours.

They claim to be a full-fledged ST of the state. In 1949, the Office of the Dewan of Manipur State recognised them as a scheduled tribe along with Kuki, Kabui, Kacha Naga, Tangkhul, Mao or (Angami), Maring, Kom, Chiru, Koireng, Maram, Lamgang, Anal, Chothe, Purum, Khoirao, Tarao, Moyon, Monsang, Aimol, Kharam, Thang-gan, Wainem and Kwatha. Later, the Government of India approved this list by a Constitutional amendment in 1951. However, in 1956, the Government of India, on behest of state government of Manipur, dropped Khoibu from the list of scheduled tribes as per modification of the list. The Khoibus were placed under the Maring tribe. The expert committee constituted by the Government of Manipur in 2002 to examine the Khoibus regarding the inclusion of the people in the list of scheduled tribes recommended their distinctive characters to be a separate ethnic identity. But, still in many writings, while mentioning the Khoibu people, the tribe name Maring is included. In the stone inscription at Khoibu Khullen, they were inscribed as Khoibu Maring. T.C. Hodson (1911: 15) also mentioned them as Koiboo Murrings.

The Khoibus, who are linguistically different from other Marings, believe to their own common ancestors with a long story of origin and migration. They are endogamous at ethnic group level organisation, but have exogamous clans. J.K. Bose (1980: 23) writes, "This, however, is not to be confused with another division of these people into two. The branch called Uipo, but referred to Khoibu by the neighbouring Meitheis, is considered elder, and the younger is called Morring. These are two strictly endogamous groups..." Their patrilineal descent groups are different from the core Marings. The Marings have four clans (*phung*) with lineages (*chakluk*)–1. Dangsawa having Khulakchim, Memangachim, Wangkhairak-ka, Rumsum-ma, Namarou-wa, Kurung-rongma, Kantim-ma, etc., lineages, 2. Makunga segmented into Wairok-ka, Muntunga, Yunglam-ma, Tampuk-ka, etc., 3. Tontanga having Hiliwa (Hleyowa), Kanshowa, Keishanga lineages and 4. Charanga sub-divided into Lamthaka, Khulpuwa, etc., lineages. Whereas the Khoibus have seven clans and thirteen sub-clans.

1. Charang: (a) Charangphungpui (b) Charang Lierpa.
2. Hongsha: (a) HongshaPhungpui (i) Hongsha Moimit; (b) Napak (i) Sangkhoi.
3. Dangsha (extinct).
4. Tontang: (a) Amethe/Malthel; (b) Tonsha (i) Toringshangthara.
5. Ronglo: (a) Ronglo Phungpui; (b) Ronglo Moimit.
6. Saka: (a) Tlangsabursom (i) Khalong; (b) Tangki.
7. Khaling: (a) Lhakpa; (b) Donpa (i) Leiti Lhoutlhun, (ii) Moda; (c) Rangson.

Some other cultural elements are also discussed here. They are agriculturists who rear mithun with different clan-wise ear cut-marks. They are also famous for making *yangkok* (a circular basketry winnowing fan). The core Marings are experts in basketry. They make conical baskets with or without lid in either one or two layers having aesthetic designs. They make a variety of basketry items. A unique cultural behaviour of the Marings is to blacken their teeth. But, the Khoibus do not stain their teeth. One of the cultural hallmarks of the Marings is the division of the ethnic group into sections based on the used shawls. These are *phingang* group owning red bordered cloth and *phimu* group possessing black bordered cloth. The Khoibus belong to the latter group. However, *khoinganglu* is a special and consecrated shawl for the Khoibu men having the extra weft motif of the head of a black monkey and antennae of bee. Earlier, it was woven by a virgin girl in the reserved forest of the village. The sacred cloth was also regarded with protective value. For instance, if a man is found guilty like the elopement with an already engaged girl, he is punishable by dismantling his house. However, the house of the man who takes the protection of *khoinganglu*, will be spared and will not be pulled down though fines will be imposed. They have their traditionalism based on ancestor worship. Their autumn festival *Haichingbawng Kachawn,* which is performed at the night of the full moon in *Yalaangpui* (October), is their remarkable festival, different from the other Marings. Traditionally, their polity depends on village level council headed by hereditary chief. The hereditary chieftainship of the Marings is succeeded in Dangsawa clan. The chief is subordinated by his council (as found at Phunal Sambum village, near Kakching). Crimes and disputes will be resolved by the court of Village Authority (V.A.). If a trial could not be solved by V.A., then the case will be processed in front of the people at community hall. If it cannot still be judged, then the case will be forwarded to 'Uparup Assembly', which is the General Assembly of all the Marings as a tribe. On the other hand, the original royal clan of the Khoibu is Charang. The chief is assisted by the council of elders selected from the clans living in the village concerned. The clan representatives are assigned with particular traditionally bounded duties. At present, 'Uipo Maruo Assembly' is the apex authority of the Khoibus at its ethnic level. Nooryeg *Naotuo Inlam* is its youth wing and *Napui Inlam* is the women's wing.

Now, the tussle in this ethnic movement is that the minority Khoibus want self-determination as a distinct scheduled tribe. Despite their claim of having the attributes of a tribe, they still suffer discrimination ranging from the absence of full cultural liberty to disprivilege as their cultural identity remains in hidden and intermingling under the shadow of the dominant Marings. The mainstream Marings think that there is minimal cultural variation, so two of them are homogenous and belong to one ethnicity. They are only a section of the Marings and instruct not to be secessionists.

Conclusion

The ethnic movements in the ethnic-mosaic of Manipur multi-pronged struggles for survival, dominancy, and self-determinacy of ethnic groups. In maintaining the ethnic boundaries to differentiate the undifferentiated, identity formation, and identity shift lead to a condition of apparent fluidity in consonance with identity delineation. In the meantime, the Chingmis under two great forces with a theme of secessionism attempts to include various ethnic groups and pulled into their respective ethno-nation in the name of cultural homogenisation. In other words, the ethno-national conflict relates to establish cultural hegemony in wider territory. A section of the Meiteis, in seeking ethnic survival, demand for their inclusion to Scheduled Tribe from the General Category. It indicates *tribalisation* due to the taxonomic system of Indian Constitution among human groups of the country. It indirectly draws the necessity of reforming the concept of scheduled tribe that expresses and privileges as if they are the exclusive indigenes lacking behind socio-economically. However, many Meiteis fear this change towards degeneration and persist to struggle their *status quo*. Thus, in Manipur scene, ethnic movements and identities of indigenes change in establishing favourable socio-political supremacy as well as in engineering strategies for ethnic survival.

References

Bose, J. K. (1980): *Glimpses of Tribal Live in North-east India.* Calcutta: ISRA.

Brown, R. (1975): *Statistical Account of Manipur*. Delhi: Sankaran Prakashan.

Chen, Liu Chuen (2015): 'What is the Inner Line Permit Controversy in Manipur?' <http://indiatoday.intoday.in/story/what-is-inner-line-permit-people-manipur-are-demanding/1/63114.html >(Retrieved on 15.12.15).

Cheung, Y. W. (1993): 'Approaches to ethnicity: Clearing roadblocks in the study of ethnicity and substance abuse', *International Journal of Addictions, Vol. 28*(12): 1209-1226.

Das, N.K. (2001): 'Regionalism and ethnicity in North East India', *The Journal of the Anthropological Survey of India*, Vol. 50 (4): 1-16.

Das, R. K. (1985): *Manipur Tribal Scene.* Delhi: Inter India Publication.

Fearson, James and David D. Latin (2000): 'Ordinary Language and External Validity: Specifying Concepts in the Study of Ethnicity', Paper presented at the October 2000 meeting of LICEP, University of Pennsylvania, Philadelphia, 20-22.10.2000.

Grierson, G.A. (2000): *Languages of North-Eastern India: A Survey.* Delhi: Gyan Publishing House.

Grosby, Steven (2005): *Nationalism: A Very Short Introduction*. New York: Oxford University Press.

Hasnain, Nadeem (1992): *General Anthropology.* New Delhi: Jawahar Publishers & Distributors.

Hodson, T.C. (1911): *The Naga Tribes of Manipur*. Delhi: Low Price Publication (Reprint 1996).

Kamal, Syed M. (2014): 'Ethnic Groups in Conflict in India's Manipur', *South Asia Journal,* Issue 10-Winter 2014.

Kamkhenthang, H., W. Nabakumar Singh and P. Binodini Devi (2002): *A Report on Khoibu.* Unpublished Report submitted by the Commissioner, Tribal Development Department, Government of Manipur to the Hill Areas Committee, Manipur Legislative Assembly.

Rabikanta, Thiyam and Arundhati Maibam (2013): "The Ethnic Conglomeration in Manipur with Special Reference to Textiles and DNA", In H. Dwijasekhar Sharma (Ed) *The Other Manipur.* Delhi: Akansha Publishing House.

Shakespear, John (1912): *The Lushai-Kuki Clans.* London: Macmillan and Co. Limited.

Sharma, S.K. (1996): Introduction. In K. Sharma (Ed) *Multi-culturalism and Ethnicity in Global Context*. Delhi: Rawat Publications.

Singh, T.R. (2012): "Identity Issues of the Tribes of Manipur". Paper presented at International Seminar on Resources, Tribes and State, AITS, Itanagar, India, 13-15.2.12.

South Asia Terrorism Portal (2015): 'Terrorist/Insurgent Groups–Manipur' http://satp.org/satporgtp/countries/india/states/Manipur/terrorist_outfits/index.html (Retrieved on 22.12.15).

Times of India (2015): 6 Assam Tribes May Soon Get Scheduled Tribes Status (19.5.15).

Tontang, A. and Deben Sharma (2004): *A Development Perspective of Khoibu: A Critical Study on Development Perspective*. Imphal: Tamthin Ruivanao for Development of Human Potential of TTA.

Yinger, J. Milton (1997): *Ethnicity: Source of Strength? Source of Conflict?* New Delhi: Rawat Publications.

Chapter - 2

Living on the Edge: An Anthropological Study on the Mishing of Arunachal-Assam Borders

—*Ratna Tayeng*

Introduction

Every borderland is unique in a particular way and each has its own unique problems. Uniqueness of Arunachal-Assam borderlands is characterised by fluctuation, contradiction and constant transformation (other regions have, of course, experienced similar fields). The interstate border, imposed on the landscape more than 50 years ago, gives life to new world that stretches across and away from it. The inhabitants of this transitional zone constantly shape and reshape their own identities vis-à-vis on the opposite and same side of the border.

The interstate border between Arunachal Pradesh and Assam was first established in 1954 with the creation of NEFA (North East Frontier Agency), now Arunachal Pradesh. But, it was in 1914, the hill areas of the northern districts of Assam were separated to form the North East Frontier Tracts, which, 40 years later, became the North East Frontier Agency (NEFA). This border was delineated to protect the developmental interests of hill people against the plain people, testaments to the legacy of colonial empire, India's colonised history and British governments' struggles for control over people, land, and resources. At first, the border was more or less only a line on the map. With the passage of time, however, it became infused with social and cultural meaning as the dividing line between the two worlds.

A further consequence of the demarcation was that it inflicted suffering and deprivation on some cultural minorities inhabiting in the border territory of Arunachal Pradesh. Concurrently, various socio-political movements emerged partly from believing that their ethno-nationalistic identity gives a sense of social security, distinct identity and opportunity, which keep them vigilant to stress on protection against the taking of scarce resources by the others. As a result, members of Mishing population inhabited in the border regions found themselves trapped in a dilemma of marginalisation and deprivation; they were isolated in the context of state policies, which is a state of their own. This is an ongoing process so it is hard to forecast the future for these communities since changes are taking place so fast and frequently.

This paper deals with the lives of marginalised people who live at the interstate border of Arunachal Pradesh and Assam and pledge to contribute to the understanding of cross-border identity and dilemma of such a borderlands community within an essentially tribal state run by their dominant tribal brethren. It is about displacement and fragmentation of unified and cultural politics through the creation of borders. It is an analysis of the processes that emerge when territorial borders become infused with social and cultural meaning to become lines of division between discrete groups.

During the last two decades, there has been considerable amount of literature published by anthropologists of borders and borderlands on territorial dimensions of borders, for examples, J. Borneman (1992), Thomas Wilson and Hastings Donnan (1998, 1999), Berdahl Daphne (1999), Micheal Rosler and Tobias Wendl (1999), H. Vermeulen and C. Govers (2000), and Pablo Vila (2003), among others. According to Berdahl Daphne (1997; 24), "Anthropological interest in borders stems from the fact that though borders as understood logically as physical entity in nature, they are related to people's socio-political system.". In the same way, Thomas M. Wilson and Hastings Donnan (1998: 6) speculated that "it grows from the tradition of social anthropology that focuses on local constructions of social and symbolic boundaries. Their prime focus for developing this field was to examine the ways in which living near political borders between states affect border communities' constructions of themselves and the people on the other side.

So far as representation of India in borderland studies is concerned, Willem Van Schendel pointed out that "South Asia as a whole is poorly represented in borderland studies" and tells that "South Asian borderlands appear indispensable because here a major and intensely contested experiment in twentieth-century border making took place" (Schendel, 2005).

India and it subcontinent is one of the most populous region of the world; it is also the region where millions of population lived in the thousands length of international as well as interstate political borders. Today, the reality of these borderlands is that both the international as well as interstate border disputes seize the attention. So, it is obvious and crucial to understand this plight and the processes of borders and borderlands in this part of the region. As a matter of fact, the field of anthropology of borders and borderlands is still not born in India. In Indian Anthropology, these issues are rarely discussed in research. And, therefore, I consider it as an attempt to understand socio-political scenario of Indian borderlands and to find out its interrelatedness with global borderlands from an emic perspective and most importantly how people of this region interpret/recognise their borderlands.

In this paper, I raise the following questions: how do people react to enforced political boundaries? Do these imposed divisions gradually become accepted as the social lines between distinct states and their peoples? Are the ties between and within ethnic, social and cultural communities across border stopped or persisted? In other words, I ask over what happens to ethnic minority people's sense of identity that has cross-cultural ties across the inter-state border when a new socio-political system emerges? And the objective is to demonstrate how the Assam-Arunachal Pradesh border comes into being and how borderlanders and their respective governments construct, negotiate and experience this reality and how people, who live along and are divided by state borders, have adjusted to the borderland situation and what strategies they have adopted in their socio-cultural life. As rightly pointed out by Michael Kearney (2004; 253), "Understanding the borders and it process will help us in recognising what are state and the people and their corresponding socio-political behavioural pattern and it is the task of anthropologists to clarify how people arranged and located themselves in these extended communities."

Assam-Arunachal Borderland

The borderland to which the paper focuses is not in the borders–in the territorial sense–of the nation-state, they are within the single nation state. Nonetheless, they own the same, if not more, power of segregation and filtering and are neither uncommon nor in danger of disappearing than their nation-state counterpart. It a restricted zone within a single nation, even people of own nation-state need pass to reenter this region. It is a borderland appearing to be one of the most backwards and most ignored.

In one sense, this border is about a border between Arunachalee and non-Arunachalee and, in other sense, it is a border between interstate-states-Arunachal Pradesh and Assam of India. Arunachal Pradesh as a union of Indian state was granted statehood on the basis of its diverse ethnic make-up and on the basis of linguistic homogeneity (Deepak K. Singh, 2001; 95) and also on the basis of being backward area and, most importantly, the compelling situations after 1962 border war with China plagued the region which threatened the integrity of the country. Since the times of statehood in 1987 and till today, state enjoys a unique status in terms of various legal and constitutional safeguards provided to it under the Indian Constitution. The underlying logic behind the introduction of these constitutional safeguards was to protect the indigenous culture and identity of the people from the attack of external influences (D. K. Singh, 2001; 95). Thus, making this interstate border as a border which divides people territorially, ideologically-it is a border politics of the tribal state from the non-tribal state over power and resources.

Interestingly, with the passing of time, the political influence of "dividing line" has grown stronger. Moreover, it also helps in developing a sense of distinctiveness among the people and a sense of imaginative communion among every Arunachalee person. Self-identification and identification of others is a part of boundary making. Fear for other and hatred for other is often part and parcel of every borderland's reality. Tribal population of the state argues that they are quite distinct from others (plain people) in many respects. Fredrik Barth argues that "even if people cross their own community, and get contact with other community, social process of boundary maintenance will continue to persist" (Fredrik Barth, 1969: 9).

The people of Arunachal, having lived for centuries in isolation from rest of the Indian society, developed a strong sense of attachment towards their ancestral territories and their resources. This attachment let them to argue that their land, river and forest must be protected and kept away from outsiders who are not "Arunachalee". Today, the people of the state argue that peace, development and prosperity of the state lie in this border. It gives them a sense of security and freedom. And so the dominant tribal leaders in power have sought to continue and even strengthen the exclusionary line. According to the natives, this "Inner Line" is the lifeline of Arunachal, keeping the people safe and has its relevance intact even today. According to Sanjib Baruah, "The politics of territoriality and indigeneity often becomes an exercise in defending the fences and walls that colonial rulers had erected (2008: 15)."

Borderland Community

The Mishing, earlier known as Miri, and mentioned as such in the Constitution of India, are the present Mishing people of Assam and Arunachal Pradesh, and they belong to one of the aboriginal tribes of North-Eastern region of India. These people have recently started calling themselves as Mishings, in preference to their former appellation Miris, which to their minds, means somewhat derogatory one (N. N. Lego, 2005;8). According to Lakhi Nath Pegu (2005; 22), "Miri is a name used by non-Missing to refer to them, while Mishing is a name they use themselves since the days of Abotani" (Abotani is a mythical ancestor of all Tani group of Arunachal Pradesh which includes Adi, Apatani, Bugun (Khawa), Galo, Hill Miri, Miji (Sajolang), Nyissi, Sulung (Puroik), and Tagin). Similarly, The Missing Agom Kebang (the apex body of the Mishing working for the development of Mishing language and literature) has been spelling the name of the community as 'Mising' since the early part of the 1970s. There is no foolproof explanation of the word 'Missing'. Some think the word is a blend of 'mi' meaning 'man' and 'asi' meaning 'water'; others consider it to be a blend of mi 'man' and yasing meaning 'white, *i.e.*, 'good (figuratively)' Talin Pao (2009). While according to N. Lego (2005), the word 'Mishing' stands for MI (Man) +SHING (Pure) = Mishing (pure man) or the pure sons of Abotani.

Presently, in Arunachal Pradesh, they inhabit the districts of East Siang, Lohit, Lower Dibang Valley and Changlang. However, they are mostly concentrated in the Mebo circle of Pasighat sub-division and Sille oyan circle of Ruksin sub-division of East Siang district. In Assam, they live in the eastern region of the Brahmaputra valley, with concentration scattered in eight districts of the state, viz. Tinsukia, Dibrugarh, Dhemaji, Lakhimpur, Sibsagar, Jorhat, Golaghat and Sonitpur, and Dhemaji district has the highest concentration.

Ethnically, the Misings of Arunachal Pradesh and Assam belong to the Tibeto-Chinese of Mongoloid stock. Linguistically, they belong to the Tibeto-Burman language speaking group of Upper Assam. They have common ancestor with the Adis, Apatanis, Buguns (Khawas), Galos, Hill-Miris, Mijis (Sajolangs) and the Tagins of Arunachal Pradesh, who is called "Abo-Tani" (N. Lego, 2005). However, linguistically and culturally, they are more in close proximity with the Adis of Arunachal Pradesh (Pegu, 2005).

As per the constitutional or government records, the state is having as many as 26 major tribes and more than 110 sub-tribes. Here, the question of a person's nativeness is listed on official documents and is a constitutional criterion. With the passage of time and the uninterrupted continuance of aforesaid protectionist measure, today natives of this region materialised their political space into what once B. K. Roy Burman pointed out as infra-nationalism (1989; 693). As rightly pointed out by Kristof Van Assche, Petruta Teampau, Patrick Devlieger, Cristian Suciu (2008: 119), "Social identity and place identity are often interlinked, with groups defining themselves of shared in terms of places, and/or defining place and self by member elements."

Thus, it appears true that with increasing ethno-political consciousness among the natives of this region and, to some extent, interesting reality emerged what once Benedict Anderson (1991) also termed "imagined communities", arguing that what we think of as nations are imagined communities, "because the members of even the smallest nation will never know most of their fellow-members, meet them, or even hear of them, yet in the minds of each lives the image of their communion" (Benedict Anderson, 1991; 6). If we look closer to this so-called project of state making and project of representation politics of what I termed "imagined Arunachalee", one can see how this project set the interests of the dominant ethnic group as state's goals at the expense of the borderland ethnic minority who had cross-cultural ties before the existence of the state. In other words, today Arunachal has become ethnically oriented state which uses state institutions to favour the Arunachalee majority. As also rightly, speculated by Sherry Lawrence (2006:171), that "Nationalising state," places the interests of the dominant ethnic group highest among the state's goals. Although the dominant group's collective self-esteem is enhanced through the state's use in this way, minority groups suffer from powerlessness, a lack of collective self-esteem, and identity confusion.

As a result of this project of state making, natives of this land stressing on the protection of their border so that outsider or non-native cannot infiltrate into their region, thus border protection policies emerges. As also pointed out by Anderson, James and O'Dowd, Liam (1999; 598), "the state projects of internal homogenisation stress proper drawing of state borders". Similarly, Ferguson and Gupta (1992: 16) also argue that "borders represent a physical manifestation of the social construction of space, and of a dominant group's attempt to control people through the restriction of space." Thus, it also appears to be true what Michiel Baud and Willem Van Schendel (1997; 211) once speculated that "National borders are political constructs, imagined projections of territorial power". Here comes the interesting point how borderland minority has played a pivotal role in influencing and constructing contemporary Arunachalee society and identity.

Living on the Edge

Entitling "Living on the Edge", I essentially want to convey a kind of unequal location as well as of unequal relations (Gupta and Ferguson, 1999b: 3–17; Clifford, 1997: 2–3 via Sarah F. Green, 2005; 1), where a segment of group alienated both from the territorial and the social space (Diana Mata-Codesal, 2007; 9). They can't influence (people who live on the edge), the definition of public goods or enjoy them within their mother nation (Dan Rabinowitz, 2001; 64 emphasised added). As Kristof Van Assche, Petruta Teampau, Patrick Devlieger, Cristian Suciu (2008:117) speculated that "Spatial and social marginalities can reinforce each other". I consider this concept quite appropriate when we observe how minorities such as Mishings of Arunachal Pradesh, on whose case I mainly draw here, excluded from political debate and power, including rights in their land in their very homeland.

Definitely, a people without home have no identity; the questions "Who am I" and "Where am I" are inseparable as "places shape the social identity" Akhil Gupta and James Ferguson (1992: 13). Aivars Tabuns (2005; 60) argues that "the attachment to place is an essential element of self-identity, an integral element part of being in the world". It is very interesting to point out that after the demarcation of this political border, today Mishing of Arunachal identified themselves as a sub-tribe of Adi community, it is justified by the fact that ABK (Adi Bane Kebang-the apex body of Adi community) recently submitted a memorandum to Hon'able Chief Minister of Arunachal Pradesh claiming that Mishing of Arunachal Pradesh as a group of Tani group of people having ancestral blood lineage with Adis and further pointed out that any policy to differentiate Adi and Mishing living in Arunachal Pradesh for centuries together shall be on wrong footing (p.1). What is most interesting is that they (Mishing) themselves organised to be in Adi and simultaneously they define and defend themselves from other Mishings (Assam Mishing) to accrue benefit and amenities provided by the state government. Here it appears true what Michele Lamont and Virag Molnar speculated that "States not only impose the boundary on the local community, but local community themselves made use of the states and its boundaries in pursuit of local interests" (2002; 183).

Mishing people have no other choice but to accept the new identity. In one of my interviews in March 6, 2011, the following account was made by an elderly Mishing person (Komol Noroh) who has lived in

Itanagar (state capital of Arunachal Pradesh) for over 25 years. It raises the whole issues of this paper:

"...Mishing-Adi de atel e, agomei atel dung. Kerengpe Mishing Adi yang kamang, Arunachal ko lenrong em min Mishing ko lenkan. Ngom Oyan lo oto, ngok abu neku ekom Assam lo dumang. Idokom yenam em duk la yeto, ome oo kidar e aipe yepe lagido emla midung. depe-epe ilia ngolu dan yenamem jenetene yeto... nyampo ke ngoluke ome o yepe gipe namem na pokan lukan man. (Mishing and Adi are one...our language is testimony to this. In earlier days, there was no Mishing or Adi. It was only after demarcation, I came to know about Mishing. I was born and raised in Oyan village of Arunachal Pradesh and we were never been a part of Assam. Arunachal is to the Mishings what Arunachal is to the Adis. It is also true that most of our kinsmen were expelled from this state to Assam but we were not...it's quite annoying to say that we too are the sons of this soil though we are treated as outsiders. So we are not confident that our coming generation would achieve what we have not achieved today).

This note simply speaks the difficulties and suffocation that they face day-to-day and their perceptions of a future. And according to Diana Mata-Codesal (2007; 9), "Whatever may be their real impact, 'Marginality' is the starting point and the battleground for the "border/margin people"– both in relation to the territorial and the social space–to resist and contest the main narratives, images and discourses, those that enclose them to the "border". In similar line, Julie Matthews and Kwangsook Chung (2008; 4) argue that "often, displaced borderland people encounter dilemmas of identity, selfhood and naming. They are renamed and rename themselves."

The demarcation of Arunachal and Assam border was started in early 1951, but still many parts of the border are yet to be demarcated. As a result, there are still many areas where the exact location of boundary is not yet clear, for instance, Kimin areas, Likabali areas, Dullongmukh areas, Jonai areas etc., where still both the states have strike argument. But, as a matter of fact, this issue is yet to be studied carefully, and here I am not concerned with this issue; rather my issue is how this border between two states created marginalisation of borderland communities, particularly in Arunachal Pradesh.

During the demarcation of Jonai areas in 1951, according to Tator Darang (2006), "a plebiscite was taken up at Sadiya under the chairmanship of the then Chief Minister of Assam, Gopinath Bordoloi, in which many Mishings of Assam insisted to be in Assam side and consequently many Mishing territories of Arunachal were transferred into Assam.

Nevertheless, since those times many Arunachal Mishings insisted to be in Arunachal Pradesh."

Today, the reality is that, some sections of Mishings, who remained within Arunachal, are stateless. Actually, dominant natives of this state misrecognise the rights of the Mishings and overlook the misfortune that took place among them when the state of Arunachal Pradesh was established. They are not claiming for political space but they are claiming for equal rights and dignity. These experiences of marginalisation, which actually trigger off with the creation of state, are not only confined to Mishings of Arunachal, but it is also experienced by their relatives in Assam. The only difference between them is that the Arunachal Mishings were unable to articulate them not like their counterparts in Assam.

There is also some political aspiration among Mishings to reunite Mishing land, but as a matter fact, it is not achievable as both the state governments are radical and inclined towards accommodation of them within their respective territories. Moreover, the Mishings of Arunachal perceive themselves as a native of Arunachal Pradesh despite the fact that they are not considered to be a native, may be due to their relatively small numbers or fewer representatives in decision-making bodies. Till today, they are not constitutionally specified as APST. Interestingly, in recent years, as I have already mentioned earlier, the natives (common people) of this land granted them as a genuine Arunachalee on the condition that they should identify themselves as Adi. Thus, they are and already some of them redefine their position by constructing new identities—Sub-tribe of Adi or Arunachalee.

It is also important to point out here that dominant Arunachalee and, particularly All Arunachal Pradesh Student Union (AAPSU, the highest apex body of students union of the state), view Mishings' complaint negatively, considering it to be much more threatening than their protest since they imagine themselves as a minority in the national context and this in turn determines its treatment of the domestic minority such as Mishings. For them, Mishings (*i.e.*, Non-Natives) are a threat to their resources, land and jobs etc. In a recent newspaper report, president of AAPSU pointed out that "Mishings are not an STs of Arunachal Pradesh" arguing that "a person belonging to a Scheduled Tribe in one state cannot ipso facto claim the same status in another state unless his/her tribe is declared to be a Scheduled Tribe in relation to that state under Article 342(1)" and further "according to a government directive of March 3, 2005, sixteen major tribes and sub-tribes have been recognised as Scheduled Tribes of the state and clearly notified according to the Supreme

Court ruling of February 2, 2001 that Mishings are not STs of Arunachal Pradesh" (*The Arunachal Times*, 28 September 2010). Here, it is also quite interesting and revealing that Mishings' protest came about peacefully and legally; on the other hand, dominant people, particularly AAPSU, protest violently against them.

However, recently, in a newspaper it was reported that "the Arunachal Pradesh government has decided to grant Scheduled Tribe status to Mishing communities as a sub-tribe of the Adis residing in Arunachal Pradesh and it would be granted to those members of the community who settled in the state before 1947" (*Arunachal Times*, Itanagar, July 14, 2010, UNI). Whatsoever the truth, the reality is that Arunachal borderlands and their people continue to suffer because of neglect and a complete blankness of governance in the borderlands. They are still struggling to get recognition as a Scheduled Tribe of Arunachal Pradesh despite the fact that they too are aboriginal inhabitants of this land. In addition, many of the areas inhabited by Misings (mostly border regions) are far from parallel development like other counterparts of Arunachal Pradesh. This is the reason which led to much confusion, now some of them started considering themselves as "second class citizens".

Definitely, the state has brought previously divided society into united cultural, social and political space, but it also brought marginalisation to minority borderlanders, which still suffered from lack of development and social and political deprivation. Here, the dominant natives have to accept the fact that India as a great nation known for democratic and multi-cultural-multinational setup, re-accommodates their fellow minority citizen such as Mishing borderlanders. And, therefore, if the state government or common native does not interfere and provide them better socio-political space, nothing is going to be changed.

Concluding Remarks

The democratic principle of India talks about preservation of the cultural diversity and strongly emphasises cultural tolerance, but what is actually emerging out of ethno-political consciousness in Arunachal Pradesh is that the dominant natives articulate the issue of outsiders or non-natives as a threat to their identity and culture. As a consequence, borderlanders community like Mishings, who actually are uprooted people with very little or no state protection and it is still continuing as many of them in Arunachal live without any formal identity, call 'APST', unlike refugees such as Chakmas and Tibetans (who are at least formally recognised as refugee), and most unfortunately, they do not get any national coverage or publicity like other refugees such as Chakmas are getting. Their 'Mishings' sense of communal harmony and their ability to form a coherent identity within Arunachal has totally injured, although they were deeply aware of their belonging to their homeland with pride and dignity. The fact that the Mising is from Arunachal is known to everybody, but there has not been any serious effort to end this problem. The efforts of the state government for identification of Misings have not met with much success. The fact remains, that the Mishing citizens of Arunachal have yet to claim their rightful share in the discourse of Arunachal's public memory. As rightly pointed out by Robbins Burling (2007), "a people with no dream and vision cannot preserve a memory", they are day-by-day losing and suppressing their own history.

As a result, the state borders continue to instill confusion, inferiority complex and social stigma to many communities living across Assam-Arunachal borderlands. The magnitude of the problem and its implications are such that there seems to be no easy solution to it. Open acceptance of the reality by the political forces in both the states is also unlikely.

References

Books and Articles

1. Acharya, S.K., "Ethnic Processes in North-Eastern India", *Economic and Political Weekly*, Vol. 23, No. 21 (May 21, 1988), pp. 1068-1077.
2. Alvarez, Robert R. Jr., "The Mexican-US Border: The Making of an Anthropology of Borderlands", *Annual Review of Anthropology*, Vol. 24 (1995), pp. 447-470.
3. Anderson, James and O'Dowd, Liam (1999), 'Borders, Border Regions and Territoriality: Contradictory Meanings, Changing Significance', *Regional Studies*, 33: 7, 593-604.
4. Assche, Kristof Van, Petruta Teampau, Patrick Devlieger, Cristian Suciu, Liquid Boundaries in Marginal Marshes; Reconstructions of Identity in the Romanian Danube Delta, Studia Universitatis Babes-Bolyai, Sociologia, LIII, 1, 2008.
5. Baud Micheal and Willem Van Schendel, "Toward a Comparative History of Borderlands", *Journal of World History*, Vol. 8, No. 2 (Fall, 1997), pp. 211-242.
6. Burling, Robbins (2007), 'Language, Ethnicity and Migration in North-Eastern India', South Asia: *Journal of South Asian Studies*, 30:3, 391-404.
7. Burman, B.K. Roy, "Problems and Prospects of Tribal Development in North-East India", *Economic and Political Weekly*, Vol. 24, No. 13 (Apr. 1, 1989), pp. 693-697.
8. Daphne, Berdahl, 1999, *Where the World Ended: Re-unification and Identity in the German Borderland*, University of California Press, London.
9. Gupta, Akhil, and James Ferguson, "Beyond "Culture": Space, Identity, and the Politics of Difference", *Cultural Anthropology*, Vol. 7, No. 1, Space, Identity, and the Politics of Difference (Feb., 1992), pp. 6-23.

10. Kearney, Micheal, 2004, *Changing Fields of Anthropology from Local to Global*, Rowman and Littlefield, Lanham.
11. Lamont, Michele and Virag Molnar, "The Study of Boundaries in the Social Sciences", *Annu. Rev. Sociol.* 2002. 28:167-95.
12. Lawrence, Sherry, "Identity, Grievances, and Political Action: Recent Evidence from the Palestinian Community in Israel", *International Political Science Review/Revue internationale de science politique*, Vol. 27, No. 2 (Apr., 2006), pp. 167-190.
13. Lego, N. 2005, *History of the Mishings of Arunachal Pradesh and Assam*, Mrs. Ponung Lego, Peregrine Graphics, Itanagar.
14. Parker, Bradley J., "Toward an Understanding of Borderland Processes", *American Antiquity*, Vol. 71, No. 1 (Jan., 2006), pp. 77-100.
15. Rabinowitz, Dan 2001, "The Palestinian citizens of Israel, the concept of trapped minority and the discourse of transnationalism in anthropology", *Ethnic and Racial Studies,* Vol. 24, No. 1, January 2001, pp. 64–85.
16. Schendel, Willem Van 2005, "The Bengal Borederland; Beyond State and Nation in South Asia", *Anthem South Asian Studies*, London.
17. Singh, Deepak K., 2001, "The Refugee question in Arunachal Pradesh: Some conflicting currents", *Journal of Anthropological Survey of India* (2001), 50: 95-102.
18. Wilson, Thomas M. and Hastings Donnan, (Ed), 1998, *Border Identities: Nation and State at International Frontiers*, Cambridge University Press, Cambridge.
19. Zartman, I. William, (Ed), 2010, *Understanding life in the Borderlands: Boundaries in Depth and Notion.*

News Articles, Memorandum, Websites and Journals

1. A memorandum submitted by Adi Bane Kebang to the Hon'ble Chief Minister, Arunachal Pradesh.
2. Arunachal Pradesh DATA HIGHLIGHTS: THE SCHEDULED TRIBES, Census of India 2001.
3. Asian Borderlands Enclosure, Interaction and Transformation Asian Borderlands Research Network.htm
4. Bina D'Costa, Strangers within our Borders: Human In (security) in South Asia, Centre for International Governance and Justice Issues, Paper No. 5 September 2008, Regulatory Institutions Network, The Australian National University.
5. Codesal, Diana Mata, 2007, "Where we can meet" From borderlands to contact-zones, Brighton, United Kingdom.
6. Green, Sarah F., 2005, Marginal Margins: Notes from the Balkans, Princeton University Press.
7. Httpwww.accessmylibrary.comarticle-1G1-92528463study-boundaries-social-sciences.html
8. Kashyap, Samudra Gupta (2000-07-10), More reconversion stories, this time from Assam "More reconversion stories, this time from Assam", The Indian Express, http://www.expressindia.com/ie/daily/20000710/ina10046.html More reconversion stories, this time from Assam, retrieved 2007-12-07.

9. Mising people-Wikipedia, the free encyclopedia.htm
10. Pao, Talin, 2009, Origin of Miri (Mishing Tribes) of Arunachal Pradesh http://themishingofarunachalpradesh.blogspot.com/
11. The Arunachal Times-Archives-Sep 30.htm.

Chapter - 3

Knowing the Less-known: An Ethnographic Exploration of the *Bangru* Community in *Arunachal Pradesh*

—*Tame Ramya*

1. Introduction

The Bangru is a small, less-explored community living in the northern part (in Kurung Kumey district) of Arunachal Pradesh. Most of the people of Arunachal Pradesh do not know much about them. Normally, Bangru people are known as part of the major Nyishi tribe. In fact, the Bangrus are a specific group of people, at least linguistically. The meaning of the word 'Bangru' is dubious. It is a term given by neighbouring Nyishis and Puroiks. The origin of the Bangru is not apparent, but it is certain that its origin is unparalleled with the Nyishi, though they are similar in their physical appearance and are well versed in Nyishi dialect. It is believed that they were the descendants of the children who were born out of the *Ju,* the Mother Sun (Ramya, 2012:2). Earlier the word *Ju* was suffixed with every clan name. Accordingly, they were identified as *Phujoju (*Pisa), *Milliju* (Milli), *Malloju* (Mallo), *Tagangju* (Tagang), etc. But, with the passage of time, this '*Ju*' word was gradually avoided by the people and in contemporary situation only the clan name remain such as Pisa, Milli, Mallo, Tagang, etc.

They are seen spread in Sarli town and in few villages, *viz*., Bala, Lee, Lower Lichila, Upper Lichila, Machane, Milli, Molo, Nade, Namju, Palo, Rerung, Sape, Sate, Wabia, and Walu. Although Nyishi and Bangru have differences in perception about origin and language patterns, yet, it is evident that both have some similar socio-cultural traits, which may due to their long historical contacts. Ethnically, Bangru could not be called

Nyishi; nor are they Puroik; rather they are more similar to Sajolang (Miji), a tribal community inhabiting the East and West Kameng districts of Arunachal Pradesh, to whom, they call *Wadu-Bangru*. To prove this, they gave an example by comparing their *Phojoju* and *Milliju* with Sajolang's *Rijiju* and *Khonjuju*. Though, they live in along with Nyishi and Puroik, they are different from both Nyishis and Puroiks in language, customs, and the way of life.

In physical features, Bangrus look more similar to Nyishi than Puroik. A good number of Nyishi people live in Bangru area and they have been living alongside Bangru people from time immemorial and referred to them as *Kadai*[1]. Although they are considered Nyishi, marked differences exist between them in physical traits, dress, customs, and their dialects. The Bangru origin myths and linguistic peculiarities show that they are a Mongoloid, Tibeto-Burman language speaking indigenous people. Bangrus can be identified as belong to Tibeto-Burman linguistic family with as its closest genetic relatives Miji and Hrusso, spoken further to the southwest in East and West Kameng districts (Bodt and Lieberherr, 2015:66).

2. Objectives of the Study

While this study is an ethnographic in nature, it is based on the following basic objectives:

(i) To know who are the Bangru people - their origin, migration, and oral tradition;

(ii) To provide a basic ethnographic understanding of their social institutions–religion, marriage, village administration, etc.; and

(iii) To understand subsistence economy and other livelihood strategies.

3. Methodology

This study is carried out in 15 Bangru villagess at Sarli Circle of Kurung Kumey district, where the Bangru community lives and maintains their ethnic and cultural identity. Researcher gathered information over a year from 2010 to 2011. The field study was conducted through ethnographic approaches, including participant observation, in-depth interviews, unstructured and open-ended interviews, and other tools and techniques by considering *emic* and *etic* perspectives.

This is an exploratory inquiry, used qualitative methods to generate data based on the live experiences, views, attitudes of Bangru existing customs and behaviour. For this study, respondents were chosen from the study area based on convenience sampling with the help of community leaders and aged community members with differing backgrounds and histories including the cultural dynamics of the Bangru. During the selection of the informants, gender-and age-wise division of population has also been taken into consideration.

4. Universe of Study

Bangru, a tribal community spread over 15 villages in Sarli circle of Kurung Kumey District of Arunachal Pradesh, constitutes the universe of the study. The socio-economic status of the inhabitants of these areas varies greatly due to a number of factors, *e.g.*, transportation and communication facilities, agricultural practice, availability of resources, exposure to the modern development, cultural contact with other communities, etc. Since the Bangru constitutes unit of study, basic information was collected in respect of the universe through a comprehensive household survey schedule. Further, detailed information in respect of villages was collected using multiple data gathering devices, to make an in-depth investigation of the issues concerning people's participation and development of the target group. Selection was made to all the Bangru inhabited villages because Bangru people are solely concentrated in these villages, though some people have migrated out of their villages in recent times.

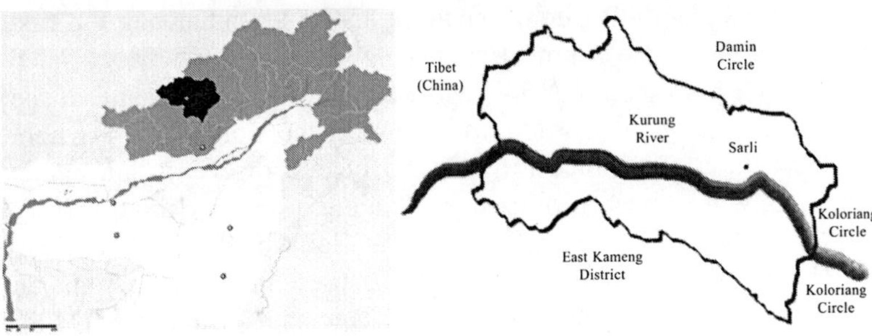

Figure 3.1: Map Showing the Study Area (Bangru Inhabited Region).

5. Bangru: An Ethnographic Profile

This paper investigates the inherent position of Bangru way of life—how they lead traditional and modern life in keeping with other communities. It also examines their origin, histories and existing trend of cultural dynamics. It is believed that based on origin narrative and linguistic background, the Bangru is a distinct ethnic community. Now the Bangru custom, ritual, and belief are reformed through Christianisation. Traditional ritual is being changed by outer influences. Social, political, and economic institution bring forth the overall change of the Bangru contemporary culture, including Christianity and traditional religiosity.

5.1 Origin and Migration of the Bangru

Like most of the tribes in Arunachal Pradesh, the history on the origin and migration of the Bangru is vague and documentarily absent for lack of written script culture. There is no earlier reference made to these people for documenting their histories, customs and traditions, which are very unique in it. Non-documentation is due to the fact that no scholar has ever paid a visit to the land of Bangrus, who inhabitate one of the most remotest and inaccessible regions of Arunachal Pradesh. What little is known about the history of their origin and migration comes from their oral tradition, which are well profound among the tribals across the world.

The Bangru believe their migration to the present habitat in Sarli Circle of Kurung Kumey district from a place called *Neto-Nello Puko*, a place where the people believe to be falling/bring down from *Ludlu* (Sky/Heaven) by *Aneya Ju* (Mother Sun). Unlike many tribes of Arunachal Pradesh, they traced their origin directly from the Ju (Sun). It is to be noted here that within Bangru, there are two factions/clans, *i.e.*, general Bangru (*Phujoju* and *Milliju* and other minor groups) and *Sape* who have different route of origin and migration. According to the legend among the first group, over the course of time, Bangrus moved to areas nowadays called Sarli from a place called *Neto-Nello Puko*. According to some of the respondents, earlier the word Ju, which implies the Mother Sun, to whom they believe as their ancestor, was suffixed with every clan name. Accordingly, they were identified as 'Phujoju' (Pisa), 'Milliju' (Milli), 'Malloju' (Mallo), 'Tagangju' (Tagang), etc. But, with the course of time, this 'Ju' word was gradually avoid to be used by the people and in contemporary situation only the clan names remain such as Pisa, Milli, Mallo, Tagang, etc.

According to Bangru mythology, thousands of years ago, the Bangru migrated somewhere from Tibet and set up their inhabitation in the place that we now call Sarli and in its adjoining areas. The Bangrus prefer to call themselves '*Taju-Bangru*', but till date all these people are known as a sub-tribe of Nyishi to the outsiders. Indeed, it is not ascertained as to when Bangrus have entered in the present location; the most popular belief is that Bangrus have migrated from Tibet, although there is no historical evidence to support this belief. People believe that there is another branch of Bangru which they call as *Wadu-Bangru*[2]. Those people are believed to be moved towards the western route, *i.e.*, the present East and West Kameng districts. Through this they believed that Aka and Miji (Sajolang) tribes are their same descendants which come under *Wadu-Bangru* branch. To prove this, they gave an example by comparing their Phojoju and Milliju with Miji's (Sajolang) Rijiju and Khonjuju.

On the other hand, the second group, *i.e.*, Sape clan traced their migration route from a place called Jiila-Ralla. This group is considered to be a late entrant in the present habitats who came to help the first group during warfare. These people assumed themselves as of same descendants to Memba and Khamba who were migrated towards east, *i.e.*, present Mechuka and Tuting regions of West and Upper Siang, respectively. Here it is pertinent to note that the two groups have different migratory routes with different ancestral history. But after reaching and settling in the present place, both the groups are speaking same language and following same customs and traditions, though with little variation.

5.2 Structural and Demographic Analysis of Bangru

Bangru, numbering about 1,023[3] (39.35 per cent), out of approximately 2,600 persons in the Sarli Circle, is one of the lesser-known tribes of Arunachal Pradesh, presently dwelling in one administrative centre i.e. Sarli Town and in more than 15 villages of the circle in Kurung Kumey district. Although there is no separate census record on this community, however, according to the data gathered, the Bangrus account for about 1.14 per cent of the total population of Kurung Kumey district. The present Bangru population in different villages of Sarli Circle is alphabetically presented in the following table.

Table 3.1: Distribution of Bangru Population in Different Villages

Village	*Total Population*	*Male*	*Female*
Bala	10	5	5
Lee	64	36	28
Lichila (Lower)	72	32	40
Lichila (Upper)	54	29	25
Machane	65	35	30
Milli	102	45	57
Molo	22	12	10
Nade	12	5	7
Namju	33	18	15

(Contd...)

Palo	30	11	19
Sape	152	75	77
Sarli Town	306	134	172
Sate	28	7	21
Wabia	66	24	42
Walu	6	2	4
Total	**1023**	**471**	**552**

***Source*:** The Electoral Registration Office, Koloriang.

5.3 Language

The Bangru is a Tibeto-Burman language of northeast India, classified as a distinct language which shares a common custom with Nyishi. The Bangrus speak their own language even though they can understand and speak the Nyishi and Puroik languages as well. For long, it was considered to be a dialect of Nyishi. Bodt and Lieberherr (2015) demonstrate that it has correlation with language of Sajolang (Miji), spoken in East and West Kameng districts of Arunachal Pradesh. However, there are many words which are believed to be borrowed from neighbouring Nyishi and Puroik due to long contact among these communities. Bangrus do not have their own script. They use the Roman alphabet for writing.

5.4 The Settlement Pattern and Housing

The Bangru settlement is small in terms of its size and population. As per my field records, the total population of the Bangru villages varied between 6-306 persons, the highest being the population of 306 persons observed at Sarli Town, while the lowest is 6 persons in Walu village. This is because a person is living with his Nyishi relative in the village. However, a typical Bangru settlement usually consists of 50 to 100 people. Each of these small settlements inhabited by about 10-20 households is known as *Neye* (village). It is also found that 5-10 hamlets on a particular hill are combined and given a village name.

The typical Bangru settlement is characterised by sparse distribution with little disorderliness. The houses are distributed unevenly in the settlement area. Many a time, the houses are constructed wherever a place is available. Traditional households in the Bangru settlement are thatched and uniform in their structure. However, with the passage of time, such traditional thatched houses are replaced/being replaced with modern day's CGI sheets (tin sheets) to whom people deem more comfortable and secure to use. When the sons separate from their parents usually after marriage, they construct another house adjacent to their parents' house. If there is no space available, they may construct at some other place nearby.

6. Social Organisation of the Bangru

Bangru society is patriarchal with a distinctive character of tribal endogamy and clan exogamy social system. We have already noted that the Bangru tribe is divided into five clans and each clan into few minor clans. The Bangrus' tradition is unanimous in talking of five clans, although the number of sub-clans differs. The Bangrus accept the rule of the clan system and the myths, which form its background, are a key to the understanding of almost everything that is distinctive in their way of life. Violation of tribal endogamy and clan exogamy are the crimes in the Bangru society and those who break these rules are dealt with exemplary penalties. The fundamental and primary feature of social organisation is represented in every Bangru village. The presence of different clans in a village demonstrates obviously the democratic character of Bangru society.

The Bangrus constitute a well-defined and homogeneous group of people. Although their villages are scattered over a wide area, the Bangru people everywhere speak the same language and follow the same customs, have the same traditions, beliefs, rites, and ceremonies. Such small differences as they present from place to place are hardly greater than those obtaining between the villagers of adjoining regions. All are bound together by a common sentiment for the tribal name, reputation, tradition, and customs. At least five clans of Bangrus, each bearing a distinctive name, are recognised. The word *Neye*, which appears in the names of each group, means village or settlement, and it seems probable that these five clans represent 15 original Bangru villages viz. Bala, Lee, Lichila (Lower), Lichila (Upper), Machane, Milli, Molo, Nade, Namju, Palo, Rerung, Sape, Sarli Town, Sate, Wabia and Walu, which have contained the whole Bangru population.

6.1 Gyaiidya (Marriage) among Bangru

Marriage in Bangru society, as in all other societies, is a turning point in the life history of an individual from where he branches off from the parental roof and establishes a new unit. A girl on her marriage abandons her parents' home and goes to live with her husband.

It is worth mentioning here that the Bangru, Nyishi and Puroik intermarry frequently and have some close socio-cultural relations. These intermarriages and close socio-cultural contacts have smoothened out any much difference in their marriage system, although we find finer dissimilarities among them. Marriage among the Bangrus generally involves the following considerations:

(i) Enhancement of social and economic status in the society.

(ii) Addition of a working hand in the *Wua* (fields).

(iii) Housekeeping partner.

(iv) Meeting the biological and psychological needs.

(v) Procreation.

(vi) Financial gain to the bride's in-laws.

(vii) Increase in sphere of influence and cooperation through new relationships.

Among the above considerations, the priority is given for procreation, to meet the biological and psychological needs, to need helping hand in the domestic works and for housekeeping.

Marriage in Bangru society is traditionally arranged by the parents, preferably with the people of equal social status. The Bangrus do not prefer marriages between specific kinsmen, for in olden days the alliance of the two families called for mutual support in fends and raids (Haimendorf, 1982:64)[4]. Matrimonial alliances were a means to gather allies to defend itself against attack from enemies. Marriages are also arranged to obtain some valuables of fine quality and repute which the girl's family may be having.

6.2 Lameii (Family) in Bangru Society

Lameii (Family) in the Bangru society is the outcome of marriage. The family is a universal institution and has existed throughout the history of human society. It is the smallest social unit consisting of parents and their unmarried children. Such is a nuclear type of family which is most commonly found among the Bangrus. The family is the simplest and the most important primary group in the society. It is the most basic of all social groupings. It is also the first and the most immediate social environment to which a child is exposed and it is in the family that the child develops its basic attitudes.

But, with the passage of time, family has undergone changes, gaining and losing valour, shapes and characteristics. The present age of economic development and cultural revival has posed some new challenges to the institution of family; leading to radical changes in the structures and functions of family. However, the institution of family is surviving and will survive for the survival of the society itself.

6.3 The Clan System

The basic feature of social organisation depends on the division of the community. In Bangrus also, there are two distinct groups; they are *General Bangru* and *Sape.* These two groups are endogamous divisions of Bangru. Within *General Bangru* also exogamous practice is prevailing. This means a man with a particular clan identity marries a woman with a different clan membership, though both of them belong to same group. For instance, a member of *Pisa* clan could marry a member belonging to *Milli* clan, though both the clans have identical affiliation within *General Bangru* group. Each clan holds a village or group of villages and have the names from the name of place where they presently inhabit. The *General Bangru* group is divided into four major clans, with some minor clans, and *Sape* group is considered to be existed with only one clan with same name of the group. The *General Bangru* group is consisted of clans like *Pisa, Milli, Mallo or Mullo or Mullong, Tagang,* and few minor clans.

6.4. The Village Administration

Anthropologists have, from the very beginning, studied the village as an autonomous human institution from the point of view of political institutions and processes, social interactions, inter-personal and inter-family relationships, etc., and have come to the conclusion that the village, despite various influences and changes, has retained its particular traditional institution. The Bangru village, being the most traditional and ancient institution, crystallised a whole system of social, political, and ritual structures.

While the clan is the most important social unit in Bangru society, the traditional polity is based upon the village. The village is a territorial unit claiming an exclusive right to a tract of land with clear boundaries. On occasions, the village drew from its members a strong spirit of cohesion, and there is considerable local patriotism based upon a host of legends and colourful history of the village's past exploits. Another important aspect of the village is its function as a unit of defence. Most villages (or its member clans) are sometime in state of feud, and there is a need for perpetual alertness and vigilance, as well as for strong defences that would enable the villagers to resist attack without inordinate difficulty or great loss of life. For this reason, many villages are built on the summits of hills, while a convenient source of water enhanced the selection of the site. The villages are permanent and they are encased in extensive and impressive circumvallation, which represented the efforts and innovations of many generations.

6.5 Bangru Guii-Koro (Kinship) System

Kinship system is usually seen as a method of organising marriage relations between groups. Through marriage, members are recruited to kinship groups. The kinship is helpful to study the means of genealogies. The Bangrus are having a well-planned kinship, which has got some interesting features also. The most important feature is the use of the same term *Alo* for grandfather, on the one hand, but, on the other, for father-in-law (of both man and woman). Another feature may be found in the using of term *Ako* and *Mesebya* for all brothers and sisters (elder or younger), respectively. *Mesebya* is also used to refer to father's sister. The important features of the Bangru kinship are the system of existence of two well-marked groups of terms expressing bonds of kinship. Similarly, with regard to grandfather and grandmother, they call *Alo* and *Asse,* respectively, and it is used to refer to both paternal and maternal grandfather and grandmother. *Asse* is also simultaneously used for both grandmother and mother-in-law or wife's mother.

Another interesting point is that the Bangru system has two set of kinship terms, those used in direct address and those used when speaking of relatives who do not correspond closely with one another. This system distinguishes widely between elder and younger member of the family and clan. The Bangrus never mention their *kiini* (mother's brother) and *alo* (wife's father). Similarly, a man is also prohibited in mentioning the name of the father-in-law and mother-in-law (*asse*). The Bangru terms of address and their equivalent words in Nyishi and English are given in the Table 3.2. I have included the Nyishi here only to find out the similarities and dissimilarities of wordings within them.

Table 3.2: The Bangru Terms of Addressing and their Equivalent Words in Nyishi and English

Bangru Terms of Address	*English Equivalent Words*	*Nyishi Terms of Address*
Achowa	Mother's Sisters (common)	Amu/Mu
Aneya	Mother	Ane
Ako	Brother (common)	Achi/Abang/Buru
Alo	Father-in-law	Atu
Asse	Mother-in-law	Ayu
Juchobii	Sister's Son and Father's Sister's Son	Ku
Juchobya	Sister's Daughter and Father's Sister's Daughter	Ku

(Contd...)

Kiini	Mother's Brother	Akh/Kiigh
Mechemya-Nyiib	Grandson	Ku-Nyaga Huiish
Mechemya-Nyiiwai	Granddaughter	Ku-Nyeme Huiish
Melgya	Husband	Nyulu
Mesebya	Sister (common)	Anyi/Barme
Mii	Wife	Nyahang
Miibi	Father	Abu
Miibo/ Miwo/Mibow	Daughter's Husband and Son-in-law	Magbu/Magtey
Minyii	Son's Wife and Daughter-in-law	Nyaahang
Muju-Nyiib	Son	Ku-Nyaga
Muju-Nyiwai	Daughter	Ku-Nyeme

Source: Fieldwork (July 2011)/Bangru Villages.

7. Bangru Political Organisation

Whether it is a *state* or *stateless* society (Fortes and Evans-Pritchard, 1940) or a *minimal* or *diffused* government (Mair, 1965), there exists some form of political organisation in every society. This organisation carries out the functions of social control in the society at large. It is not necessary to differentiate between the social and political control and identifies politics as the function of society. But who controls whom, who is a leader, who are his followers, and how a leader assumes a position of control over others are crucial in the understanding of any political system, whether it is traditional or modern. In the study of a political system of a group or society, the first thing that singles itself out is *authority* or *leadership*.

The political organisation of the Bangrus is run on democratic lines unlike some tribes of Arunachal Pradesh where autocratic chief is the sole authority of the community. The important affairs are decided by village councils consisting of elders or heads of families. The pattern of social organisation of Bangrus is not much different from the neighbouring Nyishis and Puroiks. They are dividing into five clans, which are further divided into several families. The clan-wise division of the Bangrus is as follows: *Pisa*, *Milli*, *Sape*, *Mallo* and *Tagang*. All clans mentioned marry with each other. But they do not marry within themselves, *i.e.*, they practice clan exogamy (Discussion with Bangru community leaders/elders, January, 2011).

In parallel with the other tribes of Arunachal Pradesh, Bangrus also have certain legal system of their own, *i.e.*, customary law. Bangru customary law in its traditional manifestations is not embodied in any formal codes. There are no written laws; and although many rules of conduct are epitomised in proverbs and kindred sayings, there is also no well-defined corpus of legal maxims and principles. The laws of the Bangru are to a considerable extent inherent in the social system of the people. They exist as rights and duties developed through the course of time out of man's efforts to adjust his behaviour in relation to his fellows and to the physical environment he shares and exploits with them; and have become accepted from their very nature, from the fact that they satisfy the more fundamental and common needs of life in society, as binding and obligatory.

In contrast to the earliest norms of justice dispensation in the Bangru society, the roles of village council including the role of Gaon Burahs (GBs) are diminishing. The factors behind such changes are clear. The introduction of modern electoral political system in the form of Panchayati Raj System and the abrupt coming of Christianity are responsible for the diminishing role of village council. People nowadays approach directly to village panchayat as the panchayat has also right of framing rules and regulations for the welfare of the villagers. On the other hand, those who are converted to Christianity have no more belief in the customary law; due to which they didn't approach the village council for resolving any dispute.

However, there is no instance of influencing the functioning of the village council by any political parties. They are not able to influence the functioning, as the political parties are mostly seasonal. Government has taken steps to stimulate the village council by announcing allowances and honorarium for Gaon Burahs (GBs). This seems to be a kind of reorganisation of the village council. On Independence Day, the District Administrator recognises the Gaon Burahs (GBs) by awarding red-coat and other honorarium.

8. Subsistence Economy and Livelihood Strategies of the Bangru

The Bangru people mostly resided in close proximity to forest and fringe of the river in the past. This is so due to their dependency on products for firewood, close access to wild medicinal plants used to cure disease, and fishery as their alternative source of income for livelihoods. They started practising shifting cultivation. They have generated enormous knowledge on a large number of plants species on which they have depended for centuries. Due to this, forests were most important resources for them in terms of food, fibre, medicine, housing materials, fodder and various other needs.

As information from Bangrus[5], people lived in the group near the forest and fringe of the river because their life is depended on the forests and rivers. They practised shifting cultivation, hunting wild animals and gathering wild fruits and herbs. The Bangrus are expert in capturing wild animals, perfected in hunting and fishing. They used various traps and tools and natural poisons while fishing in rivers and streams.

Agriculture is of the utmost importance to the Bangru economy. The Bangrus depend upon their plots not only for the major part of their sustenance but also for a cash income since few years back. The staple crop cultivated by the Bangrus is *eay/eaii* (paddy); but there are other crops like maize, *tamai* (millet), finger-millet which supplement the rice at regular interval. Other than all these crops, there is one such tree called *Lavo*[6] known as famine food which supplement their foods at very difficult time like during famine like situation very often due to bamboo flowering. This tree is particularly predominant among the neighbouring Puroiks, for whom, it is serving as staple food.

Briefly, the Bangru farming practices are as follows: a plot is planted with paddy, maize, and other eatables for one year. In some of the villages, plot is allowed to lie fallow for years. After the years of fallowing, it is again put back into cultivation. In other words, plots carry crops on alternate years. The fallow periods of the plots ranges from 4-5 years. In theory, the cycle of fallow and carrying crops continues indefinitely but the Bangru people perceived that some plots "tire" more quickly than others and these, after a few years, must be allowed a longer period of rest than the usual one year.

9. Bangru Religious Beliefs and Ritual Practices

Belief system and ritual practices play an extremely important part in the religious life of the Bangru. There is a well-defined belief in certain supernatural beings able to influence for good or for evil the destinies of the living. Their religious beliefs and practices have a basic similarity with those of their neighbouring tribes like Nyishi and Puroik. Like other tribes, they have also developed myths about the creation, the Sun and the Moon, the origin of man and about death. Their concept of the soul, which they call *arey*, is that a separation of the soul and the body takes place at the time of death.

The traditional Bangru religion is *Donyi-Polo* or *Donyi-Poloism*[7]. They believe that some trees, stones and hills are the abodes of the spirits. Like all animistic religions, that of the Bangrus consists of the belief in a multitude of beneficent and malevolent spirits, to some is attributed the creation of the world, to the others the control of natural phenomena, and the destinies of man from birth to death are governed by a host of divinities whose anger must be appeased by sacrifice through a ritual ceremonies.

9.1. The Bangru Religious Beliefs

The whole belief systems of Bangru religion may be categorised as follows:

(i) Belief in Supernatural Powers.
(ii) Belief in the Supreme God.
(iii) Belief in Spirits World.
(iv) Belief in Magic and Witchcraft.
(v) Belief in Worship, Prayer and Sacrifice.
(vi) Belief in Life after Death.
(vii) Belief in Soul.
(viii) Belief in T*yameii* (Dream).

9.2. The Bangru Religious Practices

The Bangru religious practices are inherent in their day-to-day ritual performances which can be categorised into following:

(i) Ritual to Vindicate the Truth.
(ii) Ritual Related to Agriculture.
(iii) Ritual Related to Evil Practices.
(iv) Ritual on Human Death.
(v) Ritual for Immediate Healing.
(vi) Ritual Related to Creation.
(vii) Ritual Related to Purification and Divine Favour.

9.3 Bangru Festivals

Like many tribal societies, the Bangru also have their festival system. The complexity of the many clans and their interlocking nature are crucial aspects of the festival system, and notable when found at the Bangrus' technological level of development. The major agricultural festival of the Bangrus is similar to Nyishis of Koloriang area where they celebrate *Longte-Yullo* or simply *Longte* or *Lungte* as major festival. More interesting fact is that the myth behind the festival is entirely of Nyishis; and Bangrus have no independent myth on the origin of this festival though they are entirely a different ancestral group.

Literally, *Longte* means a large wooden barricade/fence which is erected on community basis in the belief that this demarcates the domain of humans and spirits from ill-intended trespass. This festival is celebrated on the advent of spring season in the month of April (*Lachar-Polu*). The festivals, an aspect of Bangru religion in the broadest sense, are ceremonies that instil, especially in the young, profound feelings for and beliefs in the Bangru way of life. The festivals provide guidelines for acting out traditional roles, thereby sanctioning them, as well as social settings in which the individual can experience joy and express love. The festivals contribute in this way to the high social cohesion that is characteristic of the Bangru socio-cultural system.

9.4 Christianity among the Bangru

The study of the Bangrus' traditions and institutions would be incomplete without taking into account the influence of Christian missionaries. Christianity has a significant influence upon the Bangrus and, apart from missionary activities, they undertakes many welfare activities towards the people. Actually, Bangrus' conversion to Christianity started in the later part of the last century and during the earlier part of the present century when Baptists Christian Missionaries under the aegis of Kurung Kumey Baptist Mission Field (KKBMF) had set their foot at the Bangru inhabited regions and then some other missionaries started to work. With the influence of Christianity, they shifted from their old beliefs on *Ju-Libaying* (Donyi-Poloism), but they attend mostly their basic traditions and social customs.

The recent exposure to Western and Christian ideas, especially education and religious practices, has resulted into a change in the Bangru way of life. This change caused a division into traditionalists and non-traditionalists. The traditionalists are being those regard themselves as the custodian of tribal customs, and the non-traditionalist being those who have changed their traditional way of life to adopting Christianisation/ Westernisation. It is, however, important to note that these group are not geographically distinct, but they live side by side in their communities and share many aspects of their social life. It is important to note that there are also those who have been Westernised/Christianised, but they are still interested in maintaining a typical traditional Bangru way of life.

10. Conclusion

Every tribal group or society has its own unique characteristics, value-systems, traditional mores, life-attitudes, social hierarchies, religion and traditions. It has its own approach to life and death, disease and sickness, individual and community, and above all, a sense of identity. This sense of identity or cultural self-image always has positive and negative facets;

it defines the traits of solidarity and uniqueness of the tribal group, and also seeks differences with other groups in the larger society around.

The study of this closely knit tribal group termed *'The Bangru'* is of importance from the point of sociological and anthropological insight into their social system and other overt aspects of their society cannot be denied for the simple reason that no study had ever previously been undertaken. The Bangru society needs to be more profoundly studied and analysed from other socially scientific aspects.

As this is the first study on Bangrus, difficulties in drawing conclusions from the empirical evidences collected through various ethnographic methods and techniques naturally presented themselves; but, I had also simultaneously taken great care in recording the data of my participant and non-participant observations, it may venture to claim that the data are fairly accurate and may be relied upon as adequate insights into the workings of the Bangru societal constitution.

This ethnographic piece of writing on Bangru is a humble attempt to highlight the earlier history and culture of the people which is not available as yet. In this study, I have focused on traditional Bangru society and culture as it existed long before. Today much has changed, and much is changing, for the Bangrus find themselves confronted with new social, political, and economic circumstances.

Notes

1. A name given to Nyishi people by Bangru.
2. There is no evidence on the relations of the first group with Aka and Miji and second group with Memba and Khamba. The information is entirely in accordance with the narrations of the informants.
3. This is in accordance with the recent revised electoral rolls carried out in the month of January, 2011. This is exclusively the population of persons having 18 years of age and above. No separate population statistic for Bangrus is available yet.
4. This refers to the Nyishi society to whom Bangru society has basic similarities in their marriage customs.
5. Based on the interviews held during the fieldwork period (January, 2011).
6. This was the staple food of the Bangrus before they shift for contemporary modes of cultivation. The term is called as *Tasse* and *Bey* among Nyishis and Puroiks respectively.
7. These terms in Bangru language are known as *Ju* for Sun and *Libaying* for Moon respectively. Since Bangru does not have a religion with their terms; so the *Donyi* and *Polo* is being used.

References

Bodt, Timotheus A. and Ismael Lieberherr (2015). "First notes on the phonology and classification of the Bangru language of India", *Linguistics of the Tibeto-Burman Area*, 38(1), 66-123.

Ramya, Tame (2012). "Bangrus of Arunachal Pradesh: An ethnographic profile", *International Journal of Social Science Tomorrow*, 1(3), 1-12.

___________(2012). "Brief mythology of Longte-Yullo festival of the Nyishi tribe", *Asian Journal of Research in Social Sciences & Humanities*, II (VI), 5-8.

___________(2013). "Health care perception and illness among Bangrus: A study in Kurung Kumey district of Arunachal Pradesh", *International Journal of Research in Sociology and Social Anthropology*, *1*(3), 53-58.

___________(2015). "The Bangru: an ethnography of a lesser known tribe of Arunachal Pradesh", *Rajiv Gandhi University Research Journal*, 11(2), 85-106.

___________(2015). "The Bangru: the lesser known tribe of Arunachal Pradesh", In Cheithou Charles Yuhlung and P.G. Jangamlung Richard (Eds.), *North East India Tribal Studies: An Insiders' View* (pp. 3-22). New Delhi: Regency Publications.

Chapter - 4

Land alienation among the *Mising* Tribe: A Case of Dhemaji District in Assam

—Tanuj Tayeng

Introduction

Dhemaji District is situated in the remote corner of Assam in the North East part of India on the north bank of river Brahmaputra. The boundaries of the district are the hilly ranges of Arunachal Pradesh to the North and the East, Lakhimpur district in the West and the river Brahmaputra in the South. There are numerous rivers and rivulets that flow down from the hilly ranges of Arunachal Pradesh in the north to the south which causes regular floods in the district. The main rivers are Subansiri, Gai, Laipuliya, Jia, Lali and Simen. The district is divided into two sub-divisions viz., Dhemaji and Jonai, comprising of five blocks (Dhemaji, Sissiborgaon, Morkong-selek, Bordoloni and Machkhowa) and 1150 revenue villages. As per 2011 census, the district shelters a population of 888,077, which comprise of schedule tribe, schedule caste and general population of the district works out to be 70 per cent, 5.33 per cent and 24.67 per cent, respectively of the total population. Among the schedule tribe population, it consists of *Mising* 48 per cent, *Bodo* 18 per cent and others 8 per cent. The urban population is only 1.85 per cent, which indicates the predominantly rural character of the district. The literacy rate is 41.69 per cent while the female literacy rate is 13.6 per cent.[1] Geographically situated between the 94° 12'18" E and 95° 41'32"E longitudes and 27°05'27" N and 27°57'16"N latitudes, the district covers an area of 3237 sq. Km and is basically plain lying at the altitude of 104 m above the Mean Sea Level.

The district is in a strategic location where steep slope of Eastern Himalayas abruptly drop forming a narrow valley, which widens towards the western side. Numerous drainage systems originating from the hills of

Arunachal Pradesh flow through this narrow valley ending at the mighty river Brahmaputra. In general, the slope of the triangular district drops from northern and eastern corners towards south and western sides. After the confluence the three mighty rivers, *i.e.*, Dihing, Dibang and Lohit from their hilly course to the valley exert tremendous impact of peak runoff at the easternmost corner of Dhemaji district, making the district vulnerable to annual flooding. After the great earthquake in 1950 the Brahmaputra riverbed is rising continuously due to deposition of sand carried down from upstream. This has led to the formation of a saucer shaped low-lying zone in the plains of the district.

Who are the *Misings?*

The *Misings*, a schedule tribe (ST) under the Constitution of India, is the second largest plains tribe of Assam after the *Bodos* having a total of 679,824[2] souls. Previously called the *Miris*, though never identify themselves by the people, are a Mongoloid ethnic group falling under the Tibeto-Burman linguistic group inhabitation in eight districts of present-day Assam. viz., Lakhimpur, Dhemaji, Dibrugarh, Jorhat, Sivsagar, Sonitpur, Golaghat, and Tinsukia. Some of them are also found in the Arunachal Pradesh. They mostly inhabit the riverine areas of the Brahmaputra, Dishang, Subansiri, Dhansiri, Bharali and so on. The *Misings* are closely related to *Adis(Abors)* and *Nyishis(Daflas)*, and the Hill *Miris* all belongings to Arunachal Pradesh. They are believed to have first migrated to the plains of Assam in the thirteenth -fourteenth century A.D. in search of the fertile land which also gave protection from enemies. (Bharali, 2006; Sharma and Sarma, 2014) After building up such a close affinity with rivers over the centuries it is not surprising that many *Mising* are accomplished boat and fishermen, however sadly some of the villages are being forced to relocate away from the rivers due to soil erosion. A large numbers of *Misings* are found settled on the Majuli Island of the river Brahmaputra. Out of the total 243 villages in Majuli, the *Misings* are dominant in 108 villages. They speak their own language though has no written form. The *Mising Agom Kebang*, which is the highest literary society of the tribe, has adopted Roman script for the written form and with their initiatives the government once accepted to promote *Misings* as one of the subject in Lower primary schools in *Mising* dominated area.

A folktale exists that says although the *Mising* wrote the alphabet given to them by their god of learning on a sheet of deer-skin over time, it slipped their mind and they ate the deer-skin, losing their script forever. Therefore, although the tribe has its own language they have no authentic written records and so the story of their exodus was passed on verbally. (Doley, 1986; Identity and Society, 2014; Society and Britain, 2014).

Settlement and Livelihood

The *Mising*s are mostly settled in the riverbank of the numerous rivers that flows down from the neighbouring Arunachal Pradesh, which make them the most vulnerable to annual floods. They are predominantly rural settlers with only 2.43 per cent of the total population settled in urban area that too mostly males, which implies temporary for livelihood purposes. The traditional house of the community is *Taleng Ukum* or *Chang Ghar*, *i.e.*, house with raised platform. The construction materials are used from the locally available resources like bamboo, wood, plank and thatch etc. Since their habitats are near the rivers that are prone to regular floods as a result they have to shift from time to time to the safer places, therefore people do not have any permanent settlement/house. In recent time people of affluent group started building permanent houses even than they would have the kitchen in the traditional stilted form/ *Taleng Ukum*/ *Chang Ghar*. Those houses are more convenient as well as prevent from floods waters.

Socio-economic background of the study area

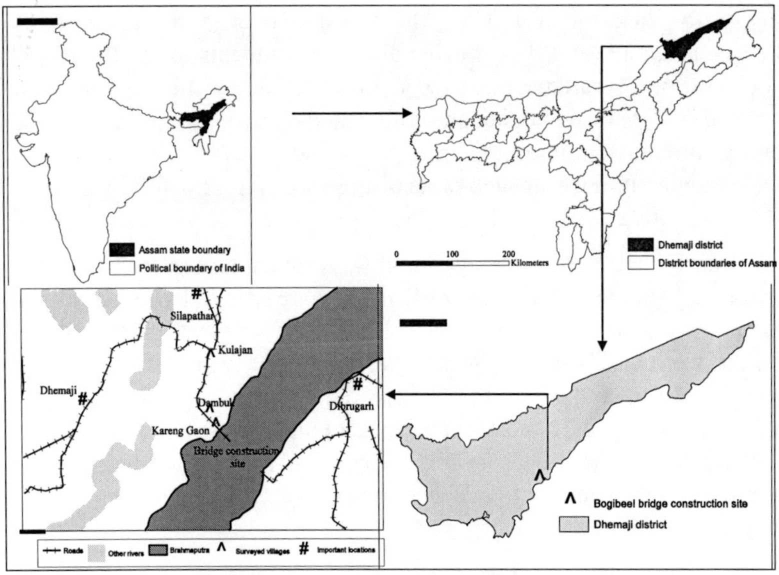

Figure 4.1. Location map of Bogibeel Bridge and the surveyed villages.

The study area comprises of two villages viz. Kareng and Dambuk which has a total of 347 households, consisting of 90 and 257 households respectively. In order to collect the primary data 120 households from both the village are selected randomly combining household who have lost land and those have not lost. The populations in the area are dominated by *Mising* tribe and the main occupation is cultivation. The mode of production is primitive i.e. solely dependent on the natural cycle. Only a few of the household has arable lands but due to the regular flood the crop are destroyed almost every year which result low yield.

Traditional livelihood of the Tribal in India vis-à-vis the *Mising* Tribe

The life style and tradition of each indigenous community is unique and is related to the utilisation of particular natural resource and particular type of work. They had been collecting resources from forest without causing any damage to it. The forest provides them with food and livelihood security.

Since tribal communities live in close proximity with biodiversity rich landscapes, they have evolved local specific and novel livelihood strategies based on their indigenous knowledge. This knowledge was passed on through generations and it played an important role in the conservation and sustainable use of biodiversity. By and large, they were depending on nature for their survival. Thus, there always existed an organic unity between humans and their surrounding environments in the traditional societies. As a result, there existed an intricate relationship between their culture and nature. Social and cultural diversity, coupled with the environmental complexity, have generated diverse approaches and technologies in the management and use of different natural resources (Mishra, 2007).

Like other tribal groups, agriculture and animal husbandry is the main livelihood source of the *Mising* tribe. They are solely dependent on the land which is the only property as well as livelihood source. Though they follow wet cultivation for sustenance, a few dry crops (Rabi) are also cultivated to meet the day-to-day cash requirement. Since these people are inhabitants of the almost all the banks of the majors rivers and rivulets flowing from the neighbouring hills of Arunachal Pradesh and their habitats are prone of the spurting floods that often damages their crops leaving no way out for their survival.

In addition to those issues, the introduction of different developmental policies and programmes, and changes in the land tenure have brought certain changes in the traditional system of resource management among

Mising tribe. Further, the intrusion of non-tribes into tribal areas has disturbed the age-old organic unity of tribes.

Methodology

The study adopted qualitative method and used both primary as well as secondary data. The primary data were collected through extensive fieldwork using tools like in-depth interview schedules, focus group discussion (FGDs), personal observation, and so forth. And the secondary sources such as related literature in printed/published/unpublished documents, report, meeting proceedings, government and non-government records, etc. were used. The field work was conducted in two different fringe villages of the Bogibeel Bridge and Rail-cum-road construction area in Sissiborgaon Block in Dhemaji District.

Pattern and causes of land alienation

The area of study for collection of empirical data is Sissi Borgaon Block, which has a population of about 1,61,657. Majority of the population comprises of Scheduled Tribes (*Mising*) and few non-tribals. According to official report, there are 2310 landless families within the block due to flood and erosion alone. As stated above, there is no much development in the area of study. The few development projects in the form of infrastructure are the Bogibeel Bridge, Railway Gauge conversion and the approach road construction that are ongoing projects in the area.

The bridge will improve the communication network between the North and the South bank of Brahmaputra in general and Dhemaji and Dibrugarh in particular. This will also be of great importance for the other parts of Arunachal Pradesh in improving the mobility and development of the entire region. However, the development projects have posed many problems for the already poor indigenous communities in the project area. These development projects have cost the people of their only source of livelihood in the form of land acquisition for the construction activities. It has alleged that the people have not received proper compensation for the land that has acquired for the projects. Because most of the people do not have land-holding document (patta) for which the land becomes government land. The Bogibeel project alone has affected as many as 19 villages in the form of land acquisition. There different causes of land alienation among the *Mising* tribe. A few of those are listed below and their consequences on the life and livelihood of the people.

Figure 4.1: Road breached due to flood.

Figure 4.2: Sand deposition after flood.

Figure 4.3: Inundation due to guide bund.

Figure 4.4: Bogibeel construction site.

Figure 4.5: Land under acquisition for stocking boulders

Figure 4.6: Land under acquisition for stocking boulders

Alienation by leasing out of land: *Mising* people generally leased out there land to fellow affluent members within the community or members from other communities for certain economic requirement/ other such purposes, which they could not repay and gradually lost it to the member leased. Moreover, they also have the tendency of secondary privatisation. As a result, people migrate from the developing urban/centres to rural places. Such instances are Silapathar town, Dibrugarh, etc., which were predominantly settled by *Mising* tribes.

Alienation through flood and erosion: Floods occurs almost every year in the area. People are alienation due to such perennial flood and erosion. (Fig. 4.1 and 4.2.) There are 2310 landless households in the study areas as per official report. That keeps rising every year after the flood. In recent flood, a total of 14 lakhs people are reported to be affected and Dhemaji district is one of the most affected in the state. According to the people's understanding, flood not only means inundation, it also causes losts of land, lives, livelihood due to flooding and sand deposition. It also degrade the fertility, yields and crop cycles.

Alienation by acquisition of land: Acquisition is the most recent and severe cause of land alienation among the Mising tribe. The under construction Bogibeel bridge and the Service Road has acquired around 251 bighas (1 bigha = approx. 0.76 hectare) land. There no compensation as people do not possess land patta. Land without individual patta is Government Land (Land Acquisition Act of 1894). Fig. 5 and 6. In the study areas 136 houseshold's arable land have been acquired.

Alienation by development of township centre: It is apparent that the *Mising* tribe retreats themselves in the interior area with the development of township and trade centre. It might due to cultural causes and most importantly livelihood issues. Since these people are solely dependent on land for livelihood.

Impacts of Land Alienation

Impact on land and livelihood: Agriculture and allied activities are the main sources of livelihood among the people. The development projects and other interventions have led to the lost of land, which is the only source of survival. And moreover, they are not adapted to secondary and tertiary sources so far.

Lose of culture: The cultural practices of tribal groups are intricate with the natural environment. The cultures and festivities are based on the day-to-day uses of the land and livelihood practices. The losts of land has detached them from their own culture.

Rural out migration: The land alienation has also intensified the rate of rural outmigration among the male folks from those villages. One can find this from the fact that in most the villages affected by the bridge construction male (young /old) migrated to towns and cities in others state like Kerala, Karnataka, and so forth. They are reported to work as security guards, night watchmen, etc. with little or no education. The family in the village depends on the meagre amount of remittance from the migrants.

And the female folks work as daily labourers in the construction with little wages, with no skills to substantiate daily sustenance.

Loss of alternative sources: *Mising* tribe, as mentioned above, inhabits the riverine areas and has developed symbiotic relationship with the nature. They are pretty well in fishing activities. These not only serves as food for sustenance rather is an alternative livelihood for them. Moreover, these people are well versed with the making of indigenous fishing tools. But due to the construction of guide Bund on both sides of the Bridge, the wetlands /Beels are inundated and restricted the fishing area where people use to substantiate their livelihood. People alleged that due to high water level it risk their life as well as the catch. It also inundates the entire village in the peak of monsoon. (Fig. 4.3)

Impact on agriculture: Flood is a regular phenomenon in the study area. Most of the land (homestead/agricultural) are affected by flood every year. People lost their crop as well as soil become unsuitable due to coarser sediment deposition. (Fig. 4.2.)

Conclusion

Mising community with diverse problems ranging from natural, economical, social, is living in acute poverty. There is political organisation that raises voices for the communities though not articulating all the sufferings of the people as they are busy in fulfilling their vested interest. The *Mising* Autonomous Council, the sole responsible for development of the people, is reported to be drowned in corrupt practices and mismatching funds mean for the development of the people. National and regional parties remember these sufferings of the community only at the time of elections and the people too, with little or no knowledge of politics, overwhelmed by the speech and election manifesto of their popular leaders. It has been observed that, the people are tempted by the few feasting and partying with those leaders or parties. But there is no different between those who ever may be in power. Amidst such sufferings of the people, the state continued to imposing development initiatives causing loss of land and livelihood to the people. The essay does not mean that development initiatives should not be undertaken by the state; but is the development at the cause of land and livelihood of people justified? At this juncture, many questions may comes up. Development for whom? Is this development bear in the real meaning? Do such development really required at cause of the rural poor? If it is the case of development for whose sake? Will such development really benefit the people who bear the lost?

Development is the most appropriate word of today's world. Though it has its own vested interest and network. It benefits a countable group at the cost of the others. There is also evidences of marginalisation and victimisation of development projects. (Banerjee, 2011; Fernandes, 2003). Here the development authority or the state should go for inclusive approach, where all the stake holders are taken into account in all respect of the project. The authority should also sort out the pros and cons of the project and take up proper solutions in mitigating those. Such an approach will lead to a participation of all stakeholders and eventually ownership feelings and the benefits will be shared. Such development will serve the real purpose that will not victimise any marginal groups for the development benefit of a handful of vested interest groups. As a result, this will minimise the conflicts between the development authority and the affected communities.

References

Doley, D. (1986). "Pattern and Causes of land Alienation of the Mishing Tribe of Assam", in B.N. Bordoloi (Ed) *Alienation of Tribal Land and Indebtedness*. Tribal Research Institute, Assam.

Bharali, Gita (2006). *Development Projects Threat to Tribal Livelihood: Case Study*. Guwahati: Assam Institute of Research for Tribals and Scheduled Caste. Print.

Cernea, Michael M. (200). 'Risks, Safeguards and Reconstruction: A Model for Population Displacement and Resettlement'. *Economic and Political Weekly*, Vol. 35 (41).

Bordoloi, B.N. (Ed) (1986). *Alienation of Tribal Land and Indebtedness*. Guwahati: Tribal Research Institute, Assam.

Fernades, Walter (2003). "Development Displaced and The Right To Life: Implications For the Northeast". In Tanmoy Bhattacharjee (Ed) *Problems of Internally Displaced Persons in Assam with Special Reference to Barak Valley.* Silchar: Department of Political Sciences, Assam University.

Fernandes, Walter (2008). *Land as Livelihood vs Land as Commodity in India.* Guwahati. Working Paper.

Gadgil, Madhav and Ramachandra Guha (1992). *This Fissured land: An ecological history of India.* USA: U of California Press.

Gohain, Hiren (2008). 'Big Dams, Big Floods: On Predatory Development'. *Economic and Political Weekly*, Vol. 43 (30).

Good, William.J and Paul K. Hatt (1952). *Methods in Social Research.* USA: McGraw-Hill Book Company.

Hussain, Monirul (2008). *Interrogating Development: State, Displacement and Popular Resistance in North East India.* New Delhi: SAGE Publication India Pvt Ltd.

Mahanta, Chandan and Anjana Mahanta (2006). 'Bridge over the Brahmaputra', *Economic and Political Weekly,* Vol. 41 (7).

Rao, P. Jaswantha (1998). 'Tribals' Struggle against Land Alienation', *Economic and Political Weekly*,Vol. 33(3).

Sharma, Chandan Kumar (2001-2002). 'Tribal Land Alienation: Government's Role', *Economic and Political Weekly*, Vol. 36(52).

Sharma, Chandan Kumar (2012). "The State and the Ethnicisation of Space in Northeast India", In N.G. Mahanta and D.Gogoi (Ed) *Shifting Terrain: Conflict Dynamics in North East India*. Guwahati/Delhi: DVS Publishers.

Sharma,Chandan Kumar (2014). 'Issues of Conservation and Livelihood in a Forest Village of Assam', *International Journal of Rural Management*, Vol.10(1).

Fernandes, Walter and Geeta Menon (1987). *Tribal Women and Forest Economy*. New Delhi: Indian Social Institute.

Gadgil, M. and R. Guha (1990). *Ecological prudence and modes of resource use*. Centre for Ecological Science, Technical Report 59.

Chapter - 5

The Marriage System and Religious Beliefs and Practices among the Ponthais of *Changlang District, Arunachal Pradesh*

—Bikimoni Gogoi and Satyawati Mili

Introduction

Several scholars have carried out innumerable studies on the various vibrant ethnic communities of North-East India. A humble endeavour has been made in this paper to present an ethnographic account of the Ponthai Tangsa, with special reference to their religion and marriage system. The paper is primarily based on a fieldwork among the Ponthai people in a village named Wagun Ponthai of Changlang district of Arunachal Pradesh, which is seven kilometres away from Bordumsa circle of the district.

The Tangsas are one of the colourful tribes of Arunachal Pradesh. They belong to the Tibeto-Burman linguistic group occupying the eastern hills of Changlang district. The word "Tangsa" means 'hill people' (*Tang*- hill and *Sa*- people). The Tangsa story of migration alludes to the fact that search for cultivable land and inter-tribal feuds compelled them to migrate from their abode across the Patkai hill range and settle in Tirap a few centuries ago. It is certain that the Tangsas came before the arrival of the Singphos, as some groups of them are said to have been conquered and subjugated by the Singpho chiefs, named Sombianong, Ningru, Bisa and Kheryam. The Tangsa tribe is divided into several sub-tribes and clans. Some of the sub-tribes are are *Tikhak, Muklom, Kimsing, Sangwal, Ponthai, Lungri, Tonglim, Ronrang, Lungphi, Mossang, Lungchang, Havi, Jugli, Yongkuk, Sanke* etc. The sub-tribes are again divided into a number of exogamous clans, such as *Thancing, Khusue, Mokham, Thancing Khusung, Logyung, Mowing Kengya, Simian Mailung, Yumpla, Taichu, Thankhu, Thancing Wabon* and *Hangyung*. Physically, the Tangsas are medium-statured and have a well-built body. They are fair-complexioned with a slight yellowish tinge and they belong to the Mongoloid stock. Agriculture is their main occupation and shifting cultivation is the traditional method of subsistence (Patir, 1996-97).

The Ponthais are one of the major sub-tribes of the Tangsas, who were earlier called *Phong* or *Nokta,* but in the course of time came to be known as Ponthais. As per the sources available, it has been known that the term '*Ponthai*' means 'people whose decision was found to be correct'. Ethnically, the Ponthais belong to the Mongolian stock of human race. They are believed to have come from the southern route of Burma advancing towards the Indo-Burma border. Initially settling at Waktham (now in Myanmar), they migrated to several places, *viz*., Changrah, Phongsa, and Raktong and then settled down in a few villages in Changlang, such as Yumchum, Phonsok, Longkom and Samlam. Search of plain and fertile land for better habitation later compelled them to settle in Bordumsa of Changlang. At present, they are the inhabitants of a few villages, including Wagun Ponthai, Longkom Ponthai, Balijan Ponthai and Galenza Ponthai of Changlang district of Arunachal Pradesh.

Marriage is a universal institution, so is religion. Marriage merely means a socially approved union, usually between a man and a woman which is presumed, by both the couple and others, to be more or less permanent, and it subsumes reciprocal rights and obligations between the two spouses and their future children. Religion may be marked as any set of attitudes, beliefs and practices pertaining to supernatural power which may vary within a culture as well as among societies and may change over time. We do not find any primitive as well as modern society without religious beliefs and practices.

Review of literature

Literature review evidences that there are many studies on marriage. However, there seems a research gap in the area of studying marriage pattern and their effects on family satisfaction. To understand the marriage scenario in the human population, some significant studies have already has been carried out by a good number of scholars.

K. S. Singh, in his book *People of India: Arunachal Pradesh,* incorporates several dimensions of the marriage system of the different sub-tribes of Tangsa, such as Havi, Jugli, Mosang, Tonglim, Tikhak, Muklom, Lungphi, Ronrang, Lunchang, Kimsing, Sangwal, Yongkuk, and Sanke (p. 31).

The book, *Marriage and Culture,* by Tamo Mibang and M.C. Behera, contains several aspects of marriage and culture of different tribal societies of Arunachal Pradesh. The aspects include marriage and culture, marriage rules and regulations, marriage rituals, emotions, entertainment and songs and marriage and social relations. Wangru Taidong in his paper highlighted some aspects of marriage practices of the Jugli sub-tribe of Tangsa in Arunachal Pradesh.

Jeuti Barooa, in her book *Customary Laws of the Tangsas of Arunachal Pradesh: With Special Reference to their Land Holding System,* discusses various aspects of marriage of the Tangsas. Different types of marriage, such as arranged marriage, marriage by elopement, etc., marriage proposal, bride price and divorce are the highlights of her study (pp.12-18).

B. Tripathy and S. Dutta, in their edited book *Religious History of Arunachal Pradesh* containing twenty seven research papers of several noted researchers, throw light on various aspects of tribal culture with emphasis on spirits and deities, sacred specialists, sacred rituals, etc. The Theravada and Mahayana Buddhism, as practised by a number of Arunachali tribes, have been presented in a historical setting. The impact of Brahmanical culture in the foothill areas of the state has also been analysed. It was an attempt to understand the religious history of the people, and their cultural interaction with Brahmaputra valley of Assam, Tibet and Myanmar throughout the ages.

Aims and Objectives of the Study

Following are the specific aims and objectives of the present study:

- to examine the tradition of marriage in the study of community, the type, the form, ways of acquiring mates etc.;
- to examine the impact of marriage in the socio-cultural life of people;
- to see the changing trends in marriage ceremonies in other inter-tribe marriages;
- to examine the existence of bride price and dowry system;
- to observe the change in case of marriage feast;
- to study the role of religion in the socio-cultural life of the people of the village;
- to study the rites and rituals observed by the community under study;

- to study the newly adopted system of worship and prayer of the people of the village; and finally
- to study the traditional beliefs and practices of the community under study.

Methodology

During the present investigation, standard anthropological techniques such as observation, interview and collection of relevant concrete cases etc., were followed in the field to generate the desired mass of data depending on the nature of the data. The techniques were used either independently or in collaboration. More emphasis was put on the techniques of observation and collection of concrete cases.

On the whole, all efforts were made to generate data on the problems from a cross-section of people representing various strata. The description and the interpretation have been done depending upon the etic and emic nature of the data.

Ponthai Marriage System

Marriage is an accepted form of union between man and woman among the Ponthais. They view marital union as a blessing bestowed to them by God. They don't regard marriage as a casual affair; in fact their outlook on it is to strictly adhere to the laws prescribed by nature.

They have their own distinct ways of solemnizing the marriage ceremony like other tribes of Tangsa. The Ponthai observe clan exogamy. Marriage within the clan is strictly prohibited and is not permissible. The couples who are involved in such prohibition are liable to face the village council and the prescribed punishment. Their residence is patrilocal; therefore, the children take their father's clan. They call marriage in their language as *Me-rigmoi*.

The rules and regulations of marriage among the Ponthai are also significant. The Ponthais are traditionally monogamous. Among the Ponthais, polygamy is strictly prohibited; in no circumstances it is permissible. If any individual of the society is found to break the rule prescribed by the village council, then they have to face severe punishment. But, in certain specific cases, such as, for instance, if after marriage, wife is found to be barren the husband can go for second marriage with the consent of his first wife. Normally, polygamy is completely discarded among the Ponthais. On the other hand, junior and senior levirate is in practice among them. Cross-cousin marriage is a favoured form of marital alliance, but parallel cousin marriage is strictly prohibited. The marital relationship between the parallel cousins is incest among the Ponthai people as they belong to the same clan.

The most accepted forms of marriage among the Ponthais are negotiated marriage, marriage by mutual consent and marriage by purchase. Marriage by elopement is strictly prohibited among them. Earlier, child marriage was also practised, but the system no longer exists today. They also prefer widow remarriage. Divorce cases are rarely found in the society. Divorce system doesn't exist in their customary law. According to them, once married, the couple remains together till death separates them.

Generally, the accepted age for marriage of both sexes among them is 20-25 years. Mostly they prefer to perform their marriages in the month from December to March. After attaining puberty, the Ponthais consider a girl as eligible for marriage. Dowry is not followed by the people. In every form of marriage, earlier among the Ponthais, bride price was mandatory, but now it is not. Those who were capable pay the bride price handsomely, but those who were economically poor had the option of avoiding it. Marriage by exchange among the Ponthais is not accepted. Extramarital relationships are prohibited in the society. Adultery is regarded as a punishable offence and if anyone of the village members is found to be caught in the act of adultery, they are punished by the village council as per the customary law.

The most accepted and socially recognised marriage is customarily performed by an individual after complete negotiation between the intending parties. There are many rituals among them regarding their marriage. A couple has to live in the parental house of the husband in the Ponthai society.

The Ponthais are divided into various clans, viz, *Longkho, Bo, Sumta*, *Bolok,Santheng, Katang, Chillom*, and *Sowen*. As they strictly follow clan-exogamy, marriage does not take place among the clan groups like *Longkho*, *Katang* and *Chilom*. They have to marry from other clan groups. Similarly, marriage among the clan members like *Sumta, Somen, Bolok* is also prohibited, because they consider themselves as having originated from the same descent and that they are brothers and sisters.

Among the Ponthais, monogamy is legally recognised in the society. It is not because of poverty or scarcity of girls, but is considered as acceptable norm of the society. They believe that prosperity and happiness can be maintained in monogamous family and their children will get more love and care from their parents.

As polygamy is strictly prohibited in the Ponthai society, for the second marriage, the husband has to pay penalty to his first wife's parents. As a penalty, he has to give rice-beer (*Kham*) and 5 rupees. After that, again he has to give a cow or a pig as a bride price for his second marriage.

Arranged marriage is the most preferential among the Ponthais. In this type, marriage of the children is arranged by the parents. In the Ponthai marriage, *Kamwa* (middleman) plays a very important role. The *Kamwa* goes to the girl's house by taking the boy's proposal for negotiation of the marriage. The middle man's role is performed by the paternal uncle of the boy, or in some cases, maternal uncle also acts as the middleman. In some cases, in the absence of paternal and maternal uncle, any respectful person of the village acts as a middleman. Among the Ponthais, there is a rule, if the girl's family refuses the proposal brought by the negotiator on behalf of the boy's family, they have to go to the girl's house for three times by taking the proposal. If the girl's family refuses the proposal for three times then only the proposal becomes cancelled. After the cancelation of the proposal, the boy's family searches other girl for their son.

Marriage by elopement among the Ponthais is strictly prohibited by the society. But, still some cases of marriage by elopement are found in the village. When a girl and a boy well deep in love with each other and want to marry, but the parents of both girl and boy raised objection or disapprove their relationship, the couple elopes to some other village and stays as husband and wife. As no parents want to lose their children and can't live without their children, therefore, both of the families try to locate them with the help of village people and take back them to the village. After that, the couple must perform the customary rites; until they perform the customary rights, the marriage is not socially recognised. Therefore, the parents of the couple become bound to legalise the marriage by paying the bride price and also by offering a feast to the society. The couple who elopes may not be of same clan or family with whom marriage is restricted. They consider it as a serious crime which cannot be forgiven. Such marriages are recognised as incestuous by the village people.

Widow re-marriage is socially sanctioned among the Ponthais. In such cases, the unmarried youngest brother of the deceased husband is the preferable choice for the widow. In case, if a widow does not have clan brothers of her deceased husband, then she could walk out of the family and marry another person as per her wish. If there is no youngest brother of the widow's husband, then also the widow can marry another person according to her wish. Again, if the widow is pregnant during the time of her husband's death and she wants to marry another person according to her choice, instead of her brother-in-law, then she cannot marry during the period of her pregnancy. She has to wait till the birth of the baby. The widow cannot carry her deceased husband's child to the second husband's house; she must hand over the child to her deceased husband's family. After that she can marry any person of her choice. According to their customary law, the boy who will marry the widow have to give a buffalo to widow's father-in-law. Widow's father-in-law will perform a small ceremony and invite all the village people along with the *Lowang* (village chief) and other respectful persons of the village and offer meat and rice beer. At that time, the father-in-law will declare that their daughter-in-law (widow of his deceased son) will be no longer his daughter-in-law and set her free from their rules and relationship. All the people of the village, along with the village chief, agree with widow's father-in-law and give her freedom to marry with the person.

On the other hand, if the widow agrees to marry with his brother-in-law and the boy is also agree with his father and mother's decision, then a small ceremony is held in order to recognise their marriage socially. All the village people are invited to the party and offer a feast with rice beer and pork. After that the couple will be recognised as husband and wife.

The children of the elder brother are accepted by the younger brother as his own children and he cannot make distinction between his elder brother's children and his own children.

However, if the widow does not agree to marry the youngest brother of her deceased husband, then the bride price taken by the parents of the widow at the time of her marriage has to be returned to the family of the deceased husband and only then they will set the widow free and allow her to go back to her parent's house. In case of failure to pay back the bride price by the widow's parents, it remains as the obligation for the family to pay back by the next generation. If the younger brother of the deceased husband refuses to marry the widow of his elder brother and does not want to take care of his elder brother's children, then he has to pay five rupees to the parents of the widow and whatever they demand. When the widow goes back to her parents' house, she has to leave the children behind in her in-law's house. She can take the baby with her, if any, but when the child grows up, she has to return the child to her deceased husband's parents.

Generally, among the Ponthais, the young widow returns to her parents after her husband's death, but those who have children prefer to stay back with her in-laws and look after children.

Among the Ponthais, bride price is mandatory in every form of marriage. It is known as *Zyada-Ngun*. According to their customary law, bride price is not fixed, it is finalised by the bride's family through negotiation. They give a pig (*wak*) of big size, cow (*maan*), buffalo (*lo*), *kham* (rice beer) in containers made of bamboo, and quantity depends upon the demand of the bride's family. The bride's parents demand either buffalo or pig. If buffalo and pigs are not available, the groom's party may respond to this demand in cash in the present day society.

Earlier, it was customary for the bridegroom to pay cash to following persons, viz., *Ngi-ku* (maternal uncle) ₹ 15, *Ngi-to* (father's brother) ₹ 10, *Wa Wa* (father-in-law) ₹ 10, *Nu Nu* (mother-in-law) ₹ 7, *Ngi-Ni* (father's sister) ₹ 8 are given as bride price in cash. But nowadays, it is increased to ₹ 215 for *Ngi-ku* (maternal uncle), ₹ 210 for *Ngi-to* (father's brother), *Wa Wa* (father-in-law) and *Ngi-Ni* (father's sister) and *Nu Nu* (mother-in-law) are given ₹ 207. There is no strict rule to spend huge amount in the marriage party, but depends on the capabilities of the families of the bridegroom and the bride.

The pigs or buffaloes provided by the groom's family on demand are consumed on the marriage ceremony. In return, the parents of the bride give rice seeds, foul cage, ornaments made of beads and coins, cloth, utensils and other belongings as a token of love to their daughter. It is not compulsory to give all the bride price at a time because of economic condition. They can also pay the bride price in the form of instalments even after marriage.

The Ponthai society is patriarchal as well as patrilineal in nature. Father is considered to be the head of the family. They usually prefer clan-exogamy system of marriage. If any member of the society violates the rule of clan exogamy, he or she is punished by the society and have to pay fine to the village council according to their demands. More often, social restrictions lead to ostracisation from the society.

Among them, adultery is regarded as an offence. It is restricted in the society and the adulterers are punished by the village council (*Ngung thut*).

In the Ponthai society, no divorce system exists in the customary law. According to them, once married, they remain together till death separates them. But nowadays, many cases of divorce are found in the society. When a wife divorces her husband, there is a rule that the parents of the wife must return the bride price taken during the marriage to the divorced husband. But when the husband divorces his wife, he has to pay compensation to his father-in-law.

Once a girl is married to a family, there is a strict rule that, no boys of the bride's family, can marry any girl from the groom's family.

In the Ponthai society, there is no hard and fast rule regarding the residence of the newly-wed couple after marriage. The Ponthais are mainly patrilocal; therefore, the newly-wed couple mostly prefers to live in the groom's parents' house. However, they were also set free to set up new household and live there separately from their parents. Neolocal pattern of residence is favoured among them, as the father divides the property among the sons in order to avoid quarrel and misunderstanding among them.

Among the Ponthais, the parents of the boy takes initiative for marriage of their sons. When they think that their son is of marriageable age, then they look girl for their son. The girl whom they select must be of well behaviour, having knowledge regarding household activities and also help them in the field. She must have educational knowledge to help her husband in his work. After selection of the bride for their son, the parents of the boy send a middleman to the girl's house.

Sometime boy expresses his feelings to the parents either by himself or through friend or relatives. Accordingly, the boy's parents consult with their relatives and send a middleman to the girl's house to offer the proposal of marriage. The middleman carry *Kham* (rice beer) in a jar, which is made of bamboo and *Kham Tee* (rice beer juice), to the girl's house as a token for marriage proposal as per their norm. Both the parties sit together, then the middle man tells them the reason of his visit and also offers the token to the bride's parents. If the parents of the girl accept the rice beer and rice beer juice then it indicates that they agree on the proposal. If they do not accept the items, then it indicates that, they disagree the proposal. According to the norm, the mediator should take the proposal to the girl's house for three times even after the girl's refusal. They think that repeated approach may bring positive result.

The Ponthai bride wears dresses and ornaments like ***Samsung-sah*:** It is kind of blouse, worn by the bride. It is white in colour. ***Nug-sah*** is a long piece of cloth worn by the bride. It is wrapped from the waist to shoulder. Its colour is white. ***Kineh*** is a kind of wrapper worn by the bride around the waist extending down to ankle. It is also white in colour. *Kineh* is woven by the Ponthai girls themselves in their personal handloom. It is specially worn by the bride. ***Jak-Phan* (Bangles)** is a kind of bracelet worn by the bride in her hand. ***Nah-cho* (ear ring)** is a kind of earring worm in the ear by the bride. **Nagun-lek (Necklace)** is a kind of necklace made of *Ngun* (coin). ***Nek-sang* (necklace)** is made of beads, worn by the bride in her neck. ***Kholat*** **(hair bend)** is a kind of hair bend put by the bride in her hair to keep her hair light. Dagteip **(ring)** is worn by the bride in her finger. It may be made of gold and silver.

Dress and Ornaments of the Groom

A checkered *lungi* worn down the waist extending towards the ankle by the groom. ***Samsung*** is a shirt, which is white in colour worn by the bride. **Coat:** A kind of half jacket with open front and short sleeve. In the jacket, traditional symbols are designed over the back.

Among the Ponthais, marriage ceremony is of four types. First one is the *Ronghon*. It is more elaborate form of marriage ceremony when large amounts of articles are needed like buffalo (lo), cattle (*Maan*), pig (*wak*) and huge quantity of rice-beer (*kham*). Second is *Wakbot*, which is a bit simple than *Ronghon*. Third type of marriage ceremony is *Pong dok,* which is a bit simple than Wakbot, and the fourth one is *Pongsa dok*, which can be performed only by *Roomthat* (traditional household ritual to their deity *kathak Rong*), where one pig is sacrificed. Performing marriage ceremony depends upon the socio-economic conditions of the village people; respective family decides the ways of marriage.

On the day of marriage, activities start from early in the morning at about 4.00 A.M. The invitees and relatives of the groom gather at the groom's house for the marriage ceremony. The villagers also come to the groom's house early in the morning to help them in other works. The *Makwa* (person appointed for cutting meat), along with two or more persons, sacrifice a pig for the ritual. They also slaughter more animals like buffalo, pig, goat, cow for community feast. But, for marriage ritual, only pig is required. The appointed person for cutting meat (*Makwa*) and his friends ready the *sokut* (meat bundle) according to the demands of the bride parties before the arrival of bride. The meat bundle is made differently for different categories of bride's relatives, such as *Thangsah* which contains 15 pieces per bundle are for bride's maternal Uncle, Aunty, Uncle, Mother, Father, *Kamwa* and *Lawang*. *Suwang*, which contains 10 pieces of meat in each bundle are for other close relatives of the bride. The *Makwa* (meat cutting person) and *Makwa* (woman appointed for distributing rice beer) also get *sokut* (meat bundle) which contains 10 pieces of meat. The other near relatives of the groom are engaged in performing the rituals. After the completion of preparations in the groom's house, the *Kamwa* will go to invite the bride party for the marriage ceremony along with rice beer. Invitation is specially made to the girl's uncle, aunties, father, mother and her other family members.

The *Kamwa* brings the bride party to the groom's house. Bride, along with her two friends of her village, Mother (*Nu Nu*), Father (*Wa Wa*), Uncle (*Ngi ku*), Aunts (*Ngi-nie*) and other blood relatives proceeds to the groom's house for the marriage ceremony. On the way, nearly one km. away from the groom's house, some of the elder persons of the groom's family stop the bride party to perform a small ritual. They give rice-beer to the bride's party in the *Ladak* (kind of leaf). They just take a bit of the rice-beer and throw the rest to the road side. After the ritual, they were welcomed at the groom's house. Inside the house, ritual for their new *Ngam-Nu* (daughter-in law) is performed by sacrificing a cock. This ritual is performed by the groom's father. In the absence of him, any elder male blood relative of the groom can do this ritual. It is done in the centre post of the house. They believe that God and Goddess reside in the post; on the one side, there is God and, on the other side, there is Goddess (*Theng Khong and man-rong*). Different clan members call their clan God differently, but Goddess is the same for all clans of the Ponthais. The middle post of the house is decorated by *Ladak* (sacred leaves), three *Ladak* leaves for the God and three for the Goddess on both sides of the post. Blood of the sacrificed cock is put on the *Ladak* leaves and it is hook up in the post. A jar, full of water, is kept on both sides of the post. The groom's father takes six pieces of cock liver in his hand and yells the name of their clan God to inform him about the arrival of their *Ngam-Nu* (daughter-in-law). He throws rice for three times to the post and three pieces of cock liver. After that, by pouring water in the post, groom's father declares the respective bride as his daughter-in-law and gives her permission to do all the household activities, also asks blessings for her longevity, good health, prosperity, etc. Same thing is done at the other side of the post. After finishing the ritual properly, they proceed to the next ceremony.

Bride's father, mother, uncle, aunty, *Kamwa, lawang, makwa, maknu* and groom's relatives make a circle and sit in the kitchen. Groom's parents distribute rupees to the bride party according to their custom; maternal uncle of the bride gets ₹ 15, father ₹ 10, mother ₹ 7, aunty ₹ 8, father's brother ₹ 10. Again *Cho-tuk* is distributed as, bride's maternal uncle, father, mother, aunty, *lowang* (village chief), *makwa* (meat cutting person), *maknu* (rice beer distributor female) as 15 pieces per bundle, and 10 pieces per bundle are given to *kamwa* and other close relatives of the bride. After the distribution, *maknu* (woman who is appointed to distribute the rice beer) serves rice beer with pork meat. Before taking the meat, they recite *Rumtam* (prayer) in the name of clan titles of the bride and groom, wishing a happy conjugal life for the couple. Only after distributing the articles to the respective persons, the community feast is arranged. Subsequently, bride and groom, with their companions, are invited inside the kitchen to perform *Chamron-cham shah* ceremony. Groom with his two friends and bride with her two friends sit opposite to each other. Family members of groom serve three plates of rice with chicken curry to groom and his friends, and also to bride and her friends with three glasses of water. The bride and the groom eat together in the same plate and other two friends of groom and bride also eat together in the same plate. According to their custom, little rice should be left in the plate for *Chamdakhang* (Goddess of wealth). The Ponthais believe that sharing rice plate with each other makes their relationship more strong and their love becomes more for each other. After finishing the *Chamron-chamcha* ceremony, father-in-law ties thread in both hands of the bride. They believe that sacred thread will help them in their future life and help the bride and groom for her longevity, good health prosperity. With this formal ceremony, the first day of marriage rituals gets over. After the feast, singing and dancing continues along with drinking rice beer in the groom's house, it is continued till the next day.

The bride, with her friends and relatives, returns back to her home. In the midway, bride's mother performs a small ritual; she throws four pieces of meat by chanting mantras to four directions, so that no evil spirit can harm them. After this, the bride, accompanied by her friends and relatives, moves to her house.

On the same day, another pig is slaughtered, the meat of this pig is divided into three parts. The first part, *i.e.*, the neck portion, is for the maternal uncle of the bride. The second part, comprising one hind leg and one fore leg, is separately kept for bride's parents. Again, three pieces of meat, three pieces of liver and big size meat from the fat portion is covered with leaves (*ladak)* is given for the ritual called *Chimphkhon*. Along with the meat, rice-beer in a big size container is also sent to the bride's house from the groom's as a gift. This portion of meat and rice-beer is carried to the bride's house by the *kamwa* along with his two or more friends. The third part, comprising one hind leg and one fore leg, is cooked at the night at the groom's house and served to active workers who help the groom's family in the management of marriage ceremony. After the feast at night, the villagers and groom's relatives enjoy singing, dancing, and drinking rice-beer with pork. Groom is too involved in the party; he drinks rice beer. In this way, the villagers create an enjoyable moment at the groom's house.

Next day, a grand feast is arranged by the bride's parents where the villagers and the close relatives of the groom's parents are invited. A pig is slaughtered for the feast. The chest portion of the pig to the groom's relatives and friends and rice-beer, pork, and rice are served to the groom's party. The token, which is brought by the *kamwa* from the groom's family, such as meat neck portion, is given to the bride's maternal uncle to show respect from the groom's family and other half is distributed among the bride's close relatives. After the distribution, bride with her friends and groom with his two friends are invited to the kitchen and same ritual *chamron-chamsah* is performed. Subsequently, father-in-law ties sacred thread to his son-in-law for his bright future, happiness and prosperity.

After the completion of the marriage ceremony, the bride and the groom, along with groom's father, mother and relatives, returned back to the house. On return journey, *kamwa* leads the party. On the way, relatives of the groom crack jokes, make fun of them, dance and sing song, they make the way a joyful journey. The bride carries with her the items of her daily needs, such as clothes, utensils, ornaments, etc. On the next day, a small feast is arranged at the groom's house where the villages and blood relatives are invited.

The Ponthais of the Wagun Ponthai village are the followers of *Rangfraism*. Earlier, they were animist and nature worshipper. They practised marriage according to the customs prescribed by their ancestors, but now-a-days, they practise marriage according to *Rangfraism*. As the Ponthais presently practise marriage ceremony and rituals according to the *Rangfraism* custom, some rituals from their ancestral period are still followed by them. But, like earlier, they don't sacrifice animal in the marriage ceremony. Animal sacrifice is strictly prohibited according to *Rangfraism.*

Ponthai Religion

Religion plays an important role in the socio-cultural life of the Ponthais of the Wagun Ponthai village. Traditionally, they were animists and worshippers of nature wherein they believed that the supernatural power had its manifestation in the things of nature. Epidemics, fire, earthquake, flood, storm, crop failure, etc, were believed to be the expression of wrath of supernatural power. Some common diseases of mankind and of livestock were believed to be effects of wrath of some of the deities. Therefore, propitiation had to be made by sacrificing animals such as cattle, fowls, etc.

The animistic faith of the Ponthais was characterised by belief in the existence of soul, which was conceived to be of two kinds, *viz.*, *tchikkhang* and *jakhang*. In aspects of one's desire, egoism and wants, the former was conceived to proceed towards evil and so was regarded evil. The latter, on the other hand, was considered as the good one. The conception of a high impersonal God, whom they regarded as the Creator of the universe, was mainly based on their belief that He is the impersonal principle of justice and also the upholder of moral order of creatures. The Supreme Creator was known to them as *Khotak Rangwa*. Besides Him, there were two benevolent and malevolent Gods who for all practical purposes had direct influence upon their lives. As per this connotation, these two Gods were *Hahnuta*, the one who was believed to bring happiness and prosperity, and the other *Hahkhoh* who brought distress and misery. It was believed that *Hahnuta*, the God assigned as good sometimes exhibited evil actions by imparting curses to people. They regard *Chamdakhang* as their Goddess of wealth. The Ponthais believe in a number of deities, *viz*., *Ho Chang Jong, Khotak Ta Sa*, *Theng Khong* and *Manrong*. These, however, collectively are named as *Chongrang* whom they worship as their household deity even now.

Pertaining to such animistic faith, the Ponthais also believed in the existence of evil spirits whom they held responsible for their diseases and ailments as well as other misfortunes. Hence, in their endeavour at propitiating these spirits, they had to resort to sacrifice of animals such as fowls and cattle.

But since the inception of the socio-religious reform movement, *i.e.*, the *Rangfraa Social Reform Movement (RSRM),* the religious life of the Ponthais is marked by the adoption of a new system of worship and prayer, *i.e.*, *Rangfraism.* The Supreme God whom their ancestors did worship was *Khotak Rangwa*. Their new faith also acknowledges the same God in the name of Almighty *Rangfraa*. They, only for their convenience, brought the formless *Rangfraa* into form, *i.e.*, in the form of idol (and also image) in accordance with the description depicted in the *Rangfraa* mythology. The adoption of the new system of worship and prayer resulted in deviation from many of the traditional beliefs as well as the ways of performing rituals. The belief in the existence of evil spirits no longer prevails and as such most of the traditional rituals performed for the well-being of the people lack the concept of animal sacrifice for the propitiation of the spirits. Even now, for the recovery of ailing people, prayer to God is done, but neither food nor drinks are offered, for the people now believe that the very question of offering these to God does not arise for He is purely celestial, hence perfect and complete in itself and therefore neither food or drinks are offered to Him nor are animals sacrificed.

To eliminate the prevalent system of worship predominantly characterised by animal sacrifice, they began worshipping Lord *Rangfraa,* with a newly formulated system devoid of animal sacrifice, where purification with holy water and chanting of prayers mark an important aspect of almost all the rituals of household as well as community level and also during the rituals associated with the principal events of life, *i.e.,* birth, marriage and death. The ritual for chicken pox is performed at present. However, the hunting and fishing rituals as well as Rangsang are no longer in practice. Again, some of the people have also accepted Christianity of various denominations. The people who got converted to Christianity have deviated themselves from their pristine traditional ways of life and faith.

According to a textbook, published by the Rangfraa Faith Promotion Society (RFPS*)* to the *Rangfraites,* man himself is a perfect model of the universe but in smaller size. Therefore, man is inclusive of all the levels of manifestation. Man, actually, is the interplay of two elements, *viz.*, celestial and earth. The earth component of man is his body, while the celestial component is his soul.

The *Rangfraites* believe that soul is basically God Himself, so it merges with God after death. By God, the *Rangfraites* mean the existence of the non-manifested which is all pervading and a self-effulgent substance called *Rangfraa* or simply Rang i.e. the celestial. After death, the soul is believed to merge with the celestial (Rang) and the body with the nature or earth. However, this is true only for the liberated soul (*Jakhang*). In case of an unliberated soul, preferably called *Tchikkhaang,* it goes to the land of the dead, called *Honglowlom,* which they believe to be an intermediate stage of life (*The Second Coming of Rangfraa*, Vol. I, 2006).

The Ponthais of the study village also have beliefs regarding life after death. They are of the view that the welfare of people after death depends on the rituals carried out during funeral rites and sometimes on the possession of objects to be buried with them. It is believed that the ritual actions of living relatives and descendants, which if not performed correctly, may anger the dead who may send disease, disaster or death to the living. The dead sometimes visit their descendants and relatives in dreams where they are told about unclear debts or unreturned things and so forth. In response to such dreams, the relatives of the deceased do everything in accordance to the instructions they are given in their dreams. If in any case the dead person is seen to be unsatisfied with anything, he or she may torture the family members in their dreams. In earlier times, propitiations were made in the name of the deceased, but as per *Rangfraism,* it is not done now.

In the studied village, the role of guiding these practices belongs to the *Tengwa* (priest). He is also addressed as *Tengwa* by the villagers. He is the socially initiated and ceremonially inducted member of the religious organisation of the village. He is a full time ritual specialist as well as the custodian of the *Rangsomchem* (temple). It is believed that the *Tengwa* is the messenger between man and God, so his role is very important in the society. He performs all the religious activities of the village.

Along with the *Tengwa,* there are two other categories of persons who are believed to be endowed with spiritual power. They are called *Rang-samaal* and *Kayechu-samaal*. The *Rang-samaals* are the spiritual practitioners. The *Kayechus-samaal*, the spiritual leaders of the temple, attain their spiritual power from Almighty *Rangfraa* to bless and cure ailing people due to varied reasons. Firstly, to protect the lives of people who are loved by God, emergence of *Kayechuhood* takes place. Secondly, in order to eradicate evils, God (*Rangfraa*) emerges as *Kayechu*. They do not perform miracles, but predicts future events and heals patients, either directly or through medicines collected from the jungle. On Sunday service days, Lord *Rangfraa* is believed to come into the *Kayechu-samaals* and gives spiritual healing powers through which they heal the people suffering from any ailments. The *Rang-Samaal* and the *Kayechu-Samaal* occupy distinct places in the temples services.

Besides them, there are several other members of the temple who are responsible for various duties and responsibilities of the temple. They are President, Vice President, Secretary, Assistant Secretary, Preceptor, Assistance Preceptor, Treasurer, Social Service Secretary and Secretary of games, sports, culture and literary affairs. The Preceptor is also referred to as *Kayechu* who infuses the teachings of *Rangfraa* to the devotees.

When a Preceptor or *Kayechu* attains moral perfection, he or she becomes a *Kayechu-ayong, i.e., Ming Kayechu*. The President, Preceptor and *Mingkayechu* are the members of the administrative council of the temple who are selected on accounts of good moral behaviour and conduct with no age bars. The term of service of these members is generally three years. However, their terms can be extended on the basis of their performances. None of these positions is hereditary (not even that of *tengwa*). They are not paid for their services because they believe that service to god has no pay.

With regard to taboos observed by the experts, there are certain restrictions they have to follow such as they cannot take any intoxicants like tobacco, opium, and cigarette or any kind of alcoholic drink, nor betel nuts and leaves and so on. They are even prohibited to consume any items from a household where meat and rice-beer are prepared. If possible, these should be maintained by them daily.

On prayer service days, *i.e.*, Sundays, Wednesdays and Saturdays, they must however strictly follow these restrictions. The people of highest spiritual level, *viz.*, the *Rangsamaal*, *Mingkayechu* and *Kayechu-samaal* must strictly adhere to the restrictions. As regards personal rituals of the experts, they must undergo fasting and practise meditation twice or thrice in a week and a full fasting (12 hours) in a month.

Sacred objects may be the objects of cult, *i.e.*, objects that are worshipped or to which reverence is paid and ritual objects, *i.e.*, objects used in the rituals. Among the Ponthais of the study village, images and idols of Lord *Rangfraa* fall in the former category and vessel such as small pot of bell metal, stand on which incense sticks are lit, earthen lamp, etc., fall in the latter.

The language used in rituals is different from that in everyday use. The people of the village are found to practise their own Ponthai dialect as their ritual language.

The temple, *Rangsomhum* (also *Rangsomchem*), is the common place of worship of the people under study. Besides, every household has its respective altars of Lord Rangfraa where they worship and offer prayers.

Observances of religious rites are an integral part of the religious life of the Ponthais. Through prayer and general ritualistic activities, the people appeal to their supreme God Lord *Rangfraa* for aid and His blessings. The people of the village observe various rituals both in their common place of worship, *i.e.*, the *Rangsomhum/Rangsomchem* (temple) and in their households. Most of the responsibilities to perform the rituals belong to the *Tamwa* (priest). The other members of the Administrative Council of the temple such as the Preceptor also assist him in the performance of the rituals.

There are several rituals performed at the household level on various occasions, such as during construction of dwelling house, thunder strike, etc.

The Preceptor or the Priest (*Tamwa*) takes part in the ritual before construction of a dwelling house. At first, a few chunk of soil is taken in a plate from the spot identified for the position of the main health of the house. An image of *Rangfraa* is placed on a raised platform or a wooden board on that spot. The plate with soil is kept before the feet of *Rangfraa*. Then the owner of the house burns three incense sticks and prays by sprinkling holy water for three times. Some amount of soil from the plate is put back to the place wherefrom it was taken and some is spread over the area meant for construction of the house. Then the priest sprinkles holy water in the area by chanting prayer.

After the completion of the construction, the new house is purified by sprinkling holy water to the walls and roofs of the house by the priest or the owner of the house by around in anticlockwise direction by chanting prayer. This marks the end of the ritual during construction of a dwelling house.

Rituals are also performed for thunder strike. The rituals performed when there is thunder strike in a paddy field or farm somewhat differ from the rituals done in the case of a house or granary. The prayers (*Rumtam*), however, are the same in both the cases.

In case of paddy field, the priest, accompanied by the owner of the paddy field or farm and other fellow villagers, at first goes beneath the thunder strike tree and offers prayer to Lord *Rangfraa* that He has come in the form of thunder and seeks His blessings for their well-being. The priest (*Tamwa*) erects two wooden posts on the western side of the tree and pours *kham* three times and chants prayer. Then an egg is placed on one of the posts and on the other some quantity of rice is placed in a *ko*-leaf (*naap-phaan*) and some are thrown over it thrice. The ritual is performed in this sequence, but it must be kept in mind that the *naap-phaan* used must not be torn or half-eaten by worms and the egg must also be pure and local. After the completion of prayer, all the members go to the temple and offer prayer for the well-being and Almighty Rangfraa's blessings. The priest sprinkles holy water upon them to purify. In case of granary, the rituals of thunder strike are performed by the head of the family; and in case of a dwelling house, the priest carries out the ritual on their behalf. The priest sits on the western side of the post hit so that he faces towards east. He then lights three lamps (or candles) and incense sticks and places them near the post hit with thunder strike. An egg and some rice are placed in a *naap-phaan*. The priest then pours *Kham* near the post by chanting prayers and it is followed by purification of the house and also the members with holy water. With this, the ritual ends. This ritual is usually carried out in the morning hours before 12 o'clock. No taboos are observed on this account.

The Ponthais, at present, celebrate only one principal festival which they call "*Hahrong Moo*" (originally called *Kuh/Mo*). The *Hahrong Moo* is a festival associated with the harvesting. It is celebrated in the first week of October.

For carrying out the rituals of the *Hahrong Moo,* the people usually select a day except Saturday, Sunday and Wednesday (because these days are considered as the days for prayer service). The rituals are performed by the priest (*chamroomwa*) in the ritual ground (*hahrongrang*), a common area selected for observation of rituals during festivals of the village.

The rituals begin with offering of cooked rice and ginger in *ko*-leaf (*naam-phaan*) in the name of *chamdakhang* (their Goddess of wealth), their deities. The priest then pours *kham* on the *naam-phaans* with the offerings and prayers for the well-being and prosperity of the people. It is followed by a mass prayer being led by the Preceptor of the temple or the priest. Then a general prayer is done praising the Almighty Rangfraa for being able to have got blessed with a good harvest the previous year and seeking blessings for better harvest of crops in the years to come. This marks the end of the rituals and after the completion of the rituals a community feast is organised.

Every year, on a full moon day of November, the *Rangfraa* Day is celebrated at community level. Lord *Rangfraa's* idol was first installed on 4th of November, 1997, a full moon day. The installation of the idol is treated to be the second coming of *Rangfraa* in the form by the *Rangfraites,* that is why, this day i.e. every full moon day of November, is celebrated as *Rangfraa* Day. It is observed throughout the day and night. A vivid plethora of programmes is organised for the celebration of *Rangfraa* Day. Programmes are also made for the previous day and the day after that day.

Programmes of the previous day begin with the gathering of devotees at the temple (*Rangsomchem* or *Rangsomhum*), where they offer their prayers before Almighty Rangfraa and seek His blessings. It is followed by a host of events, which includes reports on the activities of the Rangfraa Faith Promotion Society, selection of special devotees of *Rangfraa* for the year based on the performance of the previous year, speech from the elders, Secretary General or President or representative of the temple's administrative council and so on.

On the *Rangfraa* Day, the programmes begin with the gathering of devotees at *Rangsomhum* (temple). The invited Chief Guest lights a lamp, followed by the clan members. Then the Secretary General or President or a representative performs purification. Then a mass opening prayer song is sung. And after a few events, a community feast is arranged. Several fun games are also organised during the later part of the day; and at night, a campfire is organised where people make merry and exchange gifts.

The next day begins with the prayer and worship at the temple, and prizes are distributed among the people for their participation in the various games and competitions. After that a cultural programme is being organised, followed by vote of thanks and a closing prayer song.

Like other communities of the world, the Ponthais of the study village also perform certain ritualistic activities in important transition that affects the entire community or society at the time of birth, marriage and death. As the ritualistic aspects associated with Ponthai marriage has already been discussed earlier in the paper, accounts of the rituals associated with birth and death have only been stated as follows:

> A new life begins with conception. Every married couple expects baby to keep their lineage going. And the Ponthais of the study village are no exception to it. During pregnancy, a woman has to follow certain restrictions such as she must not go outside in the evening and early in the morning (They believe that during these times, evil spirits roam about. That is why, a pregnant woman is forbidden to go out at these times so that both the mother and the to-be-born baby remain safe from the spirits). Belief in the existence of evil spirits is not accepted by the village people as per their faith, but in this respect for the well-being of the pregnant mother, it is generally accepted as an act of precaution. As per convenience of families expecting a child, prayers are offered in the temple for their well-being.

After the birth of a child, the family undergoes a pollution period. When the umbilical cord falls after five days or sometimes a week, the priest (*Tamwa*) is invited to the home for purification. The priest sprinkles holy water upon both the mother and the new-born, chants prayers and blesses them both. All the family members, along with the house, are to be purified. Only after purification, the mother and her baby can go to the temple to pray and seek blessings of Almighty *Rangfraa.* The parents of the child make offerings in the temple in the name of their child.

In case of twin-birth, the same ritual is performed. It is usually believed that the ritual is to be performed first to the first born baby, otherwise it would be a disgrace for the first born child. In this case also, the family members and the house are to be purified with holy water.

In the matter of stillbirth, a separate ritual is performed. All the members of the house are to be seated on a mat and the priest (*Tamwa*) should stand facing them and chant the prayer (*Rangtam*) and sprinkle holy water on them after each chanting, which is to be repeated for three times. The same prayer (*rangtam*) meant for thunder strike is chanted here. After that, the house is purified with holy water all around once with the same *rangtam*. No taboo is to be observed here.

As per convenience of the parents (usually after purificatory ritual), all the village people are invited for the name giving ceremony of the child. At first, *rumtam* is performed by the villagers for the good health of the child. A prayer is offered in the name of their household deity, *Chongrang,* as well. Then a name is given to the child after consulting the parents as well as the village people. It is then followed by a feast where *Kham* and meat form the main feast items.

A series of rituals is observed by the Ponthais as regards the death of an individual. They cremate as well as bury the dead. On the death of an individual, the dead body is first given a bath (with ordinary water) and taken to the kitchen. The head of the dead person is placed towards the exit of the kitchen. It is then covered with a white piece of cloth by the maternal uncle of the deceased person and the priest (*Tamwa*) sprinkles holy water three times over the corpse and prays for his or her eternal peace and hands it over to Lord Rangfraa. A fowl is killed in the name of the deceased, which is done by the priest (*tamwa*) or any other member of the family. It is killed only by the left hand, for they believe as because it is being done for the deceased the right hand is not used. In the meantime, the villagers prepare a bamboo stretcher (*thangchang*) and the corpse is placed on it. The priest (*tamwa*) once again sprinkles holy water over the corpse for three times and prays for the departed soul's peace.

On the second day, the villagers collect firewood. After coming back from collecting the firewood, all the belongings of the deceased person, including clothes, knives and other articles, are brought down the house by the maternal uncle and a prayer is done and an offering is made of cooked rice, money, beetle nut and beetle vine leaves, sugar, flattened rice, etc. It is again taken up to the house. This rite is called *Thalok* or *Kekdaklek*. Then a daughter-in-law of the same clan of the deceased person's family prepares a meal, which is offered to both the departed soul and the villagers who went for firewood collection. They are once again brought down and a post of bamboo or wood is erected by the villagers in the front yard of the house on which an egg is placed along with the belonging. Then they move around the post with knives (*dang*) and throw powdered rice in order to drive away evil spirits. On the right of firewood collection, a person (preferably middle aged or elderly person) is selected for bidding farewell to the departed soul. This rite of bidding farewell is called *Lumwang*. A young person is generally not preferred because it is believed that the dead one may take away his soul with him.

The elderly person bids farewell to the departed soul by saying that everything (including food, money, other necessary articles such as umbrella, hand fan, shoes, clothes, knives, rice beer (*kham*), some rice in a small bamboo tube and so forth) has been given for his or her journey to eternal abode. He also requests the departed soul not to look back on this earth and thus to be at peace. A farewell song is then sung by everyone.

On the third day, the dead body is brought to the cemetery or burial ground. The maternal uncle's role is important on that day. He carries the belonging of the deceased and leads the procession with the corpse. At the cemetery or burial ground, a few coins, being the cost of land, is thrown and *kham* is poured two times before burying or setting fire to the dead body. The *Tamwa* has no role in these rites. Any member of the deceased's family can take part in the cremation rite. After the cremation, a burnt bone is taken out from the ashes with the left hand and placed in the deceased person's plate (in which he or she used to have meal during lifetime), along with some coins and *Kham* poured over them, and then at the centre place where the cremation was done they are buried along with the dish. Four posts are erected around the four corners of that area. Near to it, a small hut of bamboo is built and a doll as a replica of the dead person of bamboo is also made and put inside the hut. The doll is dressed with white and red clothes. Near the hut, some offerings, including a jug of water, vegetables, fruits, knife, umbrella, etc., are hung beneath the hut. This can be done by any elderly or middle aged person. And after that everyone returns back home.

Coming back home, everyone gets fresh and then the room where the dead body was kept is cleaned. As per the capabilities of the families, a community feast is arranged in the name of the deceased person. Some people prefer to organise the feast after completion of a week.

On the next day, all the family members of the deceased person as well the villagers go to the temple to pray for the eternal peace of the departed soul. The *Tamwa* offers them holy water to drink and also sprinkles upon them for purification. He again goes to their house and purifies it with holy water and prays for the departed soul's peace. This marks the end of all the death rituals.

During the period of cremation, no person of the village go to work in their fields, as they believe that if they work, the paddy will die, resulting in famine. So, one day is observed as tools down, when works is stopped on the agriculture field. Even weaving of clothes is prohibited on such days. Only, after one day of the cremation or burial, people can go for their usual works. Moreover, when there is a death of an elderly person of the village, in honour and as a mark of respect, the entire village does not celebrate any festival for a year.

In case of immature or accidental death, the rituals and ceremonies are not performed like that of mature death. If an accidental death takes place, the dead body is buried on the same day without any kind of offerings or customs. The members of the deceased's family leave the house and shift to a temporary house. On the third day, in the temporary house, they purify themselves by performing the purificatory rite called *Mahrongphun*. They do not use the household articles on that day.

Nowadays, due to the social and religious movement, most of these ceremonies and rituals are no longer practised. All the deaths, both natural and accidental, are treated with equal and similar rites, and rituals are performed where purification with holy water is marked as an essential part.

The people of the study village traditionally believed in the existence of evil spirits whom they held to be responsible for their diseases and ailments as well as other misfortunes. And hence, in their endeavour of propitiating these spirits, they had to resort to sacrifice of animals such as fowls or other cattle and this formed a major aspect of the varied rituals performed by them. The traditional Ponthai people performed several rituals related to hunting and fishing, for minor as well as severely ill patients, and so forth.

Invoking the deities and spirits of the jungles, a few grains of rice (preferably white in colour) were thrown at the entrance of the jungle. Then all the members of the hunting group prayed for a successful hunt.

Similarly, before going for fishing, the people used to throw some rice grains near the banks of the river or near a pond (wherever they went for fishing). Throwing of rice of other colour was believed to anger the spirits. They performed this ritual of throwing rice before going for hunting or fishing to invoke the spirits and deities of the jungles and rivers. It used to be ways of letting them know that they have come to their abode in the jungles (or rivers) and pray to them to offer or provide them with a left-over animal/fish from their kingdom.

The ritual for a sick person suffering from chicken pox is simply done by wrapping some ashes in a *naap-phaan* and tying it with a spear made of bamboo which the *Romwa* (as well as the *Tengwa*) invoking the deity and praying for the recovery and well-being of the sick person throws in a nearby big tree. The sick person has to maintain a restriction not to go out of the house for three or four days until he or she recovers.

Traditionally, the Ponthai people performed a ritual named *'Rangsang'*, a death ritual performed after the completion of a year, which was considered as the final farewell of a deceased soul for eternal peace. The *Rangsang* was a five-day ritual generally performed in the winter season, preferably during March or April when there is blooming of flowers like marigold and orchid.

On the first day of the ritual, the bunch of hair which was cut out from the dead person's head at the timc of death and stored in a bamboo tube for a year was at first taken out. Holding the hair in his hand, the *Romwa* (or any elderly person of the family of the deceased) resorts to cut the bamboo tube into two halves with a knife (*dang*) carefully, not allowing them to fall. Then he places the knife on the ground (with which he did cut the bamboo tube into pieces) and keeps the two bamboo halves upon the knife vertically and then releases them. He used to do this for three consecutive times. In each of the times, the manner in which the bamboo pieces did fall was carefully seen. If they fell in similar ways, *i.e.,* with front and front sides up or back and back sides up, it was considered to be a bad omen. But, if they fell with one side up and one side down, it was regarded as a good omen.

Followed by that, an effigy representing a model of the dead person was being made with a bamboo basket, decorated with white and red clothes and taking a king of plant's leaf which they call *Tingniko* and some strands of hair of the deceased the hair of the effigy was being tied. The ritual of the first day ended with this.

The next day, the effigy was being taken for a stroll around the village by some of the family members of the deceased and a few villagers. On the third and fourth days, the village people are entertained with a feast where pork and rice beer (*Kham*) are offered. People used to sing and dance and enjoy the feast in the name of the deceased person. The songs which were sung on that day were not ordinary songs. Those were simple conversation between the two people, one of whom acts as the dead person and the other as a fellow villager. The conversation was about whether he (the man acting or pretending to be the deceased) had a proper look at the village before his death or not and the likes.

On the third day, a small offering of *kham wa*s hung near the window of the expired person's house in the name of the departed soul. Unknowingly, if anyone consumed this hung *kham,* it was considered to be a good sign for success in fishing and hunting.

And then finally, on the fifth day of the ritual, the effigy was to be kept in the burial ground. This marked the end of the *Rangsang* ritual.

The adoption of the new system of worship and prayer by the people of the study village has resulted in deviation from many of these traditional beliefs as well as ways of performing rituals. The belief in the existence of evil spirits no longer exists and as such most of the traditional rituals performed for the well-being of the people lack the concept of animal sacrifice for the propitiation of the spirits. Even now, for the recovery of ailing people, prayer to God is done, but neither food nor drinks are offered to God, for the people now believe that the question of offering these to God does not arise for He is purely celestial, hence, perfect and complete in itself and, therefore, neither food or drinks are offered to Him nor are animals sacrificed.

The *Tamwa* now purifies the households with holy water and chants different prayers for the well-being of the people at different occasions. The ritual of chicken pox is performed at present as well. However, the hunting and fishing rituals as well as *Rangsang* are no longer in practice. Sacrifice of animals on the occasions of marriage ceremonies is not practised at present. The rituals of marriage are now rather simply carried out with prayers and few other customs completely devoid of animal sacrifice.

There are certain taboos which are being followed by the people of the villages in various occasions. When the *Tamwa* performs any ritual in a household, there is prohibition of going to agriculture field for works on that day. In case of ritual performed for the recovery of a sick person, after the ritual is performed the sick person is not allowed to get down of the house for two or three days until he or she recovers. Outsiders are also not allowed to visit that particular household on the next day of ritual. In order to signify that, a green branch of a tree named *Midmung Wang* is put in front or near the steps of the house.

In case of child birth, until the falling of umbilical cord of the new-born baby, the mother as well as the other members of the family cannot go to the temple. Menstruating women are not considered as polluted, but they cannot offer any of their offerings in the altar of the temple nor can they light lamp or incense sticks before it. They are, however, allowed to pray from a distant corner of the temple.

When any elderly person of the village expires, celebration of festive occasion is prohibited in the honour of the deceased. This, however, is not a strict imposition, but the people of the villages do it as a mark of respect. Beating drums in casual occasions apart from festival is prohibited.

In addition to these, eating of meat or fish prior to prayer service (especially Sunday service) is a taboo for the devotees. Besides, they are not allowed to enter the temple after resorting to any kind of alcoholic drink or intoxicants like tobacco, cigarette, opium, etc.

Conclusion

The Ponthai people of the Wagun Ponthai village are very humble and peaceful who have their own values and customs of marriage. Earlier, the concept of divorce was absent among the them, however, nowadays, divorce cases, though rarely, are found in the village. This might account as one of the significant changes in the sphere of Ponthai marriage. According to the norm of the Ponthais, both the husband and wife can initiate a divorce. The *Ngung thut* (village council) of the village looks upon the matter.

Although certain changes have taken place due to their newly adopted religious system, still many of their traditional customs are continued to be practised by them. Their religion is aptly marked by the adoption of a new system of worship and prayer, *i.e.*, *Rangfraism,* with observance of a vivid series of religious rites and rituals. Animal sacrifice is no longer the part of the religious activities of the people. It has been replaced with purification with holy water by the religious experts.

It can also very well be asserted that the *Rangfraa* faith is a syncretic entity because certain elements of syncretism have been observed during the study. Firstly, the design of the *Rangsomhum, i.e.*, the temple, has similarities with the temples or shrines of the major religions of the world, including Hinduism, Islam and Buddhism; the dome structure of the temple has been inferred from the similar structure of a mosque; the small structure of glass panes above the dome of the temple has similarities with the structure of a *Gurdwara*; the top portion of the dome is similar to a Buddhist monastery. Secondly, the very way of addressing their God as 'Lord' is also an inferred practice from Christianity as well as Buddhism. Moreover, the system of prayer has also been incorporated from Christianity.

The *Rangfraites* of the studied village have not given up their indigenous faith, while at the same time, impacts of Christianity have penetrated into a few portion of the Ponthai population. Believing strongly that if one loses one's own culture, one's traditional faith, one will lose one's own identity, they are found to still stick to or adhere to their indigenous faith system.

The villagers of Wagun Ponthai lead a simple way of life. Due to rapid modernisation, advancement in education and interaction with outside so-called modern world, certain changes and developments have been taking place in their socio-cultural life. We would like to urge upon for more empirical research works on such least known ethnic communities like the Ponthais of our ethnically rich North-East India. It would not only yield wide ethnographic data on them, but also open up new prospects of areas of study for the researchers.

References

Borooah, J., 2014, *Customary Laws of the Tangsas of Arunachal Pradesh: With Special Reference to their Land Holding System*, Labanya Press, Guwahati.

Dutta, P., 1959, *The Tangsas*, NEFA Administration, Shillong.

Mibang, T. and M.C. Behera, 2006, *Marriage and Culture: Reflections from Tribal Societies of Arunachal Pradesh*, Mittal Publications, New Delhi.

Patir, D., 1996-1997, *An Ethnographic Field Investigation Report on the Tangsas of Machum Village of Nampong in Changlang District of Arunachal Pradesh*, an unpublished M.Sc. Dissertation, Dibrugarh University, Dibrugarh.

Singh, K.S, 1995, *People of India: Arunachal Pradesh* (Vol. XIV), Seagull Books, Calcutta.

Sinha, R., 1977, *Religion and Culture of North-Eastern India*, Abhinav Publications, New Delhi.

The Great Third Coming of Rangfraa, 2013, Rangfraa Faith Promotion Society, Arunachal Pradesh, India.

The Second Coming of Rangfraa (Vol. I), 2006, Rangfraa Faith Promotion Society, Arunachal Pradesh, India.

Tripathy, B. and S. Dutta, 2008, *Religious History of Arunachal Pradesh*, Gyan Publishing House, New Delhi.

Chapter - 6

Death and Disposal among the *Sonowal Kacharis:* Some Observations

—Biplob Bhuyan and Anand Sharma

Introduction

Death is the termination of the biological function that defines a living organism. The word refers to both the particulars events and to the conditions that result thereby. The true natures of the latter have for millennia been a central concern of the world's religious traditions and of philosophical enquiries. Beliefs in some kind of afterlife or rebirth have been a central aspect of many religious traditions. In modern scientific enquiry, the origin and nature of consciousness has yet to be fully understood; any such view about the existence or non-existence of concourses after death therefore remains speculative.

Phenomena which commonly bring about that include prediction malnutrition accidents resulting in terminal injury and disease that of an entire species is known as extinction, concept of death is a key to human adjustment to the phenomenon. That world seems to refer to either the movement at which life ends or when the state that follows the life begin. However, determining when dead has occurred requires drawing precise complete boundaries between life and death.

Even death is not treated in the same way in the societies. The Judeo Christian tradition, for examine, views that period after form a linear perspective. Dead is considered to lead to a permanent existence in non-corporal spiritual state. To the Hindus, it is a part of cyclical process, and the spirits of the deceased will eventually be reborn.

Any of numerous ceremonial events, existing in all societies, mark the passage of an individual from special or religious status to another.

The term was coined by French anthropologist Arnold Van Gennep (1909). Many of the most important rites are concerned with the biological stages of life-birth, maturity, reproduction and death.

The Setting

The present paper attempts to focus death rituals among the Sonowal Kacharis of Kapahuwa village of Tengakhat, Dibrugarh District, Assam. This study reveals the respondents' opinion about the rituals related to normal death, suicide, infant death, and the death of pregnant women. The hamlet is approximately at 35 km distance from Dibrugarh.

Materials and Methods

The relevant data for the study was collected from the Kapahuwa village. The village posses a total of 186 households, out of which, one household belongs to the Ahom community, one household belongs to the Assamese caste population, and the remaining 184 households belong to the Sonowal Kacharis. The total population of the village is 927, out of which, the population of Sonowal Kacharis is 920 (99.24 per cent), where 467 (50.76 per cent) are males and 453 (49.24 per cent) are females. The population of the Ahom is four and the Assamese caste population is three. It is clearly evident that in spite of slightly heterogeneous, the population of Sonowal Kachari is distinctly predominant. The methods used in the field are Observation method, Survey schedule method, Interview method, Visual and photography. The data was collected from elderly and knowledgeable persons, during the month of March, 2013.

The People

Demographically, the Sonowal Kacharis form the third largest plain tribal group of Assam. They are chiefly found in the district of Dibrugarh. A few Sonowal Kachari villages are also found in Lakhimpur, Sibsagar, and Jorhat districts. They belong to the great Bodo group and nostalgically trace their close relationship with the Burmans of Cachar district, Bodo Kacharis of lower Assam district, and Dimasa of North Cachar Hill district, presently known as Dima Hasao district. In fact, it is difficult to draw exclusive ethnic line between the Bodo Kacharis and Sonowal Kacharis as both these sections originally come from the same stock like other Mongolians people of this region. The Sonowal Kacharis are short statured, flat nosed, almond-shaped eye, straight hair and scanty bearded people. It is believed that prefix Sonowal in the name of the tribe came to be used during the reign of Ahom kings when the Kacharis of upper Assam took to the trade of gold washers and collectors of gold particles.

The Kapahuwa village is inhabited by Sonowal Kacharis. As said by the village people, in ancient times, Kapahuwa was known as Siyang and was inhabited by different groups of people. But, due to the repeated floods, all the people of the village gradually eroded away. Later, during the eighteenth century, two of the Tepari families belonging to Sonowal Kacharis came from Jamirah, which is situated at about 50 km away from the present-day Kapahuwa village. They came in order to cultivate cotton plant (*Gossypium herbaccum*). After that, as time passed by, some people belonging to the same tribe from Dihingmukh, Kapahuwa, Dhemaji, and Bhekulajan came and settled there.

Different views were given by the villagers in relation with the significance and origin of the name of the village. According to some people, there were lots of *Kopou* (Dove) which were recreating in the village. Therefore, the village is known as Kapahuwa. Again, some believe that the significance of the name of the village can be traced back to the later part of the nineteenth century. During that period the place was known for the huge production of the *Kapah* (cotton: *Gossypium herbaccum*) and thus the village was named after it as Kapahuwa.

The Kapahuwa village is located at 286^0 W., 212^0 S.W., 33^0 N.E., 116^0 S.E., in the eastern part of the Dibrugarh district. The village is surrounded by Tengakhat Block in the east, Nokhangia in the west, Tengakhat town in the north and Buridihing in the south.

Present Study

The Sonowal Kacharis of Kapahuwa village have different rituals concerning the death. These are as follows:

- rituals related to normal death,
- rituals related to suicide,
- rituals related to infant death, and
- rituals related to the death of pregnant women.

These are discussed as below:

Rituals Related to Normal Death

The Sonowal Kacharis perform different rites and rituals in relation with the death. In case of a normal death, the dead body is covered in *changi* (a bamboo bier). After receiving the information of death, all the villagers gather at the house of the deceased. The *changi* is made according to the length of the person and it is made of only one bamboo plant and that bamboo plant is not used by the family members of dead person for one year. The body is kept in such a position that the head faces the east and the leg portion to the west. They put a copper coin inside the mouth of the deceased because they believe that he or she will need it for crossing the *Baitarani* River to heaven. After that, the deceased is brought to the courtyard of the house and the dead body is placed in the courtyard with the head towards the east and it is covered with white cloth. A paste is made from turmeric and black gram and it is applied to e bath the dead body. After that, a ritual called *Lakhimi luwa* is performed where one of the family members takesone small bunch of paddy from the *bhoral* and passes it through the left hand of the dead body and then this small bunch of paddy is again placed in the granary. This quality of paddy is not used for cultivation for three years. Then the dead body is placed on the pyre and new clothes are spread over the dead body. Besides the household members, the neighbours and inmates join in the disposal. After that all the family members bow down before the dead and sing a prayer meaning your and come today Editor, plz check, it makes no meaning???, you free us from all difficulties and be happy in your eternal abode. The family members do not sleep in that direction because they believe that life diminishes with the sun setting in the west. After coming back from cremation ground, the persons who carries the dead body are to take warmth of a fire in front of the dead person's house and then they can do other works.

Rituals Related to Suicide

Among the Sonowal Kacharis, if a man commits suicide in his house, one of the inhabitant members inform the villagers about the incident. The villagers then take the dead body into the courtyard, along with white clothes. Again, if a man commits suicide in the garden or in the jungle, the villagers cut the tree, under which the man has committed suicide, from the root because they believe that the tree is not favourable for other persons. This type of suicide is considered to be sinful. In such a situation, the deceased person is tied with a roof in the neck and is dragged in the ground and then is taken to the burial place. The dead body is buried like that of an animal. They don't perform funeral rites for his soul. But, on second or third day, they drink sacred water and also sprinkle it in the rooms of the household. The family members do not follow any rites and rituals in this suicide death.

Rituals Related to Infant Death

Among the Sonowal Kacharis, when an infant dies, it is buried but the child above seven years is cremated. When the child dies, one of the family members carries the dead body in a sheath of banana by wrapping it with a white cloth to the cremation ground. After arriving at the cremation ground, the villagers dig up a big pit in the east-west direction. When an infant dies, there is no such ritual as to observe fast for the purification of the family members. They do not perform any rites and rituals at the death of an infant. They simply purify themselves by the sacred water and sprinkle it in all the rooms of their households.

Rituals Related to the Death of Pregnant Women

After the death of a pregnant woman, the dead body is carried in pyre made by bamboo. They put a copper coin inside the mouth of her. They believe that in the crossing of the river to heaven, she will need it to give to the boat-man. After that, she is brought to the courtyard of the house and her body is placed in the courtyard with the head towards the west. A paste is made from turmeric and black gram which is applied to bath the dead body. After that a ritual called *lakhimi luwa* is performed by the family members. He takes a small bunch of paddy which is again placed in the *Bhoral* and this quality of paddy is not used for cultivation for three years. The dead body is placed on his change and it is carried by three kinsmen. After arriving at the place, by offering a coin in the name of land. A hollow with positive mark is digged up in the east and west direction. The change is built by using seven parts of woods and in between each part some special kind of wood, *i.e.*, *Kukura Thengia* and *maj* is used in each side of the pyre in parallel. Before the cremation of the dead woman, the fetus which is in mother's womb is separated from the womb. It is believed by the people that the two dead bodies cannot be cremated in the same pyre. After that the cremation of the woman is done. Her fetus is burned besides her cremation ground and before putting the dead body into the pyre, the person who has carried the dead body encircles the pyre seven times. After that the dead body is placed in the pyre in upward direction and some wood is placed over the dead body. Then her husband puts fire on the pyre and then the village members help in the cremation. After burning is over, by taking water in a pot it is thrown on the place of cremating and mustard seeds are sprinkled and planted a plantation tree on that place. After performing all this, they return to their home. After arriving at home, all the members take warmth of fire, which is placed at the gate, and sprinkle the cowdung water.

Conclusion

Death is considered to be natural phenomenon from which no living being can escape. Both burial as well as cremation system of the dead ones are practiced by the people. Death like illness, old age, disease, etc., is inevitable. The dead bodies are disposed by cremation or burial depending on the age or in accordance with the wish of the deceased person. But, in unnatural death such as lightning, snake bite, drowning, etc., the dead body is invariably buried. From the study, it was found that death rituals play a very significant role among the Sonowal Kacharis of Tengakhat. They have a strong traditional belief. Their socio-religious practices show all the ingredients of their traditions, which are strongly and strictly practised, irrespective of the modern influences on the other fields of their life.

References

Barua, B.K., 1969, *A Cultural History of Assam* (Lawyer Guwahati), Guwahati.

Bordoloi, B.N. and G.C. Sharma Thakur, 1988, *The Sonowal Kacharis in the Tribes of Assam*: *Part-II*, Tribal Research Institute, Guwahati, pp. 77-80.

Singh, Mutum Bokul, 1991, "Death and Disposal in the Maram Tribes of Manipur", *Bulletin of Dept. of Anthropology,* Vol.16-17, Dibrugarh University.

Sonowal, G.C., 1964, *Sonowal Kacharis in Assam Janajati*, Guwahati, Layrs Book Stall.

Chapter - 7

Tourism and Oral Tradition; Encountering Economy: A Study among the *Konyak Nagas of Longwa Village of Mon District in Nagaland*

—*Dibyajyoti Das*

Introduction

Oral tradition reveals and helps us understand humanity. Communities throughout time and space have created stories, songs, dances, music, rituals, customs, festivals and various material artistic genres to make sense of and to celebrate the world and the human condition. Our expression flourishes when tradition connects communal wisdom with innovative inspiration. As its name indicates, folklores involve both "folk" (a group of people) and "lores" (creative expression). Every community has an oral history, which is transferred from one generation to another; it is referred to as oral tradition as it doesn't have any written records. With the passage of time, the oral tradition always loses its fact(s) and it keeps on changing from time to time as it passes from one to another.

The Konyak Nagas, known for their ferocious practice of head hunting and tattooed face, also referred to as 'Tatood Nagas', are known for their rich oral history and folk lores associated with head hunting practices. The oral tradition, myth and numerous folklores associated with this violent practice have always been a wonder and interest to the outsiders. As we have mentioned earlier, the oral tradition or folk tales change from time to time for various reasons. In the same way, the oral folk tales of the Konyaks had also changed a lot. In this paper, I have made an attempt to study the reasons for the change in folktales associated with head hunting practices. It was seen that the tourist has an impact on the change in the oral tradition of the Konyaks and in the meantime their oral tradition is also becoming a medium of fulfilling their economy. Let us try to find out how this phenomena are taking place. With the help of two major objectives, which I have mentioned in the next paragraph, I have tried to study the problem. This paper is an outcome of a fieldwork carried among the Konyaks of Mon district in Nagaland.

Objectives

1. To examine the effect of tourism on the oral tradition of the Konyaks of Longwa village.
2. To understand how tourism and oral tradition are helping in fulfilling the economy of the people of Longwa village.

Universe of Study

The study was conducted among the Konyak Nagas of Longwa village of Mon District in Nagaland, India. The village is situated at the tri-junction of Arunachal Pradesh, Nagaland and Myanmar. The village lies exactly on the Indo-Burma border, rather it is scattered into both the nations. The village chief *"Angh's"* house is in such a location that it splits longitudinally between India and Burma. There is a saying that, the chief dines in India and sleeps in Burma (the present-day Myanmar).

Methodology

The present study is a descriptive research work based on both primary and secondary resources. The primary, rather first hand, information was collected during my fieldwork among the Konyak Nagas of Nagaland in the year 2013. The methods applied for gathering information was observation, semi-structured and unstructured interview with open ended questions, and case studies were also collected. The sampling technique that was used for identifying the key informants was purposive sampling and then snowball sampling technique was followed to identify the other informants. Other than these techniques, informal talks with the people were also done during my stay in the field. Information was also gathered from other secondary sources, like books, journal articles and the internet.

The Encounter

The Konyak Nagas are of two groups, namely; *"Thendu"* and *"Thentho";* the former is tattooed faced and the latter is white faced. The Konyaks are regarded the largest out of the sixteen major tribes of the state with tattooed face and passionate practice of head hunting. They are mostly spread in the Mon district of the state of Nagaland. The name

'Konyak' is derived from the local word *"Keniak"*, meaning man, during the British rule in India. The Konyaks of all the villages in Mon district had traditions regarding the origin and migration of their forefathers, and many of these myths refer also to the circumstances of the foundation of the villages. According to one tradition, the ancestors of the majority of the Konyaks came from a mountain, called *Yengyudan,* situated to the south of the present Konyak territory, *i.e.*, the village Longwa in Mon district of Nagaland.

The village Longwa, where I conducted my fieldwork, lies exactly at the Indo-Burma border, rather it is scattered into both the nations. The village chief *Angh's* house is in such a location that it splits longitudinally between India and Burma. There is a saying that, the chief dines in India and sleeps in Burma/Myanmar. The *Angh* was asked by the then officials of both the nations during the independence of India from British rule that with whom they (the Konyaks of Longwa) would like to stay. At this the *Angh* decided that on the left hand, he would hold Burma, on the right hand, he would hold India, and on his back, he would carry the Nagas, and he does not want to leave anyone. Because of these reasons, the village Longwa is set free to both the nations. Since then the Longwa village has become an interesting place for the outsiders as "one community into two nations". The geographical location of the village is also a fascinating one as it lies in the hill top that separates two nations.

The Konyak Nagas, according to McCosh, " are the wildest and most barbarous of the hill tribes, and looked upon with dread and horror by the neighbours of the plains who considered them as ruthless robbers and murderers". The head hunting practice and then the tatooed body and face make the Konyaks different from other Naga tribes. There are various motives behind the head hunting practice of the Konyaks. According to Haimendorf, it is the desire to acquire the fertility promoting force of human blood and the power emanating from human skulls. All the parts of the head were not equally valued. The parts around the eyes and the jaw were valued the most. This suggests that the connection between skull and soul substance was thought of in very concrete terms, and that a captured head was by no means regarded merely as a symbol of a victory over an enemy (Haimendorf, 1969).

Whenever a head is brought to the village, everyone, especially the elders, welcomes the hunter, which is followed by various rites and rituals; some of them are like smashing of raw eggs on the head by the clan members, pouring of rice beer into the mouth of the dead and many more. The senior males carry the head into the village and to the chief *Angh's* place, where they celebrate with dance, and then it is taken to the *morung* where the women wait with water in bamboo culmn's to wash the hunters. Towards the evening, the head is fastened to one of the main posts of the *morung,* followed by merry making and dance of the warriors. After a month or so, a grand feast is arranged to mark the final disposal of the head, either into the *morung* or in the ancestral house of the clan of the head-hunter (Haimendorf, 1969). The practice of head-huntng no more exists; it had come to an end with the advent of British rule. The advent of Christianity also played a vital role in overcoming this dreadful exercise of head-hunting.

The village Longwa is well-known for the head-hunting practices and its location with natural splendour which had added more charm to it and, on the other hand, as it is located exactly at the Indo-Burma border and the village belonging to both the nations, and the people of Longwa having free movement to either of the nations. For the above-quoted reasons, the outsiders/tourists are always curious to visit Longwa and know something about the head-hunting practices and the folklores and tales associated with it. The Konyaks have two major festivals; both are related to agriculture, namely "*Aolingmonyu*" celebrated during April 1st to 6th every year. This is a spring festival celebrated after sowing the seeds in the field. It is celebrated for seeking blessings from God for a better harvest. The other festival is *"Laolongmo"*. This is celebrated after the harvest, generally falls in the month of August. The former is a well known festival of the Konyaks. During this time, the foreign tourists visiting Longwa raise to a very good number. Other than this time, Longwa is also being visited by the tourists throughout the year, especially during winters.

The tourists are always excited and passionate to know the oral history and folklores and stories associated to head-hunting practices. At the time of my fieldwork, there were a few head-hunters in the village who could recount their experiences, but the oral tales related to those experiences, which have tailed from one generation to the other, have an important place in the society. After spending some time in the field, I realised that the stories associated with the head-hunting practices and other Konyak folklores have changed a lot and there are various reasons for the change. It is obvious that if one doesn't have a written record, then it is apparent that it will change with the change of time with different versions being interpretated by different interpretators. However, another reason that has come up is that, a few villagers had used their folk tradition as a medium of fulfilling their economy because the foreign tourists pay a handsome amount as a ransom after listening to the stories. And now it has become a practice of villagers to earn money in a short cut way. If they are being paid more, the story continues and if they are not paid the stories are cut short.

During my fieldwork, I tried to collect some of the folklores related to head-hunting practices. In the beginning I could not collect the same as I denied to pay, but after spending some time in the field and becoming a known face in the village, I finally managed to get some.

Case I : I asked why they are operating the stories to earn money? My informant, a man of around forty years of age, said that it is one of the best ways of earning money because the foreign tourists do not hesitate to pay and if we are earning money by just narrating some stories then why not make it more interesting to earn some more.

Case II : My next informant was also a man of around forty years of age. I asked him, Are not they doing bad to their society by making stories of their ancestors to earn money? At this he replied that they do not tell wrong stories to all. There are many people in the village all are not the same; some are earning money and some are earning good name, but the tourists are for a very short period of time, they are interested in listening and people entertain them and in return they earn something. But if somebody who is really interested in such information, they will cross-check the information and will spend some time in the village. But for tourist who comes and goes, it doesn't matter. He also said that there are very few people in the village who actually know something about the head-hunting practices; all others are not actual. He also said that if some poor fellow is earning something then let him earn.

Discussion and Conclusion

The village Longwa has a good number of tourists from all around the world, especially during the festival time. As outsiders, they are always curious to know whatsoever that is related to the head-hunting practices of the Konyaks and the only possible way to know this is through oral tradition. One has to narrate stories, incidents, etc. relaed to it and the outsiders generally use to pay a kind of ransom to the story teller which has now become a way of earning money for the daily livelihood. There is a rich oral tradition among the Konyaks, which has come from generation to generation, but in due coarse of time, the actual oral tradition has changed to a great extent because of various reasons and one among this is what we have discussed in this paper. It is obvious that with the change of time, the oral tradition also changes with different interpretors and interpretations. The villagers are aware that some among them are earning out of this practice, but they think that if a poor person is earning something by giving his time and energy and, at the same time, he is helping the outsider and entertaining him, nothing is wrong in it. They do not consider this way of earning money as something wrong because it is not always that they want to earn money by telling wrong tales. They usually go for those tales that they have known from their older generation, but yes, sometimes there is greed when they are paid handsomely by the outsiders. There are also people who love to narrate their history and do not accept any kind of ransom. It is not that they are harming their tradition, rather they are aware how to protect their rich oral tradition. From all these, we see that tourism has a positive as well as negative impact on the oral tradition, however, the rich oral tradition of Konyaks of Longwa in Nagaland is helping them to earn their livelihood too through tourism.

References

Furer-Haemendorf, C.V, 1938. "The Morung System of the Konyak Nagas, Assam", *Journal of the Royal Anthropological Institute*, 68:349-378.

Furer-Haemendorf, C.V, 1953. *The Naked Nagas,* Thacker, Spink and Co. Ltd., Calcutta.

Furer-Haemendorf, C.V, 1969. *The Konyak Nagas, An Indian Frontier Tribe,* United States of America.

Segal, R, 1999: *Theorizing About Myth: Amherst,* University of Massachusetts Press, Massachusetts.

www.Nagalandofficialweb_page.

Chapter - 8

Ethnographic Profile of the *Tawang Monpa* Tribe of *Arunachal Pradesh*

—Jyotismrita Phukan

Introduction

India, the federal state, is composed of twenty nine states and seven union territories. Of the twenty nine states, Arunachal Pradesh occupies the most north-eastern position among the other states of India. Arunachal Pradesh, the land of the dawn, possess a total population of 1,38,3727 (Census of India, 2011). The state nourishes different peoples in its hilly terrains. It is the home of twenty six major tribes and 110 sub-tribes and minor tribes. According to the census 2011, the Scheduled Tribe (ST) population constitutes 68.8 per cent of the total population and rest belongs to the other categories (non-APST). The state is one of the linguistically richest regions. There are about as many as 50 distinct languages, in addition to innumerable dialects and sub-dialects. There are 18 districts in the state. The state can be roughly divided into a set of semi-distinct cultural spheres on the basis of tribal identity, languages, religion and material culture such as the Tibetic area bordering Bhutan in the west. The Thanyi area is the centre, the Mishmi to the east, the Tai area bordering Myanmar and the Naga area to the south and here one finds population of related tribes speaking related languages and sharing similar traditions. So also there is a large number of migrants from diverse areas of India. There is a sudden rise in the literacy rate from 54.74 per cent in 2001 to 66.95 per cent in 2011.

Due to its rich cultural heritage, scholars show their interest in exploring these tribes from time to time. There are many anthropological studies conducted by different scholars. Those studies are very much helpful to all the researchers who are very new to the field.

The People

The Tibetic area of Arunachal Pradesh comprises the Monpa tribes. Monpas are a major tribe of Arunachal Pradesh. It is one of the most populous tribes of Arunachal Pradesh and is considered as one of the major tribal communities in the entire region. Monpas inhabit the high altitude region so also the mountainous region of Bomdila in West Kameng district. Tawang is a centre place for most of the Monpa tribes. The Monpa tribe is subdivided into six subgroups depending on the variation of their inhabitance- (1) Tawang Monpa, (2) Dirang Monpa, (3) Lish Monpa, (4) Bhut Monpa, (5) Kalaktang Monpa and (6) Panchen Monpa.

Tawang Monpa inhabits the hilly terrain of Tawang district. Tawang Monpa is one of the subgroups of the Monpa tribe. Dhar (1984) has stated that the Tawang Monpas call themselves Brahmi Monpa, who differ from the rest of the Monpas with regard to their language and culture. They belong to the Tibeto-Burman family of languages. The Monpas speak Tshangla, which is also understood by the Bhutanese and Tibetans as they share similar origin. Of the total population of Monpas, *i.e.*, 50,000, out of which 20,000 live in Tawang district, where they constitute about 97 per cent of the district population. The others are scattered in the West Kameng district and small number in the East Kameng district. The Monpas are Buddhist by religion and the Tawang Monastery, which is Asia's second largest monastery, is considered as the fountainhead of their spiritual life. The people of this tribe are generally courteous, friendly, gentle and industrious. The tribe is known for their artistic creations, including beautiful Thangka painting, carpet making, weaving and wood carving. They depend on the nature for various products. Dam and Hajara (1981) have carried out a vivid discussion on the Monpas, the utility of various plant resources in the life style of the Monpa is undeniable. Their research also shows the utilisation of diverse animals as well as their byproducts in several ways.

Materials and Methods

The research is based on the data collected through various ethnographic techniques. The techniques applied here includes the interview with key-informants in the community (such as goan bura, leaders, teachers). Questionnaire and observation methods are also being used as per the recruitment. As per the study, Tawang Monpa tribal group residing in the Tawang District of Arunachal Pradesh has been taken into concern.

This study deals with the demographic aspects of a high altitude Monpa sub-group, the Tawang Monpa, of Tawang district, Arunachal Pradesh.

For the sake of the present study, the Tawang Monpas residing in Tawang town and its surrounding areas were considered. The altitude of Tawang town is approx. 9990 ft. Altogether 500 Tawang Monpa households were covered.

Result and Discussion

Age and sex distribution:

Populations differ greatly in the way their members are distributed in various age and sex categories. Age and sex distributions are the building blocks that construct the composition of a population. The age structure and sex distribution of Tawang Monpa people as on May, 2013 are presented in Table 8.1. Of the total population, an excess of males relative to female is observed. The number of total males is 1077 and the number of females is 1005. As the age increases, the number of individuals gradually increases among the males from 0-4 years to 25-29 years age group. The number of individuals gradually decreases from 30-34 years age group in the same sex. Whereas, among the females, the number of

Table 8.1: Distribution of population by age and sex: Tawang Monpas

Age group (in years)	*Males*		*Females*		*Total*		*Sex Ratio*
	No.	*Per cent*	*No.*	*Per cent*	*No.*	*Per cent*	
0-4	62	5.76	62	6.17	124	5.96	1000.00
5-9	75	6.96	70	6.97	145	6.96	933.33
10-14	73	6.78	70	6.97	143	6.87	958.90
15-19	102	9.47	100	9.95	202	9.70	980.39
20-24	117	10.86	154	15.32	271	13.02	1316.24
25-29	141	13.09	136	13.53	277	13.30	964.54
30-34	86	7.98	72	7.16	158	7.59	837.21
35-39	90	8.36	94	9.35	184	8.84	1044.44
40-44	62	5.76	62	6.17	124	5.96	1000.00
45-49	74	6.87	89	8.85	163	7.83	1202.70
50-54	63	5.85	37	3.68	100	4.80	587.30
55-59	37	3.44	26	2.59	63	3.02	702.70
60-64	30	2.79	7	0.70	37	1.78	233.33
65-69	17	1.58	11	1.09	28	1.34	647.06
70-74	11	1.02	6	0.60	17	0.82	545.45
75-79	25	2.32	5	0.50	30	1.44	200.00
80-84	8	0.74	3	0.30	11	0.53	375.00
85-89	3	0.28	-	-	3	0.14	-
90 & above	1	0.09	1	0.10	2	0.10	492.31
Total	**1077**	**100.00**	**1005**	**100.00**	**2082**	**100.00**	**933.15**

individuals gradually increases from 0-4 years to 20-24 years age group. The number of individuals gradually decreases from 25-29 years age group in this sex. It is interesting to note that while 30 individuals are recorded among the males in 60-64 years age group, only seven individuals are recorded among the females in this age group.

Social and political organisation in the society

Monpas are simple, gentle and courteous people. The society of the people of Tawang was highly democratic and casteless. Society was patriarchal with primogeniture as the fundamental law for inheritance (Dutta, 2000, p.13). The traditional society of the Monpas was administered by a council of six members, known as Kenpo or the Abbot of Tawang, locally known as Trukdri. There is a specific Gaon Burah in every village who is appointed to look after the villagers and petty cases were decided by the village council. Regarding every aspect of religious activities, the Lamas are placed as their Godfathers. The social customs are also performed by the Lamas of Buddhist monasteries and they even performed rituals in homes, in society and in Gompas. In the case of education, monasteries performed vital role in imparting education among the Monpas, which was based on spiritual and religious teachings. There are also other educational institutes (both Govt. and Private) for pursuing education. The life of the Monpas is largely centered on the Tawang Monastery, which is not only regarded for learning, but also as the centre for Buddhist morality and culture, and it has worked as a symbol of peace and unity towards all people of Tawang.

Though they are basically patrilineal group, but the neo-local mode of residence is also prevalent. They belong to the Lamaistic school of Tibetan Buddhism of the Mahayana sect. Buddhist beliefs and traditions play an important role in the fabric of Monpa society. The man is the head of the family and he is the one who takes all decisions. But females also play equal part in decision making. There is no strict preference for a baby boy or a baby girl. However, in some cases, it is seen that preference for a baby girl is more common as she is more humble and lovable for the family.

Customs

Monpas is an endogamous group. Child marriages are unusual. Widow remarriage is also prevalent. Monogamy is commonly practiced. The people are very much loyal to each other. They show rare interest in polygyny. Marriages are fixed through negotiation and mutual consent. Though

Monpas are patriarchal social group, both patrilocal and matrilocal residences are seen. After marriage, it is the decision of the couple itself whether to live with the boy's parents or the girl's. They can also live separately. However, majority are joint families.

Food Habits

The state is rich in traditional foods and beverages and methods of processing various forest and agricultural products. The community prepares different fermented foods, boiled foods, beverages and nutritionally rich traditional foods from various indigenous crops, forest products and meat of both wild and domesticated animals. Those foods are very rich in nutrition and also benefit the tribe to cure different diseases. The diet of the Tawang Monpas consists of pulses, fish, meat, vegetables and bung chung (local beer brewed from maize, rice, millet, wheat or buck wheat). Distilled liquor known as arrah is also consumed by them. Millet is the staple food for the majority of the people. They take tea in typical Tibetan style, *i.e.,* tea mixed with butter and salt. Some specific foods are also provided on some of their cultural and social occasions to their guests. Local panner, dry meat of yak, solu krepu (dried boiled green chilly), blue green algae, ghee and churpi (paneer from yak milk) are popular foods. It is seen that the presence of chrupi in Monpa house is an indicator of social status. Yak meat and yak ghee are considered as precious food of these high altitude inhabitants. The fresh yak ghee is used for the preparation of salt tea. They are basically non-vegetarian and hence eat beef, pork, mutton and the meat of fowl and yak. The inhabitants are very fond of momos and thukpas. Generally, three types of momos are made—*pattan momo* (mann patta, lai patta, cabbage, etc.), *Chura momo* (cheese momo), and *Sha momo* (meats of chicken, pork, etc.). The fruits consumed by them are oranges, peaches, pomegranates, apples and sugarcane.

Education and occupation

Though illiteracy is seen among the Tawang Monpa, but literacy rate cannot be ignored. There are adequate facilities for primary and secondary schools. Nowadays, impact of education has changed their mind-set, which helped them to utilize their right position and status in the society. Because of it, many of them are employed, which has improved their economic condition. Monpa women are also not lacking behind. The parents are now willingly to send their daughters to schools for educational purposes, which has improved the status of women in the Monpa society.

Tables 8.3A and 8.3B Editor, plz check, there are no tables showing educational status of husbands and wives??? show the educational status of the husbands and wives in Tawang Monpa population. More than 30 per cent of the husbands are non-literate in this population. Highest per cent (40.65) of the husbands is high school level educated. A considerable per cent (9.15) of them is college and above level educated. In the category of primary level education, they recorded lowest percentage (5.89).

Table 8.2: Educational Status–Males and Females

Educational Status	*Male*		*Female*	
	No.	*Per cent*	*No.*	*Per cent*
Non-literate	157	31.91	202	41.56
Primary (I-IV)	29	5.89	20	4.12
High School (V-X)	200	40.65	179	36.83
Higher Secondary (XI-XII)	61	12.40	55	11.32
College and above	45	9.15	30	6.17
Total	**492**	**100.00**	**486**	**100.00**

Occupationally, the Monpa tribes are primarily agriculturalist and practise both shifting and permanent types of cultivation. Breeding of cattle forms an integral part of the Monpa farming economy. In the Tawang region, some villages lay at an altitude of roughly 10,000 feet where breeding of yak is far more important. They domesticate yaks, cows, horses, goats, sheep, pigs, donkeys, mules and fowls. Bhende and Kanitkar (1991) say that surroundings of a man and his occupation from which he earns his livelihood play an important role in his health habits. A man's occupation is related to his income. Both these income and education may influence his food habits and housing condition. Nowadays it is seen that Monpas have engaged themselves to various occupations like shop keeping, making brooms and bamboo products, crafting, weaving, day labour, etc., while some are engaged in private and government organisations.

Table 8.3A: Occupational Status–Husbands

Occupational Status	*No.*	*Per cent*
Agriculturists	116	23.58
Business	121	24.59
IV Grade Employees	67	13.62
Office Assistants	58	11.79
School/College Teachers	24	4.88
Skilled Workers	35	7.11
Labourers	57	11.59
Miscellaneous Activities	14	2.84
Total	**486**	**100.00**

Table 8.3B: Occupational Status–Wives

Occupational Status	*No.*	*Per cent*
Housewives	376	77.37
Service	40	8.23
School/College Teachers	19	3.91
Business	37	7.61
Miscellaneous Activities	14	2.88
Total	**486**	**100.00**

Occupational status of husbands and wives is shown in Tables 8.3A and 10.3B, respectively. The same is shown graphically in Figures 10 and 11. Editor plz check, there are no figures????

More than 23 per cent of the husbands are agriculturists and 24 per cent are engaged in business. A good percentage of them are IV grade employees (13.62), office assistants (11.79) and labourers (11.59). Among the wives, more than 77 per cent are housewives. In service and business, 8.23 per cent and 7.61 per cent wives are engaged.

Lifestyle and Economy

The Monpas live in permanent houses. They have their own land and property. They construct their houses with wood and stone masonry. The floor is made with wood as it warms the room temperature. Walls are being constructed with stones and linings of wooden planks. The roof is made with bamboo matting. Modern houses made of cement and brick are also seen in the surroundings nowadays.

Religion

The religion of the Tawang Monpa is basically Buddhism and they profess Mahayana Buddhism. The Monpas are deeply religious-minded. Their social and religious life centres around the Gompas (Buddhist monastery). It is seen that all the social and religious myths emanate from those Gompas. In the Monpa village, it is seen that there is a sanctuary consisting of several flat stones or a stone structure used for burning of incense where rites arte performed. The religious practices of the Monpas are somewhat familiar to the Bon religion of the Tibetans. In addition to the religion, the monasteries and nunneries also serve as institutions of education. In those institutes are taught the noble teachings of Lord Buddha. The students in those institutes are known as Lama. They are also taught Sanskrit and Tibetan languages, thangka paintings and other disciplines. Those monasteries are the symbol of peace and unity for all the people of Tawang. Monpas never sacrifice animals for rituals, instead they use the animal products for rituals. History tells that before the advent of Buddhism, they used to follow the Bon religion of the Tibetans.

Summary

The Tawang Monpas are one of the sub-groups of the Monpa tribe, who are high altitude people. They inhabit the hilly terrain of the Tawang district. It experiences moderate to heavy rainfall, and in the winter it experiences frost and snowfall. This study deals with some demographic aspects of the Tawang Monpas of Tawang district, Arunachal Pradesh. For the sake of present study, the Tawang Monpas residing in Tawang town and its surrounding areas were considered. The altitude of Tawang town is 9990 ft. Altogether 500 Tawang Monpa households were covered. The field work was conducted during the month of May, 2013.

It is seen that the growth of tourism has immensely helped the Monpa tribe to emerge as a friendly community to the outsiders. Due to their interaction with the outside world, the youth have managed to go for further studies and also engaged in different resourceful jobs. But in spite of all these modernisation, the Monpas have never accepted to replace their age-old traditions. Still their religious life is affiliated with the Buddhism and Tawang Monastery. Lamas are still placed as their Godfathers and they were given the authority of any religious activities. It is also seen that no matter what their educational or occupational status is, they engage themselves in various household activities like farming,

Hence, we can conclude that it is our responsibility to give much more focus on the mesmerising beauty of Tawang and its unique culture, so that the impressive high elevation scenery makes Tawang as the most magnetize tribal destination.

Concluding with Dr Verrier Elwin's description of the Monpas as;

"Gentle, friendly, courteous, industrious, good to animals, good to children, you see in the Monpas the influence of the compassionate Lord Buddha on the ordinary man."

References

Limakumla, *Asian Journal of Multidisciplinary Studies,* March (2014), "Some Aspects of Buddhism among the Monpas of Tawang in Eastern Himalaya".

Kar, R. K. (1980). "Arunachal Pradesh and Her People: A Preliminary Appraisal", *Journal: Vanyajati*, Vol. xxxviii, No. 3, July, New Delhi.

Sarkar, Niranjan (1980). *Buddhism among the Monpas and Sherdukpens.* Shillong: Directorate of Research, Government of Arunachal Pradesh.

Singh, S. (1995). *People of India, Arunachal Pradesh.* Calcutta: Seagull Books. Vol. xiv.

Norbo, Leki. (2004). "Tcharen (Rent for Grassland) practice in Domkho- A Monpa village", in Mibang, Tamo and Behera, M.C. (ed.). *Dynamics of Tribal Villages in Arunachal Pradesh.* New Delhi: Mittal Publications, pp. 191-196.

Ved Prakash. Encyclopaedia of North-east India, Vol. 3. Atlantic Publishers & Distributors. pp. *1206–7.*

Blench, Roger (2014). *Sorting out Monpa: The Relationships of the Monpa Languages of Arunachal Pradesh.*

Greener Pastures (2014). *The Monpa Tribe of Arunachal Pradesh, Celebrating Indigenous Peoples.*

PART - II

REPRODUCTIVE HEALTH BEHAVIOUR

Chapter - 9

Social Problems and Stigmas Related to Women Mental Illness: A Study of Patients Admitted at Assam Medical College and Hospital, *Dibrugarh, Assam*

—Afsana Shabnam and Somnath Sonowal

Introduction

Mental health

Mental health implies a state of mind. Mental illness is a condition of mind or a health condition that refers to one's imbalance status of mental health. It disrupts entire functioning of human mind. In Indian languages, the word *'maanasik'* is usually translated into English as 'mental'. It originates from the word 'man' which includes both emotional and intellectual capacities. However, the English word 'mental' refers to the latter and may neglect or occlude the emotional aspect. This is not just a linguistic issue because the word 'mental' has a stigma attached to it in India due to its association with colonial institutions such as mental asylums and inhuman treatment. When women suffer these disorders, they are likely to suffer far greater discrimination and stigma in the areas of life such as marriage and employment than men do. The very diverse conditions of infantile autism and hyperactivity, depression and schizophrenia, alcohol and drug abuse, Alzheimer's disease and mental retardation all fall under the broad umbrella of mental illness. Schizophrenic disorders, which are the predominant conditions in psychiatric hospitals and clinics in developing countries, are rare in a community setting.

In the Indian context, the mental health of women has emerged as an important agenda on women's health and rights-related work in recent times. Women activists see women's mental health as a result of women's inequality and political relationships. Women's mental health status is influenced by the social institutions and other cultural and political structures, which have a direct bearing on their day-to-day lives and this plays an important role in their mental well-being.

Mental health has been defined as the capacity of the individual, the group and the environment to interact with one another in ways that promote subjective well-being, the optimal development and use of mental abilities (cognitive, affective and relational), the achievement of individual goals consistent with justice and the attainment of preservation of conditions of fundamental equality (Dennerstien L, Astbury J, More C., *Psychosocial and Mental Health Aspects of Women's Health*. Geneva: WHO; 1993. 2).

Mental illness could include behavioural disturbances such as violence, agitation and being sexually inappropriate. It can affect a person's ability to perform normal day-to-day activities at home and at work. Unfortunately, people with mental illness, particularly women, are often discriminated by the community and also by their families.

The recent Global Burden of Disease (World Bank/WHO) report listed the most important causes of disability (as measured by Disability Adjusted Life Years, a measure of the number of years of life lost by disability due to a specific illness). To the surprise of many public health experts, five of the top 10 causes of disability were mental disorders: depression, alcohol abuse, schizophrenia, bipolar disorder (also referred to as manic-depressive).

It disrupts a person's thinking, feeling, mood, ability to relate to others and daily functioning. We can correlate the characteristics of mental illness with any other physiological illness, but the only difference lies in the fact that in mental illness, a person may act normally with respect to his or her physical functioning. A person having mental illness may deliver his physiological works efficiently. Mental illness is generally defined by a combination of how a person feels, acts, thinks or perceives. This may be associated with particular regions or functions of the brain or rest of the nervous system, often in a social context. Mental disorder is one aspect of mental health. The scientific study of mental disorders is called psychopathology. Mental health is not simply the absence of mental illness, but is a state of emotional and social wellbeing in which the individual can cope with the normal stresses of life and achieve his or her potential (World Health Organisation, 1999). The determinants of mental health and mental illness include biological, psychological, social, environmental and economic factors at several levels, including individual, family and community, national and global. Mental health issues vary across the lifespan from infancy to old age, across diverse groups within the population, and are strongly linked with physical health status. Increasingly, gender has been recognised as an important determinant of mental health.

Physical health and mental health

Physical health and mental health are two sides of the same coin. Mental health is extremely important in maintaining the physical health. In the course of study, the researcher has come across several cases where mental illness has resulted in acute physical illness. Because of the stress, mental trauma or for some incidence, deterioration of physical health may create problems in mental health and the vice versa. During the study, when interviewed, most of the respondents have expressed their opinions that they feel stress and depression often while facing many hurdles in life including the household one. It affects their physical health conditions too. In one instance, I have found a case of mentally ill patient, Junti Patwari of Majuli Hilikhaguri village. She has faced physical tortures and trauma from her husband and mother-in-law, which ultimately has resulted in deterioration of her mental health and now she is a mentally ill patient. About 50 per cent of the women gave opinions that sound physical health is a benchmark to maintain a healthy mind. On the other hand, around 30 per cent of the women responded that mental health conditions depend on some other factors, apart from the normal one, as in many times as they said, in spite of having a sound physical health may lead to mental illness.

Aims and objectives

(i) To find out social problems and stigma related to women mental illness;

(ii) To understand mental illness;

(iii) To understand the belief system related with mental illness;

(iv) To study the factors behind the high prevalence of mental illness in women; and

(v) To find out the change of role and status of the mentally ill women

Field of study

The study focuses at the social problems and stigma related with mental illness. The area of study is Psychiatry Department of Assam Medical College and Hospital, Dibrugarh, Assam. The patient, attendants along with department head, other doctors, and nurses were interviewed for the purpose.

A brief description of the field

Assam Medical College and Hospital

Assam Medical College and Hospital is one of the premier and oldest medical, and educational institutions and hospitals in Dibrugarh, Assam, India, established in 1947. It was the first medical college in north-eastern India. British philanthropist, Sir John Berry White, a retired Brigadier of British Army and later the civil surgeon of the erstwhile Lakhimpur district in 1870, contributed his lifetime earning of Rupees Fifty Thousand (present day valuation is more than 50 million of rupees) to establish his brainchild "Berry White Medical School" in 1900 AD. This school heralded the beginning of Allopathic Medical Education by conferring LMP Diploma in old undivided Assam. In 1938, the Assam Branch of Licentiate Medical Practitioners in its annual meeting under the chairmanship of Lokopriya Gopinath Bordoloi, the then premier of the Congress Government of Assam, decided to upgrade the Berry White Medical School to a full-fledged Medical College. Assam Medical College, Dibrugarh was established on 3rd November 1947, in the erstwhile US Military hospital of the Second World War at Borbari, Dibrugarh, through a process of up-gradation of Berry White Medical School immediately after Independence. It was inaugurated formally by the first Chief Minister of Assam, Late Lokopriya Gopinath Bordoloi.

Psychiatry Department

The Department of Psychiatry was established in 1976. It is a major centre and covers complex cases of the entire Upper Assam. The present head of the department is Dr Hiranya K. Goswami. The Department of Psychiatry has 30-40 permanent workers and 4-5 contractual workers. At present, the department has six doctors, two registrars, one clinical psychologist, two psychiatric social workers, eleven PGs, two Interns, two medical record officers, five nurses, one Sister-in-charge, three to five paramedics, 17 ward keepers, etc. The various facilities under the Department of Psychiatry include waiting room for patients and attendants, accommodation provision for patients and attendants coming from distant places, record room and enquiry, examination and care demonstration room, dispensary for outdoor patients, It also has Nurse duty room, examination and treatment room, ward pantry, Doctors duty room, laboratory for routine examination, accommodation for other supporting staff, clinical demo room, department library, seminar room as indoor services. Intake capacity for male patients is 30-40 and that of female patients is about 30-40 as stated by Dr Kamala Borah, Department of Psychiatry.

Methodology

The methods adopted by the researcher are observation method, interview method, case study method, photography method, genealogical method, narrative analysis. In case of interview method, the researcher practised informal, formal, conversational interview. While doing so, no predetermined questions were asked, in order to remain open and adaptable as possible to the interviewee's nature and priorities. During the interview, the interviewee tried to go with the flow. The description and interpretation have been done depending upon the etic and emic perspective nature of data. The study of the illness, its types and symptoms were done by interviewing doctors, nurses and consulting secondary data such as books, journals, and internet sources.

Mental Health and Gender

Sex is the term used to distinguish men and women on the basis of their biological characteristics. Gender, on the other hand, refers to those distinguishing features that are socially constructed. Gender influences the control men and women have over the determinants of their health; for example, their economic position and social status, and their access to resources. Gender configures both the material and symbolic positions that men and women occupy in the social hierarchy, and shapes the experiences that condition their lives. Gender is a powerful social determinant of health that interacts with other variables such as age, family structure, income, education and social support, and with a variety of behavioural factors. What then do we mean by gender-sensitive research and why can mental illness affect persons of any age, race, religion or income? Mental illnesses are not the result of personal weakness, lack of character or poor upbringing. They are treatable. Most people diagnosed with a serious mental illness can experience relief from their symptoms by actively participating in an individual treatment plan. A mental or behavioural pattern or anomaly that causes either suffering or an impaired ability to function in ordinary life (disability), is not a development or social norm. Mental health problems affect women and men equally, but some are more common among women. It is said that mental disorders are often remained undiagnosed and untreated. In case of women, the situation is even worse. Various studies have revealed that women are more likely to be the victims of mental disorders. Therefore, in dealing with the problem, the gender issue needs to be addressed properly. Treatments need to be sensitive and reflect gender differences. Gender differentials affect the power and control men and women have over these socio-economic determinants, their access to resources, and their status, roles, options and treatment in society. Gender has significant role to determine and formulate policy related decision-making in terms of tackling with mental health problems. Gender differences in rates of overall mental disorder, including rare disorders such as schizophrenia and bipolar disorders, are negligible. However, highly significant gender differences exist for depression, anxiety and somatic complaints that affect more than 20 per cent of the population in established economies. Depression accounts for the largest proportion of the burden associated with all the mental and neurological disorders. It is predicted to be the second leading cause of global burden of disease by 2020.

Depression, anxiety, post-traumatic stress disorders, dementia, self-harm, and eating disorders are some of the common mental diseases among the women, apart from the other such serious mental illnesses like Hysteria, Alzheimer, etc. It has been observed that, in case of women, the magnitude of the problems is higher in comparison to men. Women play several roles in the household and in the society too. The multiple roles in which women often juggle also are some of the major factors for the greater risk of mental illness among women. They may be mothers, partners and carers as well as doing paid work and running a household. Abuse is often a factor in women's mental health problems. Many renowned psychologists have opined that mental health problem can be severe among women than men as the impact and risk factors are higher in women in terms of mental illness. Sigmund Freud has rightly postulated that women are more prone to neurosis and other mental disorders as they are aggressive towards the self. Later several studies have revealed that the impacts of social factors are equally important along with the physical and psychological factors, which are the reasons for mental illness among women. The object relations theory clearly examines the cause and impact of mental illness among women. Gender-related problems are closely associated with the mental health problems. The psychological and mental makeup of women is different from men and hence it is obvious that the cause and treatment of mental disorders among women need to be taken care of separately.

Mental Health and Gender in the Developed Nations

Current evidences in many studies regarding rates, risk factors, correlates and consequences of gender disparities in mental health show that gender is an important measure and factor to study the impact of mental illness among women. Gender is conceptualised as a structural determinant of mental health and mental illness that runs like a fault line, interconnecting with and deepening the disparities associated with other important socio-economic determinants such as income, employment and social position. The socio-economic factors, which range from the income levels, working habits, nature of job among women, the social practices, customs and traditional methods of observations, are extremely important to study the multi-dimensional impact and influence of mental illness among women. For which multi-layered gender specific, gender focused mental health policies are required so as to tackle the problem of mental illness. In some mental diseases like depression in women, the economic, social factors associated with it are extremely important to determine the risk, cause and impact of the disease. The measurement of economic factors varies according to the overall economic situation and standard of a particular country with regard to the problem of mental health among women in that particular country. For example, the situation of mental illness among women in USA would be different from that of India. However, highly significant gender differences exist in different countries all over the world. Globalisation has overseen a dramatic widening of inequality within and between countries including gender-based income disparities. For poor women in developing countries undergoing restructuring, rates of depression and anxiety have increased significantly. Increased sexual trafficking of girls and women is another mental, physical, sexual health and human rights issue. The mental health costs of economic reforms need to be carefully monitored. In this regard, Freudian psychoanalysis concept is also important to know about the broad base of sexual factors in mental health problems.

Depression and other mental illness, which is a particular focus of this paper, accounts for the largest proportion of the burden associated with all the mental and neurological disorders. It is predicted to be the second leading cause of global burden of disease by 2020. In today's world, depression has become like a lifestyle disease. In this context too, gender disparities exist. The causes of depression-related disorders in women are different from men.

Despite being common, mental illnesses are underdiagnosed by doctors. A study has shown that less than half of those who meet diagnostic criteria for psychological disorders are identified by their primary care providers (Üstün & Sartorius, 1995). Patients, too, appear reluctant to seek professional help. Only two in every five people experiencing a mood, anxiety or substance use disorder report seeking assistance in the year of the onset of the disorder (WHO & ICPE, 2000). It is clear from the fact that the treatment of mental illness is still not widely held in many countries. The situation is worse in developing and under-developed countries as most of the people are not much aware about the various mental illnesses.

The ignorance among the patients and common people about the magnitude of the mental problems often bring major problems in the individual families and the society.

Mental Health and Gender in the Context of India

In the Indian context, the situation is more diverged. The age-old traditions, customs, socio-cultural practices, joint family system, and religious practices are some of the parameters along with the economic factors and social problems which can be evaluated to analyse the problem of mental health and gender. The government health policies are also needed to be monitored and revaluated so as to tackle with problem of mental health. Large scale mass awareness about the mental health problems and the importance of gender in relation to it should also be taken into account in dealing with the problem. Till date, the Indian Government does not have strategic mission to tackle with the mental health problems in multilayered and divergent medical infrastructure. In India, there are few mental hospitals or speciality institutions for mental health problems through which it is not possible to provide facilities for a large number of mentally challenged people. In case of women, the situation is even worse.

Mental Health and Gender in the Context of Assam

If we talk about Assam, then we will find out that in most of the cases, people are not much aware about the problem of mental health, both men and women. Except in some urban areas, the diseases are often remained undiagnosed and undertreated. The absence of proper treatment facilities, especially for women, in most of the places in Assam again has worsened the problem further. Therefore, a strong base study with corrective measures is required to tackle with the problem of mental health and the gender disparities within it. In Assam, we have only one fully functional and well equipped mental hospital in Tezpur—LGB. Some Government Medical College Hospitals like Assam Medical College and Hospital, Gauhati Medical College, etc., have psychiatry units and departments and those are not enough to provide mental health facilities to a large cross-section of the society. In case of private institutions too, the facilities and infrastructures are not adequate.

Factors behind the Higher Prevalence of Mental Illness in Women-From Doctors' Perspective

The prevalence of mental health problems is more in women than in men for common mental disorders as well as severe mental disorders.

Women are entrusted with contradictory roles, which is an important reason for their mental health problems. During the time of nurturing and care giving roles, women primarily are supposed to be in-charge as mothers, as wives and as women. However, the image of women is weak and she is in subordinate roles in the family. The constant change in roles leads to enormous pressures and mental health problems in women. Mental disorders have also been shown to be linked to poverty, powerlessness and alienation and these conditions affect women more than men due to the gendered roles and expectations. Some of the other reasons why women are more vulnerable to mental ill-health are as follows:

Women face more stress–Stress is not only because they play different roles at home, but also for violence they frequently experience.

Women's are not able to fulfil reproductive roles–Not producing a male offspring, or to be childless brings on a circle of abuse and violence which has been shown linked to suicide as well.

Fewer educational and economic opportunities-Though the scenario of women education and working is changing at present, yet women are susceptible to stress more in work place.

Women and men are treated differently once they are mentally ill- While women (wife, mother) care for men who are ill, women who are ill are either not married or sent back to their natal families.

Women with symptoms of mental illness are taken less seriously and are less likely to receive appropriate care.

In addition to the above, a common explanation of the greater prevalence of mental illness in women is the hormonal changes occurring during different stages of the reproductive cycle. Although genetic and biological factors play some role in the higher prevalence of depressive and anxiety disorders among women, their extent and manifestations may be mediated by the socio-cultural settings in which women live. Clinical entities include pre-menstrual syndrome, pre-natal depression, post-natal depression, post-natal psychoses and menopausal syndrome. Women may experience depression during the pregnancy or after childbirth, in the post-partum period (postnatal or postpartum depression). Some mental health conditions occur more in women and can play a significant role in the state of a women's overall health. Men experience more rate of autism, anti-social disorder, alcoholism, etc.

Institutional Aspect of Mental Illness

The Assam Medical College Hospital, which was established in 1947, has a department of Psychiatry, which was established on 1976. The OPD (Outdoor patients department) at Assam Medical College Hospital provides facilities for mentally ill patients. The Hospital OPD remains open for six days in a week, except Sunday. People from Jorhat, Golaghat, Sivsagar, Sonitpur, Lakhimpur, Tinsukia, Arunachal Pradesh and Dibrugarh come to the Hospital. As found from the record, the average number of daily patients in the OPD is 300 approximately. In the year 2014, as many as 5614 patients came for treatment in the OPD. AMCH, Dibrugarh, plays a fundamental role and it is stated that the stock and supply of medicines are adequate and regular. Authority allowed knowing that medical care provided to inmates is on the basis of weekly health checkups, fortnightly, monthly as well as daily as per the requirement of the case. On questioning as to how the institute ensures general health and proper nutritional intake of the inmates,- the Authority told about-balanced diet and regular health supplement. Moreover, regular cleaning, awareness programmes on personal hygiene among patients and hygiene awareness programmes among staff are conducted to ensure the hygiene level of the institute. The approaches/services the institute provide/undertake towards the treatment of mentally ill patients are: consultation, counselling, treatment, diagnosis and rehabilitation and social mainstreaming. In spite of the less manpower, everybody works sincerely in providing medical facilities to the patients. However, free medicine is not yet available in the hospital for mental illness.

Estimation of Mental Illness among Women

It can be said that a number of mental cases of men are found, but in comparison to women, it is far less. When some of them are interviewed, it was found that some of the mentally ill patients belong to very poor families. Vulnerability factors, therefore, affect different groups in different ways, and it would be a gross oversimplification to consider either sex as inherently more vulnerable than the other. Women and men alike are at risk of being "disappeared". Women and girls are much more exposed to sexual violence. While going through the cases of mentally ill patients admitted at Assam Medical College and Hospital, it was found that every month an average of 150 new cases of mental illness come to the Psychiatry Department of Assam Medical College and Hospital. It can also be stated that the percentage of female mentally ill persons is increasing in the last few years as stated by the doctors, yet the number of male patients is high than female patients in terms of availing treatment in AMCH.

On interpreting the data in terms of statistics, it was found that about 60:40 ratios exist in between female and male mentally ill patients.

Mental Illness: Social Problems and Stigma

Social Problems and Stigma

The impact of stigma is two-fold—Public stigma is the reaction that the general population has to people with mental illness; self-stigma is the prejudice which people with mental illness turn against themselves. Fear leads to avoidance, *e.g.*, employers do not want persons with mental illness nearby so they do not hire them. Alternatively, prejudice turned inward leads to self-discrimination. Research suggests self-stigma and fear of rejection by others lead many persons to not pursuing life opportunities for themselves. Stigmas about mental illness seem to be widely endorsed by the general public. People have stigmatizing attitudes about mental illness. Furthermore, stigmatizing views about mental illness are not limited to uninformed members of the general public; even well-trained and knowledgeable persons. The research indicates that attitudes towards mental illness vary for women and men. Several themes describe misconceptions about mental illness and corresponding stigmatizing attitude. Mentally challenged persons have to face several types of social stigma and taboos. More so when the patient is a woman as women are doubly oppressed. The researcher found in many instances that women patients are teased very openly. Even slang words are used on them in public spaces. They become subject of physical abuse as well as verbal abuse. They are counted as burden by the society as well as the family. This is truer in case of financially challenged families. Their presence is not welcomed in birth ceremonies, puberty rituals, marriage or any other social gathering. If one sees mentally challenged persons on the onset of journey then it is not counted as a good start and is believed to spoil the day. In one such case, the researcher found that when the female of the house was detected as mentally challenged then the family had to hide it from the society. There were several reasons behind it. Firstly, because they will be counted aloof from the society and they will not be welcomed readily by the society. Neighbours' behaviour will change. Again, no one will be interested in developing matrimonial terms with their family anymore. Even the fear of witch hunting was adding noise to their discomfort as it is prevalent in their society. On hearing about witch hunting, the researcher tried to penetrate into the matter, but the respondent did not cooperated much in the very topic as witch hunting is not operated openly but within definite boundaries of their societies. The problems faced by an unmarried daughter vary from that to the daughter-in-law. This is because of the social perspective towards various roles and designation of the person concerned. It was found that more than a half of respondents (attendants) are unwilling to spend an evening socialising, work next to, or have a family member, marry a person with mental illness. Social avoidance is not just self-report, it is also a reality. There is a strong social stigma attached to mental ill health, and people with mental health problems can experience discrimination in all aspects of their lives. Many people's problems are made worse by the stigma and discrimination they experience – not only from the society, but also from the families, friends and employers. Nearly nine out of 12 patients and attendants admitted at AMCH with mental health problems that stigma and discrimination have a negative effect on their lives. This is because society in general has stereotyped views about mental illness and how it affects people. Many people believe that people with mental ill health are violent and dangerous, but in fact, they are more at risk of being attacked or harming themselves than harming other people. Stigma and discrimination can also worsen someone's mental health problems, and delay or impede their getting help and treatment, and their recovery.

Society, women and mental health

Many people with serious mental illness are challenged in many folds. On the one hand, they struggle with the symptoms and disabilities that result from the disease. This may cause serious problems for the victim's family. On the other, they are challenged by the stereotypes and prejudices that result from misconceptions about mental illness. As a result, people with mental illness are robbed of the opportunities that define a quality life: good job, safe housing, satisfactory health care, and affiliation with a diverse group of people. Although research has gone far to understand the impact of the disease, it has only recently begun to explain stigma in mental illness. Much work needs to be done to fully understand the breadth and scope of prejudice against people with mental illness. Fortunately, anthropologists, social psychologists and sociologists have been studying phenomena related to stigma for several decades. On going through the statements of the patients and their attendants it was found that 80 per cent of them are not aware of mental illness, for them it's rather a matter of shame or misfortune. Some believe it's a divine punishment or curse in general and most of them feel they are considered a burden by their family. Though the rest 20 per cent are not much aware of the illness too, but they tend to show good attitudes towards the illness and the mentally ill persons. During the study, it was found that 70 per cent of the attendants of the mentally ill persons do not hesitate to stay with them. In some cases, the attendants gave opinions that mentally ill persons should get equal respect and status not only in the social sphere, but also in terms of jobs if their condition is not that bad, but unfortunately, it is not so in reality.

The study was conducted at AMCH (psychiatric department). In the course of study, it was found that most of the people that come for treatment were not aware of mental illness and mental diseases until they lost all their hopes and beliefs over traditional treatment. The most convenient place of treatment for the people living in the rural areas is faith healer rather than hospitals. In the urban areas, people seek medical treatment mostly from private practitioners. From the records available in the AMCH and other sources, we can come to a conclusion that a large cross-section of the society has been detected with mental illness. Many people find it extremely difficult to reveal about mental health of their own or anybody from their family. This creates problem for the investigators to investigate the magnitude of the problem. Similarly, the very few medical facilities available in the state cannot cater to the needs of the large section of mentally ill patients. Even in the urban areas, the medical facilities available for mental illness are not fully equipped with modern methods of treatment. The economic conditions and superstitious beliefs of the people also have hampered the situation. Studies in the area of physical health show how the organisation of healthcare in the country has been designed to privilege a certain class at the expense of others depending upon the socio-economic status and the function of individual in the society. It is well-documented that women in particular have been the enduring victims of this political organisation of health care. Statistics on the prevalence of mental illness in the community show that women are more frequently ill than men. In general, the utility of mental health services is not commensurate with the prevalence (Bhargavi Davar, 1999). In India, the proportion of women attending the facilities is very low, as compared to men. This low attendance is partly explained by the non-availability of resources for women. The traditional mental health services appear to primarily cater to the needs of male patients.

It was found that mental hospitals show gender discrimination in terms of availability of beds. In short, even though women are more frequently ill in the community, their utilisation of mental health services is lower than men. This discrimination is also visible in the access to mental health care of mentally handicapped children. Besides this, parents of handicapped young girls are less motivated to send them to these institutions for rehabilitation. There are no economic gains in doing this, as there might be in the case of boys who can still be trained for some useful employment. The mentally handicapped girl also helps out with the household chores. As she is unlikely to get married, parents would think it a waste to expend resources, material or psychological, on her.

Mentally ill people, in general, are forced to suffer a stigma in addition to their psychological suffering. Social attitudes towards, and understanding of mental illnesses in, women are much more pernicious than that towards men. A mentally ill man is an economic burden, but a mentally ill woman is an economic as well as a moral burden. Mentally ill women may be severely condemned for any behaviour that could be perceived as a violation of feminine nature and modesty, such as tearing of clothes, violence towards others, lack of attention towards the preparation or consumption of food, neglect of children, etc. Mental illness in women is seen as a moral disgrace to the family and thus censure, neglect, rejection and isolation are commonly associated with mental health. In the case of men, it is a cause for sorrow, not disgrace. Many mentally ill women receive no social support, either from their family nor from the family into which they get married. Married and mentally ill women are more likely to be sent back to their natal homes, abandoned, deserted or divorced. Our social way of life, its hierarchies, gender relations and social structure, other than our perception of mental illness, all contribute towards the large-scale neglect of mental illness in women.

Social response to mental illness

Social responses to mental illness show clear gendered differences, with greater stigma and rejection being evident in many parts of the world in the event of a woman suffering from mental illness. Mental illness in women not only attracts a greater amount of shame and dishonour, but also tends to have a more profound impact on family life, largely because of the woman's pivotal role in the running of the household (Patel and Oomman, 1999). Although the stigma associated with mental disorders often leads to a suppression of the acknowledgement of the experience of mental disorders in both women and men (*i.e.* a denial that symptoms are due to mental illness, citing instead a spiritual or religious origin), this is less likely to be the case for women. Whereas a mentally ill man may get married, mentally ill women are often left alone. Several studies, from India, have sought to investigate the differentials in the fate of mentally ill men and women. Typically, when a woman becomes ill, her own family becomes responsible for her care (SCARF, 1998). Whereas wives are generally expected to the primary carers when their husbands become mentally ill, married women face more problems with mental illness, as understood by the researcher in the field work through interviews. The field discussion agendas covered a wide range of matters starting from outlooks towards mentally ill people, stereotypes and prejudice faced in the society, to views on services accessible for people with mental health problems. Social response to mental illness is blended with mixed feelings. Some are still alien with the term "mental illness". Some have heard it, but were not in a position to comment...But, it is sad to notice that in some cases, both society as well as family members of the mentally ill patient seemed to possess negative attitude towards the illness and think it as stigma. In many a cases, it is found that mental illness is not thought as per with other kinds of physical illness. For some, mentally ill persons should be treated well and they opined that they do not dither to stay with them. Whereas, some are of the opinion that mentally ill persons are a frightful element in the society and it's hard to mingle with them as they are violent. Basically, people like to keep themselves away from the mentally ill persons and support the isolation of the mentally ill persons from society as well as from the auspicious occasions. Some even said that because of the mentally ill persons, it will be difficult to get the daughters married off. In case of patients who have recovered from the illness, they are even looked under suspect icon. The economic conditions and superstitious beliefs of the people also have hampered the situation, in general. In the opinion of AMCH, Dibrugarh, People are quite aware of mental illness and cooperate with the Department of Psychiatry from various aspects, most of the patients that are from urban settlement or semi-urban settlement agree that less awareness camps are organised by the Department as they have their technical limitations. But the researcher found that the people related with the health sector, be it the HoD or other people of Department of Psychiatry, all possessed a very positive attitude towards the research and encourager to continue for public interest and awareness.

Change in the Role and Status of Women Suffering from Mental Illness

Women perform various roles in the family. When she suffers from mental illness, her role and status declines. She is debarred of performing that work even if she is able to do in spite of the illness. She is not allowed to take care of her children, may be for the fear of hurting them. She experiences changes in the status even. She herself feels a burden to society and her family. Her family members do not allow her to perform certain rituals which she did earlier. Some are not allowed to attend social functions. Most of the mentally ill women and their attendants I interviewed say that they are sometimes engage in household activities. The married women experience negligence from their husbands, even some are threatened to divorce. Their presence at times is counted as inauspicious on many social occasions.

Finding and Analysis

The research work is conducted in the Psychiatry Department of AMCH, Dibrugarh, Assam to look on the social problems and stigmas related with women mental illness through the lenses of patients and attendants. The researcher conducted the work for fifteen days and interviewed all the patients (specifically women), those that were admitted as well as those that came to consult doctors or for counselling, and their attendants. The researcher aimed at finding the social problems and stigmas that are attached with mental illness, to find out the reasons behind the high prevalence of mental disorders among women, to find out the change of role and status of the mentally ill patient and the family. Also concern was on finding the superstitious belief that is related to such illness. The researcher found that most of the patients and their attendants were superstitious. When a person shows some kind of diverse behaviours, which are not normal, the family members take the sufferers to the local faith healer, perform various rituals, worship, etc. This is because most of them believe that the person is a victim of evil spirits. But, finally when nothing works, they are taken to the local health centres or other health centres such as AMCH, GMCH, etc.

The researcher has found that stigma is deep rooted among them and also there exist strong social problems. Mentally challenged persons have to face several types of social stigma and taboos. More so when the patient is a woman as women are doubly oppressed. The researcher found in many instances that women patients are teased using slang words in public spaces. They become subject of physical as well as verbal abuse. They are believed as burden by the society as well as the family. This is truer in case of financially challenged families. Their presence is not welcomed at birth ceremonies, puberty rituals, marriage or any other social gathering. If one sees mentally challenged persons on the onset of journey, then it is not counted as a good start and is believed to spoil the day. Sometimes the term *Pagoli* is used to threat children by the mothers when they don't listen to them. The patient becomes a matter of entertainment for others, a matter to laugh at. The researcher has found certain change in the role and status of the mentally ill patients. They are debarred of doing works which she performed efficiently prior to her disease and even can do in spite of the ill health. Mentally ill mothers are kept away from their children. They are not allowed to take part in the religious activities, or perform rituals or others. Their status also decline and, at the end, the name that remains attached with them is *Pagoli.*

The doctors say that the numbers of female patients are more, yet it is less in terms of availing treatment. During the past years, the number of admitted female patients was 3-4, but now it is 12-15. Although the authority claims to provide best care and treatment to the patients, but in the contrary, the fact lies different to the eye of the researcher. Through observation, the researcher has found that the patients depend solely on medicine. They are not indulged in recreational activities or other preferred works which they can do in spite of their ill health. They spend whole day and night with the other mentally ill patients, except those that are kept isolated or in cabin. On asked whether it is good to keep a mentally ill patient with other mentally ill patients, the doctor replied that they are bound to keep them so because of the limited intake capacity. There lacks instructor to instruct the patients or guide them to lead a normal life. The hygiene of the patients is not taken into consideration. The patient that urines in the bed or spreads stool remains so for several days. The cleanliness of bed sheet or the bed is not a concern. The premises of the department are, however, kept cleaned. Floor is washed alternately. The patients bear all the expenses of treatment, medicine along with buying toiletries. They are provided with bread and red tea in breakfast, rice, *dal* and *sabji* for lunch and dinner. Proper balanced diet is not kept in concern. On querying on the number of beds available for patients, the researcher was told that the number should be 60 but only 40 beds are there, out of which 12 are for female patients and 28 for males. This clearly shows gender discrimination in terms of bed. It was surprising to see at the security level of the patients. There is no security for the patients; they freely move out to other places, there is no watchman at the gate. There are no governmental schemes for the patients and even if there are some, they are unaware of it.

Mental illness is not different from other illness. People must be made aware of the illness; they must be educated and informed of the available treatment. The stigma and social problems are so strong in the minds of people that it needs immediate initiative to root it out from the society.

Conclusion

It is found that mental illness is a big concern of the day and little importance is paid to this, both in public as well as private sectors.

At large, the entire society is questionable for this. Mental illness is not looked at par with other illness and is not treated with apprehension. Even the academic sector is seen to limit its expansion in this zone. Economic, legal and environmental constraint perhaps is one of the cause of such negligence, and more so in case of female patients. To the understanding of the researcher, one cause of female negligence is that they are dependant financially. During field work discussions, although many are in favour of gender equality and support females out of the flavour of modernity, but the in-depth reality differs (as extracted during interview with females). Moreover, it is seen that mentally ill female patients are just taken casually and are not a matter of social concern at village level. Most of them are left abandoned and they are popular faces at every doorstep in search of food. The researcher found that although they are mentally ill, but they too have the consciousness towards meals and desire good food. For some native villagers, hunger of the mentally ill is a mean of free labour, which is beyond the question of payment. Some of the mentally ill patients who happen to be the wife of somebody and are even mother are very pathetic. Domestic violence, sexual violence, etc. are a part of their daily life. What is common in case of all patients is the lack of care and affection. If chaining up the mentally ill women, chanting spells, or beating them to force the spirits out, poking them with pins, could be replaced with medical care, the scenario would have been changed considerably. In Indian Hindu society, it could be seen that all rituals and restrictions are focused towards females, this not an exception towards mentally ill women's even. In all evil believes female serves as the protagonist and it seems the faith healer holds their command of life. Mentally ill women are also a toy for the society as they are the means of fear for young children. Mothers and relatives often warn their children that -If they don't do…he/she will be taken to the "*pagoli*", mentally ill women. Thus mental illness is a threat rather than a disease. It is not counted as other forms of physical disorder. The stigma and social problems are found high to the understanding of the researcher. In the Dibrugarh district, a good amount of medical facilities are available for mentally ill patients as compared to Upper Assam. Psychiatry Department of AMCH has resources, but caters service in a limited fashion. Overall, it can be said that in the ground of mental health, a lots requires to be done to manage the problem. More schemes are to come up, female protection is to be sought, and food security of the lower strata is to be ensured…the list just goes on. Actually, the root of the problem is poverty, lack of education, scarcity of health facilities. The issue needs immediate address at grassroots level. Still we all have miles to go….

References

Alexander, L.A., and Link, B.G. (2003). "The Impact of Contact on Stigmatizing Attitudes towards People with Mental Illness", *Journal of Mental Health,* 12, 271-289.

Bardvik, J.M. (1971). *Psychology of Women, A Study of Bio-cultural Conflicts,* New York: Harper & Raw Publishers Inc.

Bernard, H. Russell (1940). *Research Methods in Anthropology: Qualitative and Quantitative Approaches,* Rowman & Littlefield Publishers, Inc. Lanham • New York • Toronto • Oxford.

Bhargavi, V. Davar (1999). *Mental Health of Indian Women: A Feminist Agenda,* Sage Publications India Pvt. Ltd, New Delhi.

Corrigan, P.W. (2004). "How Stigma Interferes with Mental Health Care", Journal: *American Psychologist,* Volume: 59, pp. 614-625.

Corrigan, P.W, (2000). *Mental Health Stigma as Social Attribution: Implications for Research Methods and Attitude Change,* American Psychological Association, Washington DC.

Dennerstien, L, Astbury, J, More, C. *Psychosocial and Mental Health Aspects of Women's Health.* Geneva: WHO; 1993. 2.

Fink, J. Paul (1992). *Stigma and Mental Illness*, American Psychiatric Publication.

Hsu, Francis L. K., Ed.(1972). *Psychological Anthropology*. Cambridge Publishing Company, Inc.

Patel, Vikram, (2005). *Gender in Mental Health Research,* WHO Press, World Health Organisation, 20 Avenue Appia, 1211 Geneva 27, Switzerland.

Roth, Martin (1986). *The Reality of Mental Illness,* Cambridge University Press.

Thomas, S. Szasz (1974). *The Myth of Mental Illness: Foundations of a Theory of Personal Conduct*, New York: Harper & Raw Publishers Inc.

http://www.nmha.org/go/mood-disorders

http://www.nationaleatingdisorders.org/

Women and Mental Health, Mental Health Foundation.

Gender and Women's Health, WHO.

Gender Disparities in Mental Health, WHO, Department of Mental Health and Substance Dependence.

Mental Disorders and Gender, Wikipedia.

Women and Mental Health, Wikipedia.

Chapter - 10

HIV/AIDS in *Meghalaya*: Issues and Challenges

—Baphinda S. Thangkhiw

Introduction

HIV/AIDS is often seen as "someone else's problem"-as something that affects people living on the margins of society whose lifestyles are considered immoral. Even as it moves into the general population, the HIV epidemic is still largely misunderstood by many.

In Meghalaya, the true enormity of HIV/AIDS is often not fully appreciated. It is learnt that most of the people in the state perceive HIV AIDS as a disease that can be infected because of immorality, *i.e.*, on sexual lines, but most times failed to realise that it is occurring amongst the general population because of drug injectors, blood transfusion and from a mother to a child. There is a noticeable degree of denial by those people infected by the disease for fear of being outcaste from the society, which alluded to reasons of social stigma and discrimination and even on further infection to others. Undeniably, the associated factors such as those of poverty, drug abuse, prostitution, teen pregnancy, unemployment, low levels of literacy and the mobile population, which have considerable linkages to HIV affliction, have shown high vulnerability of the people to HIV infection.

The impact and consequences of People Living with HIV (PLHIV) are unavoidably confronting challenges at personal, interpersonal, family, community and societal levels. Attitudes of society, healthcare providers and others to PLHIV influenced stigma. Self-stigmatisation and self-discrimination indicate a barrier towards reaching the infected people and with a religious taboo attached to it. The HIV-related stigmas have fuelled its transmission and have greatly increased the negative impact associated with the epidemic.

The emotional trauma of HIV and AIDS is compounded by a societal reaction that judges the HIV-infected person with harshness and internalised severe reaction creating a loathing of self. HIV/AIDS is a taboo topic to many, and because of its spread during sexual contact and drug use, a large portion of the world society judgmentally regard persons with HIV/AIDS as moral degenerates and for persons who were infected by contaminated blood products are viewed as 'innocent' victims.

Aims and Objectives

The aims and objectives of the study are as follows:

1. To determine the issues and challenges faced by PLHIV in Meghalaya;
2. To find out the societal implications on PLHIV of Meghalaya and their family members; and
3. To study how PLHIV of Meghalaya cope with their HIV status.

Methods of the Study

For the purpose of this study, the ethnographic approach is based on a multi-sited intensive fieldwork focusing on the PLHIV of Meghalaya. The study area is divided into five main hill-districts of the state, comprising of the Jaintia Hills with field visits at Jowai and Khliehriat, East Khasi Hills with field visits in and around Shillong, Ri-Bhoi with field visits at Nongpoh and Byrnihat, West Khasi Hills with field visits at Nongstoin and Garo Hills with field visits at Tura. These study areas were selected because they indicate high prevalence and vulnerable areas to HIV infection.

The present study incorporates field-based data collection, published as well as unpublished data recorded and reported by the Network (MSNP+). The data collected during the fieldwork employed qualitative and quantitative methods from the sample derived using purposive and snowballing techniques. Multiple methods, including non-participatory observation, in-depth interviews, informal conversations and focus group discussion, were also used. Case studies were used to document live experiences of the infected persons. Secondary data were collected from organisational documents. Interviews were carried out based on a semi-structured schedule.

The respondents were all PLHIV selected from MSNP+, as it is the only Network of positive people in the state. Apart from field visits, most of interview process was conducted at the MSNP+ office and at the

Drop-in-Centres of the Targeted Intervention since these are the most convenient places for PLHIV to be interviewed as they are used to these places and feel comfortable and protected. The interview was carried out in English, Hindi and Khasi (mother tongue). However, in order to emphasise confidentiality and voluntary participation, the respondents were briefed with the purpose of the study to ensure their convenience and were also given a choice of opting out of the interview. With their permission, interviews were recorded and noted down in details by the researcher.

The methods employed intend to capture the point of view of the respondents and to explore issues in detail relating to the topic concerned. The respondents were given opportunity to use their own frame of reference, own language and own concept so as to uncover issues and concerns that the researcher had perhaps not thought of or had little knowledge of understanding about such issues.

Issues Concerning PLHIV

Apparently, the first HIV case in Meghalaya was detected in 1999 from an injecting drug user (IDU). Since then HIV positive cases were detected from all the districts, with East Khasi Hills and East Jaintia Hills districts having the highest prevalence of HIV cases. With more than 2000 cases tested HIV positive, this number excludes those HIV cases where testing and treatment are done in private hospitals, private centres and/or treatments which are done outside the state; which may or may not add to the existing HIV figure of the state.

The trend of the infection is increasing day-by-day, in spite of the various HIV-AIDS programmes being carried out by different Non-Governmental Organisations (NGOs), Community Based Organisations (CBOs), Faith Based Organisations (FBOs), Youth Clubs, schools, colleges and various other stakeholders, including political leaders, headmen and other different government departments of the state. Also, Intervention Programmes for High Risk Groups (HRGs) like the injecting drug users (IDUs), sex workers, men having sex with men (MSM), migrants, has been promoting for the protection of the People Living with HIV (PLHIV). Care, support and treatment services are being set up in Shillong and some other district headquarters and main towns of Meghalaya. Besides this, sensitisation, advocacy and skill development for the young and vulnerable people have been the on-going and continuous activities in the state.

The problems and challenges faced by PLHIV in Meghalaya are varied. To begin with, there is only one Anti-Retroviral Therapy Centre (ARTC) located in the state capital, this poses a much greater difficulty for PLHIV who come from the different districts of the state to undergo baseline investigation before ART initiation. Though there are three Linked ARTCs located in three districts headquarters, *i.e.*, in Jowai, Nongstoin and Tura, but all investigations and other processes have to be done first at the ARTC, Shillong. More challenging is that even after baseline investigation is done, the PLHIV who has to start ART has to take treatment in ART, Shillong, for six months and be under observation, then only the PLHIV can be linked out to other Linked ARTC. This poses a problem for PLHIV from rural areas.

Stigma and Discrimination

HIV AIDS is mostly tagged along with stigma that the illness/disease carries. Stigma and discrimination are major 'roadblocks' to HIV treatment, care and support and its prevention. In Meghalaya, stigma and discrimination attached with social, cultural and religious taboo seem to be an obstacle in reaching the infected people and also for the PLHIV to come out to seek help. During the survey, it was found out that the first thing that comes to people's mind when they heard about HIV/AIDS is that the victim or the PLHIV had involved in some kind of risk behaviours, but the fact is that most of the PLHIV interviewed and most of the clients registered with MSNP+ are those who live a simple life and have not involved in any such risky behaviour, especially the women and children. The social prejudice associated with HIV infection has helped increase the epidemic; thereby leading those infected and affected individuals to retreat into a world of silence, denial and isolation.

Stigma and discrimination is often layered upon pre-existing stigma concerning socially marginalised and vulnerable groups like the injecting drug users (IDU), the men who have sex with men or the transgender (MSM-TG) and the female sex worker (FSW). PLHIV may become implicitly associated with stigmatised behaviours, regardless of how they actually became infected.

Factors that contribute to HIV/AIDS-related stigma are:

- People's lack of knowledge of HIV is the biggest barrier for treatment of PLHIV.
- HIV/AIDS is a life-threatening disease, and, therefore, people react to it in strong ways.
- HIV infection is usually linked with behaviours or immoral lifestyle (such as homosexuality, drug addiction, prostitution or promiscuity) that is already stigmatised in many societies.

- There is a lot of inaccurate information about how HIV is transmitted, creating irrational behaviour and misconceptions of personal risk.
- HIV infection is often thought to be the result of personal irresponsibility.
- Religious or moral beliefs make people to believe that being infected with HIV is the result of moral fault and it is a punishment from God.
- Self-stigma and fear of a negative community reaction can hinder efforts to address the AIDS epidemic by perpetuating the wall of silence and shame surrounding the epidemic.

"AIDS is a war against humanity. We need to break the silence, banish the stigma and discrimination and ensure total inclusiveness within the struggle against AIDS. If we discard the people living with HIV/AIDS, we can no longer call ourselves human." - Nelson Mandela.

People, who are working directly or indirectly in the field of HIV AIDS in Meghalaya, informed that stigma and discrimination happen due to ignorance, myth, holier than thou attitudes of people and lack of responsibility in spite of continuous effort by these people to educate and sensitise the general public. Most of the PLHIV have not disclosed about their HIV status to their family as they are afraid of being rejected, isolated or even thrown out of the family or some of them do not want to put their family in shame. This concept impinged on the mind of the PLHIV, which causes them in isolation. As one PLHIV said, "*I do not tell anyone about my status. I do not want to put my family in shame. And on telling one member in the family it is no guarantee that other members will not know about my status. Instead my positive status will make them worry, depress and most of all shameful to them.*"

Almost all the PLHIV shared that they had disclosed their status only to few members of the family.

In healthcare settings, some PLHIV have experienced stigma and discrimination such as being delayed with medicines or access to facilities, verbal abuse and refusal to be touched by the staffs. Some of them had faced breach of confidentiality.

It was also found out that there are many PLHIV who self-stigmatised and are in denial of their HIV status. These are the major concern as they might give in to their problem and live in depression, fear and become less engaged in preventive behaviour or deny in seeking treatment or they can even spread the virus to others.

The following are some of the impact of stigma and discrimination on PLHIV:-

- Decrease in testing/ knowing HIV status,
- Lack of disclosure to partners/family members or others,
- Decreased healthcare and other service seeking,
- Silence PLHIV about their status resulting in invisible epidemic.

The WHO cites fear of stigma and discrimination as the main reason why people are reluctant to get tested, to disclose HIV status or to take antiretroviral drugs. An unwillingness to take an HIV test means that more people are diagnosed late, when the virus has already progressed to AIDS, making treatment less effective and causing early death.

MSNP+, which is the sole network of the PLHIV in Meghalaya, has set up one separate Stigma and Discrimination Response Team comprising of few prominent stakeholders to help the PLHIV who face stigma and discrimination.

Loss to Follow Up

One of the challenges that the service providers in Meghalaya are facing is the problem of Loss to Follow Up. As per the guidelines laid down by the National AIDS Control Organisation, that every PLHIV who are taking ART should visit and report to the nearest ARTC every month for their medicine and for regular check-ups and testing, and every PLHIV who are not on ART or in other words the Pre-ART, should visit the ARTC every six months for their baseline and for the CD4 test. But in Meghalaya, as per the report provided by the MSNP+, there were around 109 LFUs who are on ART and 256 who are Pre-ART as on June 2015 and this is the major issue because there is a risk that these people will spread the virus to others or they will be facing health problem in the future. At present, all measures have been taken to track back and relocate these LFUs and to bring them back to treatment. It was found out that the main factor determining LFUs are as follows:

- *Mobility (shifting of residence)*–Most of the PLHIV, especially those who are from the low economic background, are the mobile population as they shift from one place to another for job. Hence, it is very difficult for them to report and visit to ARTC at the same time for the ARTC to track them.

- *Poverty*–As per the information provided by MSNP+ and as per the number of the PLHIV interviewed, it is found that majority of them are from the low economic background. Hence, it is very difficult for them to visit the ARTC, especially those who are from the other districts and from the rural areas as it will involve financial expenditure and, at the same time, they will lose one day of their working. And for this reason, many of them stop coming to ARTC.
- *Side-effects of ART*–There are some PLHIV who are on ART, but have stopped coming to ARTC just because they cannot bear the severe side-effects of the ART medicines like nausea, headache, loss of appetite, sweating, insomnia, etc.
- *Time Constrains*–Most PLHIV do not have time to come and if they do come, the procedure for investigations is time consuming.
- Women bearing children find it difficult to come to ARTC.
- Self-stigma and ignorant about baseline investigation as they think that they are still healthy and does not need any kind of treatment or help.
- *Misconceptions Regarding Blood Test*–Most PLHIV think that blood is only taken from them, but no medication or treatment is given to them.

As per reported, there are also some LFUs who had opted out from the programme or treatment, others are taking treatment from other sources or private doctors and some have been transferred out to other ARTCs.

LFU is observed to be more among women since they have time constrain and family management. So, it becomes difficult for them to be regular on their follow up at ARTC.

Social Entitlements

It is learned that almost all PLHIV, especially those who were registered with MSNP+, have their monthly income from ₹ 2000 (Rupees Two Thousand) to ₹ 5000 (Five Thousand) only, and most of them are daily labourers and, most of the time, their hard-earned income is spent more on medication and treatment than on daily requirements. Children living with HIV often get infections and ailments due to their poor immunity, for which their parents' income has to be diverted towards treatments, which are always expensive. The same is the case with the children of HIV+ parents, as they are prone to many sudden sicknesses, often requiring immediate medical attention. There are some orphaned children who have lost their parents to HIV/AIDS and are residing with their relatives. Many a times, the relatives are unable to meet the requirements of these children. The reasons might be because of a large family, non-caring attitudes of the relatives towards the affected children and, most importantly, family with low income are hardly able to give attention to their requirements. This impediment is faced by both the infected and affected children.

All efforts are being taken to link the PLHIV to available schemes provided by the central and state governments so that the PLHIV can avail some kind of help and assistance for themselves and for their families. But, unfortunately, most schemes available are specific schemes that are meant only for the BPL and almost all PLHIV do not fall under the BPL category, which make them difficult to avail those schemes. The PLHIV community also finds difficulty to avail other general schemes, which everybody can apply due to the following reasons:

- Most of the PLHIV, especially those who are from the rural areas, have very little knowledge about schemes and services available.
- Most of the schemes are meant only for BPL families.
- Most of the schemes are specific schemes (age, gender, area, categories).
- Most of them also do not have proper papers and documents required for applying of schemes and services.
- In Meghalaya, to apply for any schemes or services or even to apply for bank account, gas connection, EPIC, etc, one has to produce a residential certificate from their local Headman, which is very difficult for the PLHIV, especially those who are from other states (non-locals) who did not register themselves with the respective Dorbar.
- PLHIV, who are from the FSW/IDU/MSM TG community, especially those who have had bad records in their locality, find it difficult to obtain such certificates.

One of the respondents said that if the government can declare or make a provision that PLHIV can also avail all the schemes which are meant for the BPL, it would be of great help to the PLHIV community.

At present, there are few schemes of the state government which are meant only for the PLHIV, such as the Free Transport, Free Blood and

Free Treatment for those PLHIV who are co-infected with Hepatitis-C. (As per report, at present, there are seven PLHIV who are co-infected with Hepatitis C and are eligible for free Hepatitis-C, but only six availed the free treatment).

Free transportation cards are issued for PLHIV to use them when they come for treatment or check-ups. But, as of now, these cards can be used only with the Meghalaya State Transport Corporation (MTC) and the Syndicate buses as these two units had agreed to provide free transport for the PLHIV and this has not yet benefited the PLHIV as the vehicles and buses of these units are very small in numbers and they do not ply in the city or to other parts of the state, except to two or three places.

Transit Home

Most of the PLHIV, who are from far-off places and from rural areas, face a lot of problems right from the time they tested positive as they have to do many tests, investigations and counselling, which usually take a day or two, and when they start ART medication, they should be under observation for few days. In such situations, the above-mentioned PLHIV often end up in dilemma, especially those who have no relatives in the city. There are also instances where the PLHIV were thrown out of the house by their family members or relatives and they have no temporary place to stay as there is no facility such as a transit or short stay home in the state of Meghalaya.

CD4 Machine

In the whole of Meghalaya, there is only one CD4 testing machine and this is proving to be a problem for the PLHIV in the state, as PLHIV community from all over the state has to come to Shillong Civil Hospital where ARTC is located to do their CD4 testing. There is also no viral load testing machine in the state.

Experiences of PLHIV

The incurable nature of HIV/AIDS frightened most respondents and many anticipated death when they were diagnosed to be HIV positive. Most of the PLHIV expressed fear, shock and disbelief when they first knew about their sero-positive status. Their levels of knowledge and awareness about the disease are little at the time of testing. Most of the respondents were of the opinion that they were not vulnerable and susceptible to HIV infection and it can only be infected by most 'moral degenerate' people.

One female respondent said, "*I was hospitalised for the due-delivery of my second child and was screened for HIV test. Later the doctor revealed that I am HIV positive. I was devastated, shocked and worried. With thorough explanation about the illness, the doctor assisted me on my delivery. I did not tell anyone and none of my family knows about my status till date. I only confide to MSNP Care and Support Centre. I don't know how I got infected since my 1st husband died. Then I met my 2nd husband (father of the 2nd child) who separated from me only when I was four months pregnant with this child. Now my 2nd child is one and half year old. I had her tested for HIV for which I am still awaiting for the test reports. My first child is also five years old and is negative for HIV. Since I did not reveal to anybody about my status, I bore everything by myself. I fear rejection and discrimination from my family if they come to know about my status. I am worried about my children too, since my daily earning is not consistent.*"

Majority of the PLHIV have disclosed their status according to their conveniences, while most PLHIV fear rejection and isolation to disclose. They felt that keeping their positive status a secret gave them a sense of relief from the public. The public fear surrounding HIV/AIDS as well as the moral judgment make it difficult for most PLHIV to come forward and disclose their positive status.

PLHIV response to their source of infection is minimal. Most of them do not think about the person who may have been responsible for transmitting the virus to them. Many replied that they are not concerned about who infected them since they have become infected. As one respondent said, "*There is no point to think about all those things. It is already too late. I just hope I can live a healthy life now and help others.*"

The experiences of PLHIV in health settings are not welcoming. Female PLHIV faced worse discrimination in hospitals. Most of the hospital staff perceive them as 'woman of bad character, hence the desired consequences of their behaviour'. Such irresponsible behaviour draws unnecessary attention towards those PLHIV as many have not disclosed their status in public.

The availing of treatment and medication of PLHIV hailing from rural areas is made worse. As there is only one ARTC in the whole state, this makes greater difficulty for most PLHIV to undergo baseline investigation. Most PLHIV finds it difficult to adhere to strict ART since they cannot visit the ARTC as and when advised, even though the treatment is for free, since they cannot afford the cost of travel expenses they have to bear each time they visit, for timely ART.

The perception that the community members have towards PLHIV is greatly attached to the irresponsible immoral behaviour and attitudes. What most PLHIV perceived of the community members as having minimal knowledge about HIV/AIDS. They think that because of this factor, they are discriminated. One male respondent asserted, "*Why can't people accept HIV/AIDS like any other disease? Why can't we talk freely about our positive status? People say they have diabetes, cancer, thyroid, high blood pressure, etc., why can't we say that we have HIV? I feel that if a lot of awareness and information about HIV is accelerated in a person's perception, I think people would not be so negative about it or towards us in particular. We all know that socialising with people will not spread HIV, so why should we be stigmatised and discriminated because of HIV?*"

Though experiences of the PLHIV were initially bitter after they were diagnosed to be HIV-positive, but gradually through time they recovered from their anxiety and started living a normal healthy lifestyle. The credit all goes to the MSNP+ for their immense help and support as their motto is "*Sharing Life Together*". Many PLHIV reported that coming to MSNP+ office has given them a new lease of life as they can meet people who are going through the same ordeals in life and share similar experiences. The Network provides them a platform from where they can make their bitter life better by sharing their experiences and helping each other cope with the problems. The greatest experience for PLHIV has been the protection, care and support that they perceive as being members of the Network.

Conclusion

Ever since the first detection of HIV case in Meghalaya, the trend of the HIV epidemic has increasingly become apparent with the changing nature of infection. HIV/AIDS, which was unheard of two decades ago and which was once perceived as a 'disease of others' in the state of Meghalaya, has now gain entry into the household of the general and marginalised population in which no individual and no community can afford to dismiss HIV as a condition that happens to others. HIV infections have severely affected the socio-economic structure of the whole families, communities and countries. Since AIDS is not curable and with sexual practices being essentially a private domain, these issues are difficult to address.

The perception of most people in the state viewed HIV/AIDS or PLHIV for that matter, simply as a medical issue, whereas most associated socio-economic variables are faintly taken into consideration. And with PLHIV still constituting a hidden population, it is difficult for any organisation to reach them if they themselves do not come out and voice the challenges they have experienced. The main reason of their denial, hidden and isolation from the society is undeniably the infection itself that is often stigmatised and discriminated. Those infected with the virus have not gather courage to disclose and face consequences that may arise towards or against them.

The overall response to HIV/AIDS in Meghalaya has not been very productive, though the various organisations have come together to prevent and control the epidemic. The issue related to self-stigma and discrimination is one of the most salient barriers to reach the infected. Prevalence of HIV/AIDS is mostly associated with various dimensions of ignorance and poverty, which not only increases the chances of HIV transmission, but it also increases the sufferings of the PLHIV.

List of Abbreviations

HIV	- Human Immunodeficiency Virus
AIDS	- Acquired Immuno-Deficiency Syndrome
PLHIV	- People Living with HIV
MSNP+	- Meghalaya State Network of Positive People
ART	- Anti-Retroviral Therapy
ARTC	- Anti-Retroviral Therapy Centre
HRG	- High Risk Groups
IDU	- Injecting Drug Users
FSW	- Female Sex Worker
MSM TG	- Men having Sex with Men Trans Gender
MARP	- Most At Risk Population
LFU	- Loss to Follow Up
NACO	- National AIDS Control Organisation
MACS	- Meghalaya AIDS Control Society
DIC	- Drop In Centre
NGO	- Non Governmental Organisation
CBO	- Community Based Organisation
FBO	- Faith Based Organisation

References

- Bharat, Shalini with Peter Aggleton and Paul Tyrer. August 2001. *India: HIV and AIDS-related Discrimination, Stigmatisation and Denial.* UNAIDS. Geneva, Switzerland. DOA:20/09/2015.
- Cameron, Miriam E. 1993. *Living with AIDS: Experiencing Ethical Problems.* Newbury Park, London: Sage Publications.
- Johnson, O. Mallory and Torsten B. Neilands.July 2007. *Coping with HIV Treatment Side-effect. Conceptualisation, Measurement, and Linkages.* AIDS Behave (Author manuscript).11(4):575-585.
- Mcgrath, Janet. W. March 2014. *Challenging the Paradigm: An Anthropological Perspectives on HIV as a Chronic Disease.* Website: www.tandfonline.com/doi/ DOA: 20/09/2015.
- National AIDS Control Organisation. 2008. *Mainstreaming HIV and AIDS for Women's Empowerment.* NACO New Delhi. Website: www.nacoonline.org: DOA:20/09/2015.
- National AIDS Control Organisation and Indian Nursing Council. 2011. *Nurse's Manual of HIV/AIDS and ART Training.* New Delhi: National AIDS Control Organisation and Indian Nursing Council.
- Rajamanickam, M (ed). 2006. *Psychological Perspective of HIV and AIDS.* New Delhi: Concept Publishing Company.
- Sundas, Binu. 2011. *HIV and AIDS in Darjeeling. Emerging Socio-Political Challenge.* New Delhi. Concept Publishing Company Pvt. Ltd.
- UNESCO. 2003. *HIV/AIDS Stigma and Discrimination: An Anthropological Approach Proceeding of the Round Table held on 29th November 2002.* Website :http://unesdoc.unesco.org/images/0013/001307/130756e.pdf DOA: 20/09/2015.
- Valdiserri, Ronald O. March 2002. "HIV/AIDS Stigma: An Impediment to Public Health", *American Journal of Public Health.* 20; 92(3): 341–342. DOA: 20/09/15.
- Wig, Navneet, *et al.* 2006. *The impact of HIV/AIDS on the Quality of Life: A Cross- sectional Study in North India.* Department of All India Institute of Medical Science,60 (1):3-12.
- Unpublished records from Meghalaya State Network of Positive People (MSNP+), Meghalaya.

Chapter - 11

Functional Abilities of the Ageing *Tiwas* of Morigaon District, Assam

—*Barnali Das*

Introduction

Ageing is a natural process. It begins with very birth of an individual and continues till his/her death. An individual after his/her birth gradually crosses all the stages of life and finally dies (Sahu, 1998). The process of ageing, as is now generally known, consists of progressive changes that take place in a cell, an organ or the total individual. The changes relating to ageing begin after the attainment of maturity and they are mostly degenerative and irreversible.

Ageing is a universal phenomenon. The process of ageing involves the interaction of four developmental forces. These are the biological forces, psychological forces, socio-cultural forces and life cycle forces. These forces create people's developmental experience (Cavanaugh *et al.,* 2008).

Advancement of old age is generally associated with a decline in functional capacity of different organ systems, the manifestation of which is apparent at a later stage of life. Health surveys generally have focused on social disability, especially on two kinds of daily disability i.e. personal care tasks (called activities of daily living or ADL), household management tasks (called instrumental activities of daily living or IADL).

Functional health is the ability to carry out activities and tasks that people do on a daily basis (Alam *et al.,* 2005). Sarmah and Choudhury (2010) studied 280 Assamese elderly community living in Guwahati city. They found that more women needed assistance in both personal care activities as well as instrumental activities of daily living than men.

Kammar *et al.* (2011) studied functional abilities of the aged in Dharwad district of Karnataka, with a sample size of 500 elderly from three age cohorts, *viz*, 60-65, 66-70 and 71+ years. The majority of the respondents in 60-65 years age cohorts belonged to GDTC (gradual decline towards changes). The elderly from 66-70 and 71+ years had better functional abilities as compared to early age cohorts. The 57.4 per cent elderly in the age-group of 60-65 years belonged to GDTC; 37 per cent of the 66-70 years and 23.2 per cent of the 71+ years belonged to GDTC. The association between age cohorts and level of functional ability was significant.

Material and Methodology

The present study has been conducted in two villages of Morigaon district, Assam. It is a cross-sectional study. Data for the study has been collected from 268 respondents, among them 134 were males and 134 females. The sample consists of people belonging to the age of 50 years and above. It is an attempt to assess the functional ability or the ability of an individual to carry on his/her own personal care and household management activities after he/she has attained the age of 50 and above.

The information relating to the socio-demographic factors has been collected with demographic survey schedule and the data relating to the topic has been gathered with the help of a structured questionnaire. The income group has been done on the basis of the Planning Commission Poverty estimates for 2011-12 (released in July 2013), calculated as per Tendulkar methodology. As per this calculating, families, which have an annual income of less than Rupees 49,000, fall below the poverty line.

People: The Tiwas were originally known as Lalungs. They are of Mongoloid origin. They are mainly found in the district of Nagaon in Central Assam. They are spread in Kapili, Mayang, Morigaon, Bhurbandha, Kathiatali, and Kamrup development block areas of Nagaon district. There are a few Tiwa villages in Dhemaji areas of Dhemaji, Lakhimpur district, Titabar areas of Jorhat, and Sonapur areas of Kamrup district.

The people are mainly agriculturalist. They are also engaged in masonry, carpentry, electrician, rickshaw pulling, etc. Women are predominantly housewives. The educational level of the people is low; especially among the ageing population, most of them are illiterate.

They are patrilineal, though there is also a matrilineal faction of the Tiwas. Their social organisation is based on twelve clan structure. In marriage, they follow clan exogamy and tribe endogamy. The staple food of the Tiwas is rice. Their two major meals consist of rice and vegetables. Meat, fish and eggs are also included in their menu. Fowl and pork are their delicacies. They take locally brewed rice beer (zu) in their day-to-day life.

Objectives

The study attempt to understand the functional ability of the ageing Tiwas people living in the Morigaon district of Assam. An attempt has also been made to look into their age-sex distribution, their educational level, marital status, occupational status, economic condition though their family income, living arrangement and occurrence of impairments.

Result and Discussion

Table 11.1: Distribution of Ageing Tiwas by Age and Sex

Age	*Male*		*Female*		*Total*	
Group	*No*	*Per cent*	*No*	*Per cent*	*No*	*Per cent*
50-59	70	52.24	73	54.46	143	53.36
60-69	33	24.63	38	28.36	71	26.49
70-79	22	16.42	17	12.68	39	14.55
80^+	9	6.71	6	4.49	15	5.59
Total	**134**	**50.0**	**134**	**50.0**	**268**	**99.99**

The age-sex distribution of the Tiwas population of 50 years and above has been shown in Table 11.1. There are 134 male and 134 female respondents belonging to the age of 50 years and above. The population has been shown in four age categories of 10 years interval. 53.36 per cent of the individuals belong to the 50-59 years age category out of which 52.24 per cent are males and 54.48 per cent females. 26.49 per cent individuals belong to the age group of 60-69 years, out of which 24.63 per cent are males and 28.36 per cent are females. In the age group of 70-79 years, 14.55 per cent of the individuals are found. And at the age group 80+ years only 5.99 per cent of the individuals are found.

Educational Level

Educational level of the ageing Tiwas is low. Illiteracy is high (59 per cent) and is much higher in women than men in all the age groups. 14.18 per cent of the ageing Tiwas are found in primary level. In HS and graduation level only 2.98 per cent and 2.24 per cent of males and females are found, respectively. Here no females are found in higher education.

Marital Status

It is one of the important demographic features of any population and is especially significant in the study of ageing. In the study, four types of categorisation have been done. They are those who remained unmarried,

Table 11.2: Socio-Demographic Factors of the Ageing Tiwas

Variables	*Age Group*									
	50-59		*60-69*		*70-79*		*80⁺*		*Total*	
	M	*F*	*M*	*F*	*M*	*F*	*M*	*F*	*M*	*F*
Education										
Illiterate	29(41.43)	51(69.86)	18(54.54)	28(73.68)	9(40.90)	15(88.23)	4(44.44)	5(83.33)	60(44.78)	99(73.88)
Primary	7(10.0)	10(13.69)	7(21.21)	4(10.53)	5(22.73)	1(5.88)	3(33.33)	1(16.66)	22(16.42)	16(11.94)
Middle	15(21.43)	5(6.84)	4(5.84)	4(10.43)	4(18.18)	-	222.22)	-	25(18.66)	9(6.67)
HSLC	14(20.0)	7(9.58)	39.09)	2(5.26)	3(13.63)	1(5.88)	-	-	20(14.92)	10(7.46)
HS	4(5.71)	-	-	-	-	-	-	-	4(2.98)	-
Graduate	1(1.43)	-	1(3.03)	-	1(4.54)	-	-	-	3(2.24)	-
Marital status										
Never married	2(2.86)	5(6.85)	-	2(5.26)	-	1(5.88)	-	1(16.67)	2(1.49)	9(6.72)
Married	60(85.71)	41(56.16)	29(87.88)	18(47.37)	17(77.27)	5(29.41	5(55.56)	1(16.67)	111(82.84)	65(48.51)
Widow/ Widower	7(10.0)	25(34.25)	4(12.12)	18(47.37	5(22.73)	11(64.71)	4(44.44)	4(66.66)	20(14.93)	58(43.28)
Divorce/ Separated	1(1.43)	2(2.74)	-	-	-	-	-	-	1(0.75)	2(1.49)
Occupation	Male		Male		Male		Male		Male	
Agriculture	24 (34.29)		19 (57.58)		13 (59.09)		7 (77.78)		63 (47.00)	
Petty trade	8 (11.43)		3 (9.68)		2 (9.09)		1 (11.11)		14 (10.45)	
Wage earner	24 (34.29)		10 (30.30)		3 (13.64)		-		37 (27.61)	
Service	14 (20.0)		1 (3.03)		5 (22.73)		-		20 (14.92	

(Contd...)

Income group										
Low income	19(27.14)	25(34.24)	12(36.36)	14(36.84)	7(31.82)	6(35.29)	3(33.33)	3(50.0)	41(30.60)	48(35.82)
Middle income	47(37.14)	44(60.27)	19(57.58)	21(55.26)	12(54.54)	7(41.18)	5(55.55)	2(33.33)	83(61.94)	74(55.22)
High income	4(5.71)	4(5.49)	2(6.06)	3(7.89)	3(13.64)	4(23.53)	1(11.11)	1(16.67)	10(7.46)	12(8.96)
Living arrangement										
With only spouse	4(5.71)	1(1.37)	1(3.03)	1(2.63)	-	-	-	-	5(3.73)	2(1.49)
With spouse & unmarried children	30(42.86)	18(24.66)	10(30.30)	2(5.26)	1(4.54)	-	-	-	41(30.60)	20(14.93)
With widowed & unmarried children	5(7.14)	5(6.85)	-	-	-	-	-	-	5(3.73)	5(3.73)
With spouse in extended/ joint family	18(25.71)	22(30.14)	18(54.55)	15(39.47)	14(63.64)	5(29.41)	6(66.67)	2(33.33)	56(41.79)	44(32.84)
Widowed in extended/ joint family	9(12.86)	21(28.77)	4(12.12)	18(47.37)	5(22.73)	10(58.82)	2(22.22)	2(22.22)	20(14.93)	51(38.06)
With resident in son-in-law	2(2.86)	1(1.37)	-	-	1(4.54)	1(5.88)	-	1(16.67)	3(2.24)	3(2.24)
With brother's family	2(2.86)	5(6.85)	-	2(5.26)	1(4.54)	1(5.88)	1(11.11)	1(16.67)	4(2.96)	9(6.72)

secondly, those who are no longer living with their spouses due to separation. Third category is of the individuals who are currently married and, forth is of those who had married but lost their spouses. A small proportion (4 per cent) of the ageing Tiwas have remained unmarried. More women than men are found to have remained unmarried among them. The number of males who have a surviving spouse is higher (82.84 per cent) than females (48.51 per cent). The proportion of women (43.28 per cent) who no longer have a surviving spouse is much higher than men (14.93 per cent). With increase in age, the number of widows gradually increases and in the highest age group 80+ age category their proportion is the highest. Only a very small number of aged people are found to have divorced or separated and they belong mostly to the category of 50-59 years of age.

Occupation

Agriculture is the primary occupation of the Tiwas. Those who do not have agricultural land of their own, work as agricultural labourer or are involved in semi-skilled jobs like masonry, carpentry, electrical works or were rickshaw pullers. Some of them were involved in petty business like running grocery shops, animal husbandry or selling country liquor. A very small number of males were in service such as teaching, fourth grade government jobs, etc. Women are predominantly housewives and do not have independent source of income. In the 50-59 years age category, the percentage of males involved in agriculture and wage earning is equal (34.29 per cent).

The people, who are farmers, continue to work in fields as long as it is physically possible for them to work. It is only from around the eight decades that they start gradually reducing their work in the fields. Those who are involved in petty trade continue with their business with some assistance from family members. Wage earning requires a more rigorous routine than working in one's own fields. Among the individuals working in the formal sector, the age of retirement is 60, after which they are no longer in service.

Income

The income or the economic condition of the ageing persons has been assessed on the basis of the annual family income. The categorisation of income has been done on the basis of the Planning Commission poverty estimates for 2011-12 (released in July 2013), calculated as per the Tendulkar Methodology. As per this calculation, families which have an annual income of less than ₹ 49,000 falls below the poverty line. For the study, three income categories have been classified. The first is of those who fall below the poverty line. Secondly, those who have an annual income between 50,000 and 3 lakhs rupees has been categorised as the middle income group and those who have an annual income above 3 lakhs is taken as the high income group.

33.21 per cent of the ageing Tiwas fall below the poverty line, 58.58 per cent have an annual income higher than 50 thousand but less than 3 lakhs, and only 8 per cent have an annual income higher than 3 lakhs. The number of ageing women whose families fall below the poverty line is higher than men. This is especially found in the youngest and oldest age groups. Most of the ageing males, irrespective of age, belong to the middle income group. Their income is supplemented by income of their children. Women, on the other hand, do not have any income of their own, but are dependent either on their spouses or on their children. Most of the ageing women, as has already been mentioned, do not have a surviving spouse. This may be a reason for their families facing economic hardships. Among those who fall in the high income category, the proportion is found to be highest in the oldest age category. In this situation, we can conclude that their economic condition has improved mainly from the income of the children.

Living Arrangement

Living arrangement means with whom the elderly person resides. In the study of ageing, the factor of living arrangement is important because it is a reflection of the social support and care that is available. For the elderly people, it is also related to the life satisfaction level. The living arrangements are influenced by a variety of factors, like marital status, financial well-being, health status, family size and structure, as well as cultural traditions like kinship patterns and the social supports available to the aged.

Among the Tiwas, joint or extended family is the most prevalent system. Ageing individuals live with their adult married or unmarried children. There is also the prevalence of the tradition of having a resident son-in-law. Among them, the practice of one of the daughters continuing to live in her mother's home after marriage was prevalent. A few (2.24 per cent) families having resident son-in-law were found during the field study. This is followed when the family has large landed property or does not have a son. The son-in-law gets status of a son and can inherit property. This from the point of view of the ageing individual ensures social support. Sons generally continue to live with their parents after

Table 11.3 (A): Distribution of the Elderly as per their Ability to Perform Personal Care Activity

Age Group	*Gender*	*Chewing*			*Bathing/Dressing*			*Moving Outside*			*Bladder Control*		
		1	2	3	1	2	3	1	2	3	1	2	3
50-59	M	70 (100)	-	-	70 (100)	-	-	70 (100)	-	-	65 (92.86)	5 (7.14)	-
	F	73 (100)	-	-	73 (100)	-	-	73 (100)	-	-	72 (98.63)	1 (1.37)	-
60-69	M	26 (78.79)	7 (21.21)	-	33 (100)	-	-	31 (93.93)	2 (6.06)	-	31 (93.94)	2 (6.06)	-
	F	35 (92.10)	2 (5.26)	1 (2.63)	37 (97.37)	-	1 (2.63)	33 (86.54)	4 (10.53)	1 (3.03)	35 (92.10)	2 (5.26)	1 (2.63)
70-79	M	8 (36.36)	13 (59.09)	1 (4.54)	21 (95.45)	-	1 (4.54)	16 (72.73)	5 (22.73)	1 (4.54)	19 (86.36)	2 (9.09)	1 (4.54)
	F	14 (82.35)	3 (17.65)	-	16 (94.12)	1 (5.88)	-	12 (70.59)	5 (29.41)	-	14 (82.35)	3 (17.65)	-
80+	M	1 (11.11)	6 (66.66)	2 (22.22)	6 (66.66)	1 (11.11)	2 (22.22)	3 (33.33)	3 (33.33)	3 (33.33)	4 (44.44)	2 (22.22)	-
	F	3 (50.0)	3 (50.0)	-	6 (100)	-	-	3 (50.0)	3 (50.0)	-	4 (66.66)	2 (33.33)	-
Total	M	105 (78.36)	26 (19.40)	3 (2.24)	130 (97.01)	1 (0.75)	3 (2.24)	120 (89.55)	10 (7.46)	4 (2.98)	119 (88.80)	11 (8.21)	4 (2.46)
	F	125 (93.28)	8 (5.97)	1 (0.75)	132 (98.51)	1 (0.75)	1 (0.75)	121 (90.29)	12 (8.95)	1 (0.75)	125 (93.28)	8 (59.70)	1 (0.75)

Table 11.3(B): Distribution of Elderly as their Instrumental Activity to Perform their Daily Living

Age Group	Gender	*Preparing Meals*			*Shopping*			*Light House Work*		
		No Limitation	*Limited Ability*	*Unable to Perform*	*No Limitation*	*Limited Ability*	*Unable to Perform*	*No Limitation*	*Limited Ability*	*Unable to Perform*
50-59	M	9 (12.86)	28 (40.0)	33 (47.14)	65 (92.86)	5 (7.14)	-	57 (81.43)	13 (18.57)	-
	F	66 (90.41)	7 (9.57)	22 (93.93)	8 (10.96)	22 (30.14)	43 (58.90)	49 (67.12)	22 (30.14)	2 (2.74)
60-69	M	1 (3.03)	10 (30.30)	22 (93.93)	25 (75.76)	7 (21.21)	1 (3.03)	19 (57.58)	14 (42.42)	-
	F	27 (71.05)	10 (26.32)	1 (2.63)	1 (2.63)	10 (26.31)	27 (71.05)	21 (55.26)	13 (34.21)	4 (10.53)
70-79	M	1 (4.54)	4 (18.18)	17 (77.27)	5 (22.73)	14 (63.34)	3 (13.64)	8 (36.36)	10 (45.45)	4 (18.18)
	F	6 (35.29)	7 (41.18)	4 (23.53)	-	2 (11.76)	15 (58.23)	5 (29.41)	5 (29.41)	7 (41.18)
80^+	M	-	-	9 (100)	1 (11.11)	3 (33.33)	5 (55.55)	2 (22.22)	2 (22.22)	5 (55.55)
	F	-	4 (66.66)	2 (33.33)	-	-	6 (100)	-	3 (50.0)	3 (50.0)
Total	M	11 (8.21)	42 (31.34)	81 (60.45)	96 (71.64)	29 (21.64)	9 (6.72)	86 (64.18)	39 (29.10)	9 (6.72)

marriage. If there is more than one son then they set up independent homes and the cultivated land is also divided. The son who continues to stay with the parents inherits the father's share as well. Unmarried daughter continues to live in her parents' home. After the death of the parents, the daughter gets an equal share of the property and is looked after by the brother who lives in the parents' home. The separated and unmarried ageing individuals in the villages are found to be living with the family of the married brothers in the ancestral home. No ageing individual was found to be living alone and only a very small percentage (2.61 per cent) of the ageing individuals were found to be living with their spouse.

Functional Abilities in Activities of Daily Living

The present study looks into how much the elderly are able to continue to carry on or perform different activities essential to daily living. Personal care tasks are called activities of daily living (ADL). Four essential activities of daily life were taken into consideration under personal care activities. These are chewing, bathing and dressing, moving out and bladder control. The objectives of assessing functional ability was to see the dependence level of the elderly. For each activity the elderly were asked to categorise their ability as follows.

1. No limitation,
2. Limited ability, and
3. Unable to perform.

Household management tasks are called instrumental activities of daily living (IDAL). These activities were the household management tasks, including preparing of meals, shopping and doing light house work. The respondents were asked to give their response in the same three options as activities of daily living.

In the activities of daily living, there is some difference based on both age and gender. The males from the seventh decade are found to have some limitation in chewing, but women report to have limitation from much later. Much limitation is not seen in areas of bathing and dressing. In regard to moving out, men and women face limitation from around the same age, but the number of women facing limitation is higher than men. Their proportion also gradually increases with increase in the age. In the 80+ age group, 33 per cent of the men are unable to move out. Bladder control is another difficulty faced by ageing people. People are found to face difficulties from the 50-59 age group and their proportion increases

Table 11.4: Distribution of the Impairments of the Elderly

Name of the Impairments		*Gender*	*50-59*	*60-69*	*70-79*	*80⁺*	*Total*
Vision	Low	M	1 (1.43)	1 (3.03)	2 (9.09)	1 (11.11)	5 (3.73)
	Vision	F	2(2.74)	3 (7.89)	2 (11.76)	-	7 (5.22)
	Cataract	M	-	2 (6.06)	2 (9.09)	1 (11.11)	5 (3.73)
		F	-	2 (5.26)	2 (11.76)	2 (33.33)	6 (4.48)
Hearing	Hearing	M	-	-	—	1 (11.11)	1 (0.75)
	Impairment	F	-	1 (2.63)	-	-	1 (0.75)
	Partial	M	-	-	-	1 (11.11)	1 (0.75)
	Impairment	F	-	1 (2.63)	-	-	1 (0.75)
Locomotor	Limited	M	-	-	5 (22.73)	3 (33.33)	8 (5.97)
	Ability	F	-	2 (5.26)	5 (29.41)	3 (50.0)	10 (7.46)
	Unable to	M	3 (4.28)	2 (6.06)	1 (4.54)	3 (33.33)	9 (6.72)
	Perform	F	-	1 (2.63)	-	-	1 (0.75)

with age. (Table 11.4) More women reported (59.70 per cent) to having difficulty in bladder control than men. The family members, generally daughters-in-law, unmarried daughters and even unmarried sisters are found to take care of the persons who are in need of care.

Instrumental activities of daily living have been assessed with relation to three activities. They are preparing meals, going out for shopping and doing household work. May be because of the cultural practice of not requiring to cook, more men reported to facing limitation from an earlier age. Some of the women (41.18 per cent) were able to continue with limited ability upto the eighth decade. 73.88 per cent of the total women are able to prepare meals without any limitation as compared to 8.21 per cent men. With regard to shopping, men and women show an inverse association. Most of the men (71.64 per cent) did not find any limitation. Most of the women are unable to perform this activity. Even after ageing persons retire from active work, they are generally found to keep themselves engaged in some activity or the other. Elderly men generally keep making household articles out of bamboo and women keep themselves occupied in light household religious work or other works like looking after grandchildren, etc. Most of them are found to be able to get involved in doing light house work. It is only in the 80+ age group that most of the elderly are found no longer to be able to do light household work. There is a gradual increase in number of people who are unable to work with age. Between the seventh and the eighth decade, there is a sharp rise in the proportion of both elderly men and women who are no longer able to work.

Impairments

Prevalence of impairments has been looked into among the ageing Tiwas. Impairments of vision, hearing and locomotion have been examined. Locomotor impairment is found to be more prevalent. This form of impairment can be said to be influenced by both age and sex. Women are found to be facing limited ability, but in case of men, some are found to be completely unable to move. This inability has mostly resulted from falls. Limitation in locomotion shows an association with age in both the sexes. Impairment of vision is an age associated decline and, though its prevalence is less among the Tiwas, it shows a positive association with age.

Conclusion

The Tiwas of the study area, in spite of living close to the district headquarters, follow a traditional rural way of life. The educational level of the ageing population is low. They practise agriculture as their primary means of livelihood, though a shift towards other means of subsistence is also observed. In this village, most of the families are found to belong to the middle income group. However, a gender difference is seen in economic condition. More ageing women are economically backward than ageing men. In living arrangements, most of the elderly persons reside with their spouses and children's family. The elderly from the higher age categories require assistance in their personal care activities. Women need more assistance than men in household management tasks. Women can continue to work on household management. Men, on the other hand, are able to carry on outdoor activities. The prevalence of locomotor impairment is more than the other types of impairments. Among the males, the locomotor impairment is higher.

References

Alam, M, Mukherjee, M. 2005. "Ageing, activities of Daily Living disabilities and the Need for public health initiatives: Some Evidence from a household survey in Delhi", *Asia-Pacific Population Journal,* 20:47-76.

Cavanaugh, J.C., Fields, F.B., 2006. *Adult Development and Ageing* (5th edition), USA: Wordsworth Thomson Learning Inc.

Kammar, M.R., Kamath, R. Ashalatha, K.V., 2011. "Functional Abilities of the Aged", *Indian Journal of Gerontology,* 25.1:41-50.

Sahu, C.1998. *Problems of Ageing among the Indian Tribes*, Sarup and Sons, New Delhi.

Sarmah, C., Choudhury, B., 2010. "Functional Ability and Prevalence of Disease", *On Medical Anthropology,* India.

Chapter - 12

Access to Reproductive Healthcare Services and Effect of Some Bio-Social Covariates on Prenatal Wastages and Infant Mortality among the *Rengma Naga* Women of *Karbi Anglong, Assam*

—Melody Seb Rengma and S. Sengupta

Introduction

Mortality refers to events of death occurring in population. It is a fundamental factor influencing population and is useful for determining current demographic structure as well as in understanding the prospects of potential change in the future (Keyfitz and Flieger, 1971). Mortality is demographically significant index for assessment of general health status of population. Even though the association between health and mortality might not be so direct, yet high levels of mortality suggest poor health. According to CIA World Fact Book, updated on 30th June 2015, infant mortality rate (IMR) per thousand in India was 43 in 2014. In Assam, the infant mortality rate (IMR) per thousand was 55 in 2012 and 54 in 2013 (*Statistical Hand Book*: Assam, 2014). A number of causes akin to low socio-economic condition, inadequate poor medical facilities, cultural factors, poor diet of expectant mothers are found as some of the potent factors liable for high prenatal and infant deaths. There is chances to overcome by taking both preventive measures (such as clean and safe delivery) and by proficient measures together with encouraging supplementary nutrition, prolonged breastfeeding of the infants, immunisation, simple treatment for dehydration and other infections, prevention of accidents, fostering continuity of support and helping mothers to avoid becoming pregnant once again too quickly without any healthy spacing and also to avoid giving birth to more children than the family can afford (Arora, 1980).

Reproductive health is a crucial part of general health and a central feature of human development. It is a reflection of health during childhood, and crucial during adolescence and adulthood, sets the stage for health beyond the reproductive years for both, women and men, and affects the health of the next generation. The health of the newborn is largely a function of the mother's health and nutrition status and of her access to healthcare. According to WHO (2005), an estimated 55 per cent of women do not have sufficient antenatal care. Modern contraception is often unavailable in certain parts of the world. They further state that about 222 million women worldwide have an unmet need for modern contraception, and the lack of access to modern contraception is highest among the most disadvantaged populations. Lack of access to contraception is a main cause of unintended pregnancy, which is associated with poorer reproductive outcomes. Most of these deaths can be avoided with improving women's access to quality care from a skilled birth attendant before, during and after pregnancy and childbirth.

It is now an established fact that, quite a good number of bio-social factors are responsible for prenatal and infant mortality. Human reproduction is greatly influenced by several bio-social determinants, such as age at menarche, adolescent sterility, large inter-birth spacing due to prolonged breast feeding and others, education of mother, occupation of mother, maternal age at conception, birth order, maternal health and nutritional status, embryonic wastage, pre-reproductive mortality, etc. The present study is an attempt to understand the status of reproductive healthcare services and their impact on the prenatal and infant mortality, and also to assess some bio-social factors affecting the prenatal and infant mortality among the Rengma Naga women of Assam.

Rengma is one of the Naga sub-groups found in Nagaland and some part of Karbi Anglong Assam. The Rengmas inhabit Karbi Anglong district, known as Western Rengma, and is a predominant endogamous community, notified as scheduled tribe in the hill areas of Assam. The Rengmas of Assam are sometimes referred to as "Njang Teriipunyu", which means the '*Cane Paths Rengma*' and it is conjectured that their ancestors migrated from Nagaland to the Rengma Hills of Assam in the remote past. The Rengmas belong to the Mongoloid stocks and are classified under Tibeto-Burman speaker group (Bordoloi and Sharma Thakur, 1988). Like other Naga tribes, there are very few written historical records of the Rengmas.

If local traditions are adhered to, it is believed that the Rengmas and the Lothas were once part of a single tribe.

The Rengmas, the inhabitants of Karbi Anglong, Assam, are distributed in 14 villages. They are pile dwellers. Some villages are surrounded by Government Reserve Forest. They mainly depend on agriculture. Rice is their major food crop. They are non-vegetarian. They consume good variety of fruits, which are available in their locality. They use Roman script and converse in *Nagamese* and Assamese with outsiders and Rengma dialect among themselves. Some can speak Hindi and educated section can speak English also. They have a colourful traditional dress. With the spread of Christianity, the Rengma people have become educated and aware of cleanliness. During their illness, they not only depend on modern medicine, but also on prayer and medicinal plants to cure their disease. Transport and communication system in the area is very poor and only few of the villages are linked with all weather road facilities.

Materials and Method

The present cross-sectional study has been carried out among the Rengma Nagas residing in the Karbi Anglong district ($25^{0}33'$ N to $26^{0}35'$ N latitude and $92^{0}10'$ E to $93^{0}50'$ E longitude), which is situated in the central part of Assam. According to 2011 census, the district has a total population of 9,65,280, of which male and female population was 493,482 and 471,798, respectively. The district could broadly be divided into two physiographic units viz. hills and plains. However, 85 per cent of the district was covered by hills. Moist-semi evergreen forest, moist mixed deciduous forest, river rain type, and miscellaneous type with scattered pure or mixed patches of bamboos are the forest types of the district. Presently, the Rengma Nagas of Karbi Anglong, Assam, have a population strength of 7,000 souls approximately, which is scattered in 14 villages. Out of these fourteen villages, only three villages, namely Akhoiputa-Jongpha, Choshenlari No. I and II, and Lolashonyu Tseguchangri have been considered for the present study. The villages were situated approximately 80-120 kms from the township of Diphu, the district headquarter of Karbi Anglong.

Data were collected based on household survey and interview method from among 200 ever married Rengma women of 15 years to 45 years of age in the hill district of Karbi Anglong, Assam. The selection of the universe was based on pre-dominance and homogeneity of the Rengma Naga individuals. The data were collected during the period of May 2014 to July 2015 through specially designed pre-tested fertility schedule to obtain information on fertility performances along with other demographic variables through in-depth interviews. Data on morbidity and accessing to reproductive healthcare services were collected with the help of interview schedule, on the basis of "self-reported illness and accessibility". Women whose husbands are alive and have at least one child only been interviewed. Age of some individuals was estimated with reference to some important local events and thus are approximate. While interviewing the mothers, the detailed reproductive histories, *i.e.,* the number of offspring-living or dead, abortion and still birth, including sex and age of living and dead children, and use of medical facilities, particularly with regard to tetanus toxoid, iron/folic acid tablet and safe deliveries, have been collected. Apart from these, information about age at menarche, age at menopause, age at conception, birth order was also incorporated in the study.

The necessary approvals were taken from the local community leader, village headman and relevant authorities before commencement of the study. The knowledge of Rengma language enabled the author to have an intimate interaction with the studied people, ways of treatment, and also to document some medicinal plants used by the healer.

Results and Discussion

Access to reproductive healthcare services and its impact on prenatal and infant mortality is depicted in Table 12.1. It is clear from the table that the pregnant women regularly visit the doctors for regular check-up. Among the Rengma Nagas, the highest percentage of prenatal wastages include abortion and still birth, *i.e.*, 13.67 per cent and 7.22 per cent, respectively, is found in the category of mothers who did not visited hospital at all during pregnancy. And lower percentage of it, *i.e.,* 2.77 and 1.85 is found in the category of mothers who regularly visited the doctors. In case of infant deaths, highest percentage (7.11 per cent) is also found in the category of mothers who did not visit hospital at all during pregnancy And in this category also, only 1.85 per cent mothers regularly visited for medical check-up during pregnancy. In this regard, it may be mentioned here that relatively higher percentage of infant deaths is found among the Rengma Nagas comparing to that of Kaibarta (1.24 per cent) and Kayastha (1.64 per cent) mothers, who regularly go for medical check-up during pregnancy (Baruah, 2003).

Health is equally important for both the mother and the child. Studies conducted by Ramchandran (1989), Punhari and Mahajan (1989) revealed that women who obtained antenatal, natal and postnatal services have fewer undernourished children. There is an ICMR recommendation to take a required amount of calcium, protein, iron and folic acid essential for pregnant women. A minimum of three visits to a doctor is also considered as must (Park, 2000).

Most of the villages of the Rengma are deprived of accessing modern medical facilities and only few villages are covered by *Anganwadi*. Better-off families who are staying in semi-urban areas can only have access to modern medical facilities and they are well acquainted to the use of medical facilities. Majority of them from the village area do not know the importance and knowledge of using medical facilities. The prenatal wastages and infant mortality among the Rengma women is showing higher incidence among the category of women who never visit medical centres and lower incidence is found among the mothers who regularly visit medical centres. This shows that access to reproductive healthcare service has a positive effect on their infant's health.

Table 12.1: Access to reproductive healthcare services and prenatal wastages and infant mortality

Medical visit of the Mothers during Pregnancy	*No. of Mothers*	*Percen-tage*	*Mean Conception*	*Mean Live birth*	*Abortion*	*Still birth*	*Infant mortality*
Visited doctors when called (Regular)	29	14.50	1083.72	1033.55	3(2.77)	2(1.85)	1(0.97)
Irregular	24	12.00	964.00	8233.41	9(9.37)	5(5.20)	3(3.65)
In emergency	33	16.50	1293.90	1073.24	13(10.07)	9(6.97)	5(4.67)
Not at all	114	57.00	3733.27	2952.58	51(13.67)	27(7.23)	21(7.11)
Total	**200**	**100**	**7063.53**	**5872.93**	**76(10.76)**	**43(6.09)**	**30(5.11)**

• Figures within parentheses indicates percentages.

Findings on how education level effecting prenatal and infant mortality among the Rengma women are shown in Table 12.2. Most of the Rengma women under study are illiterate. It is revealed from the table that the mean number of conception and mean number of live birth is found to be decreasing with the rise in educational level. Abortion, still birth and infant mortality rate are also found to be decreasing with the increase of educational level. Women who belong to the category of illiterate are showing higher incidence of abortion, stillbirth and infant death (12.05 per cent, 6.18 per cent and 5.97 per cent), while the incidences of abortion, still birth and infant death are relatively low among the women who attained up to the secondary level of education (6.89 per cent, 3.44 per cent and 3.79 per cent). The studies done by Patir and Sengupta (2015), and Tengaponiya Deori also show higher incidences of abortion and infant death among the illiterate mothers (10.64 per cent and 4.76 per cent, respectively), while lower incidence is found among the women who attained secondary level of education (7.74 per cent and 1.29 per cent, respectively). Again, among the Ahom population (Gogoi, 2014), higher incidence of abortion, still birth and infant death is also reported from among the mothers in the category of illiterate level (7.47 per cent, 2.14 per cent and 8.63 per cent), while it gradually decreases among the mothers who attain secondary level of education (4.03 per cent, 0.31 per cent and 3.23 per cent). Therefore, it can be assumed that education of mother is responsible for prenatal wastages and infant death. Maternal education is considered to be one of the most essential requirements to maintain the child health as well as their reproductive health.

Table 12.2: Prenatal wastages and infant mortality rate according to mother's educational level

Educational Level	*No. of Mothers*	*Mean Conception*	*Mean Live Birth*	*Abortion*	*Still Birth*	*Infant Mortality*
Illiterate	97	3073.16	2512.58	37(12.05)	19(6.18)	15(5.97)
Primary (Class I–V)	40	1734.32	1423.55	19(10.98)	12(6.98)	7(4.92)
Upper primary (Class VI–X)	36	1393.86	1163.22	14(10.07)	9(6.47)	5(4.31)
Secondary (HSLC and above)	27	873.22	792.92	6(6.89)	3(3.44)	3(3.79)
Total	**200**	**7063.53**	**5872.93**	**76(10.76)**	**43(6.09)**	**30(5.11)**

Figures within parentheses indicates percentages.

Age at marriage of Rengma women and the result of prenatal wastages and infant mortality rate are depicted in Table 12.3. The table shows that majority of women get married before 18 years of age and least number of women observed who married as late as 27 years and above.

It is observed that the mean conception and mean live birth per married woman decreases with the rise in the age at marriage among the Rengma women. Incidence of abortion and still birth and infant mortality is high among women whose age at marriage is below 18 years (15.81 per cent, 7.90 per cent and 6.70 per cent), gradually decreases then, however, sharply increases once again from 27 years and above onwards in case of abortion and infant death (17.64 per cent and 5.66 per cent), but still birth increases once again at marriage age of 21-23 years and gradually decreases at 27 years and above. Similar case is also found among the Dibongiya Deori of Assam; in case of abortion, the percentage (18.52 per cent) is high among the women whose age at marriage is below 18 years, gradually decreases then however once again sharply increases with the increase of marriage age (10.94 per cent). Still birth (7.41 per cent) remains high among the mother whose age at marriage is below 18 years which gradually decreases but once again sharply increases at 21-23 years of age at marriage (3.51 per cent). Still birth is not found to be associated with the increase of the marriage age (Patir and Sengupta, 2014).

The frequency of woman varies accordingly to the age of the mother at the time of marriage and her length of married life. It is a well-known fact that child birth at too immature age or at too late age of the mother is unsafe for both the mother and the child. Incidence of abortion and still birth and infant mortality among the women who married at relatively young age (below 18 years) is very high in the present population under study. Early marriage leads to high conception, a period where the risk of fertility is more. Children born to very immature mothers are at a higher risk of being severely under-nourished (Rajaretnam and Hallad, 2000).

Table 12.3: Prenatal wastages and infant mortality according to mother's age at marriage

Age at Marriage	*No. of Mothers*	*Mean Conception*	*Mean Live birth*	*Abortion*	*Still birth*	*Infant Mortality*
Below 18 years	56	2153.83	1642.92	34(15.81)	17(7.90)	11(6.70)
18-20 years	48	1813.77	1583.29	13(7.18)	10(5.52)	7(4.43)
21-23 years	36	1223.38	1052.91	9(7.37)	8(6.55)	5(4.76)
24-26 years	33	1203.63	1073.24	8(6.66)	5(4.16)	4(3.73)
27 years and above	27	682.51	531.96	12(17.64)	3(4.41)	3(5.66)
Total	**200**	**7063.53**	**5872.93**	**76(10.76)**	**43(6.09)**	**30(5.11)**

Figures within parentheses indicates percentages.

Prenatal and infant deaths, according to the mothers' age at first child birth, are incorporated in Table 12.4. Among the Rengma mothers, the total live birth (76.50 per cent), abortion (17.00 per cent), still birth (6.5 per cent) and infant mortality (7.18 per cent) have been assessed. The mean live birth according to the mother's age at first child birth is found to be relatively higher among the mothers who attain motherhood at the age of 21-23 years (90.00 per cent), but lower among the mothers who are below 18 years of age (55.32 per cent). In case of abortion, still birth and infant deaths, the incidence is quite common among the mothers who experience motherhood below 18 years of age (34.04 per cent, 10.63 per cent and 15.38 per cent), which gradually decreases with increase of age and then it sharply increases among the mothers who experience first child birth at the age of 27 years and above (18.18 per cent, 9.00 per cent and 12.50 per cent).

Table 12.4: Prenatal wastages and infant mortality according to the mothers' age at first child birth

Age at First Child Birth	*No. of Mothers*	*Live birth*	*Abortion*	*Still Birth*	*Infant Mortality*
Below 18 years	47	26(55.32)	16(34.04)	5(10.63)	4(15.38)
18-20 years	42	34(80.95)	6(14.28)	2(4.76)	1(2.94)
21-23 years	40	36(90.00)	3(7.50)	1(2.50)	1(2.77)
24-26 years	38	33(86.84)	3(7.89)	2(5.26)	2(6.06)
27 yrs and above	33	24(72.72)	6(18.18)	3(9.00)	3(12.50)
Total	**200**	**153(76.50)**	**34(17.00)**	**13(6.5)**	**11(7.18)**

Figures within parentheses indicates percentages.

Prenatal wastages and infant mortality according to their birth order have been described in Table 12.5. The result shows that the mean live birth increases with the increase in birth order. Incidence of abortion shows high incidence in the first birth order (17.00 per cent), gradually it decreases and then once again sharply increases at higher birth order. Incidence of still birth is found to be high at nine and above order (11.53 per cent), slightly lower at eighth birth order (10.71 per cent) and the lowest incidence of still birth is found among the sixth order (2.43 per cent). Again the highest incidence of infant death is found among the first birth order (7.18 per cent), gradually it decreases and once again it sharply increases at eighth birth order (9.00 per cent) and comes down at nine and above order (5.00 per cent). Lowest incidence of infant death is recorded at the sixth birth order (2.70 per cent).

Table 12.5: Prenatal wastages and infant mortality according to the birth order

Birth Order	*No. of Mothers*	*Live birth*	*Abortion*	*Still birth*	*Infant Mortality*
1st	200	153(76.50)	34(17.00)	13(6.50)	11(7.18)
2nd	136	115(84.55)	13(9.55)	8(5.88)	4(3.47)
3rd	101	89(88.10)	6(5.94)	6(5.94)	3(2.94)
4th	80	70(87.50)	6(7.50)	4(5.00)	2(2.85)
5th	59	51(86.44)	5(8.47)	3(5.08)	3(5.88)
6th	41	37(90.24)	3(7.31)	1(2.43)	2(2.70)
7th	35	30(85.71)	3(8.57)	2(5.71)	2(6.66)
8th	28	22(78.57)	3(10.70)	3(10.71)	2(9.00)
9 and above	26	20(76.92)	3(11.53)	3(11.53)	1(5.00)
Total	**706**	**587(83.14)**	**76(10.76)**	**43(6.09)**	**30(5.11)**

Figures within parentheses indicates percentages.

In conclusion, the incidence of prenatal wastages and infant mortality within a population is considered as a risk factor for women health. Lack of medical facilities is one of the major problems leading to increasing incidence of prenatal wastages and infant mortality. Furthermore, education of mother, mother's age at marriage, age at first child birth and birth order may not directly affect, but has high risk on infant death that cannot be ignored. Access to medical facilities, economic development, nutritional transition, improved socio-economic status is likely to lower the incidence of mortality. Furthermore, the findings of the present study may be useful for policy-makers in their endeavour to formulate various development interventions and healthcare programmes. The present study would also help enhance usefulness and effectiveness of the launched and/or ongoing intervention or supplementary programme at targeted population. There arises a need to address the challenges of establishing measures that would reduce the future ill-effects of prenatal and infant mortality rate. Finally, the results are important for effective implementation of any public health.

References

Arora, Y.L.1980. 'Infant mortality and family planning'. *Journal of Family Welfare,* 26 (4): 73-78.

Bodoloi, B.N. and Sharma Thakur, G.C. 1988. *Tribes of Assam (Part-II).* Guwahati: Tribal Research Institute, Assam.

Gogoi, Y. 2014. 'Demographic study among the Tai Ahom of Assam'. *Bulletin of the Department of Anthropology Dibrugarh University*, 42:197-206.

Keyfitz, N. and Flieger, W. 1971. *Population Facts and Methods of Demography*. Freeman, San Francisco [SD-008].

Park, K. 2000. 'Preventive medicine in obstetrics, paediatrics and geriatrics,' *Text Book of Social and Preventive Medicine,* Banarsidas Bhanot, Jabalpur.

Patir, R. and Sengupta, S. 2015. 'Effects of some bio-cultural factors on fertility and mortality among Deoris of Assam', In Aanjan Saikia (Ed): *Health Education*. A.P.H. Publishing Corporation, New Delhi.

Punhari, R. and Mahajan R.1989. *Research on ICDS: An Overview*. Delhi National Institute of Public Co-operation and Child Development 1:1975-1985.

Rajaratnam, T. and Hallad, J.S., 2000. 'Determinants of nutritional status of young children in India: An analysis of 1992-1993 NFHS Data', *Demography India,* 29(2): 179-200.

Ramachandrart, L.1989. 'The effect of antenatal and natal services on pregnancy outcome and health of the mother and child', *The Journal of Family Welfare,* 35 (5): 34-46.

World Health Organisation. 2005. *Maternal Mortality, Estimates Developed by WHO, UNICEF, UNFPA and the World Bank*, Geneva: Department of Reproductive Health and Research *www.WHO.int/Reproductive-Health.*

Chapter - 13

Reproductive Healthcare Practices among the *Idu Mishmi* Women of *Lower Dibang Valley District of Arunachal Pradesh*

—*Rakhi Rani Das and Deepanjana Dutta Das*

Introduction

Reproductive health as a whole represents the health condition of a population. The poor reproductive health status of the tribals of India reflects their poor health status, correlated with individual and household, social and economic condition. The reproductive roles of women all through the process of gestation, birth, breastfeeding and childbearing places are at the focal point of a population's reproductive health (Shankar and Thamilarasan, 2003).

The United Nations (1995, p. 2) defines reproductive health as "a state of complete physical, mental and social well-being, and not merely the absence of reproductive disease or infirmity, in all matters relating to the reproductive system and to its functions and processes". The basic definition of reproductive health encompasses the reproductive processes, functions and system of all stages of human life (United Nations Information Network [POPIN], 2010).

Throughout human history, societies have had particular perceptions of health and disease rooted in their own culture, which have had led to a plurality of practices for disease prevention and cure. Traditional approaches to healthcare are based on a culturally unique perception of the nature of illness and of healing process. Often these perspectives recognise the psychological, environmental and social contributions to disease and the active involvement of the patient in the treatment process; and places emphasis on prevention and on lifestyles that lessen the probability of developing disease (UNESCO, 1996).

Women's overall health and nutritional status, pregnancy outcomes and other reproductive health problems are considered to be the major biological causes of maternal mortality. Women's health and well-being is undetermined by a combination of social, cultural and economic factors that determine their low status in society and affect their ability to make decisions regarding healthcare. These include women's heavy workload involving domestic and income generation activities; women's lack of control over resources including cash income and capital; women's lack of access to education and information on their own health and welfare; traditional attitudes of men and community leaders towards women's well-being; and women's lack of access to health services.

The People

The present study focuses on the reproductive healthcare practices of the Idu Mishmi women of Lower Dibang Valley District of Arunachal Pradesh. They are also known as Chuli-Kata or "Cropped hair" for their distinctive hair style. Idu Mishmis are the inhabitants of the Upper and Lower Dibang Valley District of Arunachal Pradesh. Generally, it is assumed that they might have come from the north, the holy place called "Athu-Popu", situated in the border of Lower Dibang Valley District and Tibet following the course of the river Dibang, locally called Talo. Thus, the Idus have similarities with Kachins of Myanmar. They had entered their present home following the course of Ilu, also known as Lohit River. They have Mongoloid type of features. They are of medium or short stature; some of them have gracefully body-built, while some are thin. Skin colour is slightly yellowish, hair is black. All are characterised by broad face, epicanthic eye folds and presence of scanty hair on their body. The Idu Mishmis do not have any script of their own and as such things are passed on from one generation to the next verbally. They belong to the Tibeto-Burman linguistic family. Rice and millet are their staple food. They are mostly non-vegetarian. Agriculture is their main occupation. The Idu Mishmi family is of patriarchal type. The families of the villages are mostly nuclear type.

Material and Methods

The present study has been carried out in the six Idu Mishmi villages, namely, Mayu-I, Mayu-II, Cheta-I, Cheta-II, Koronu and Abango of Lower Dibang Valley district of Arunachal Pradesh. Data collection was carried out during the month of February, 2013. We have conducted intensive in-depth, informal interviews to collect data in the Idu Mishmi dominated villages of Lower Dibang Valley district. The data were collected from

300 local Idu Mishmi ever married women. A number of group discussions were also conducted during the period of investigations.

Results and Discussion

The Idu Mishmis, like many other tribes of India, practise indigenous method of reproductive healthcare, along with availing of the advantages of medical facilities available in their area. In the present paper, an attempt has been made to record some of the reproductive healthcare practices among the Idu Mishmis. Earlier, in the Idu Mishmi society, the traditional method of reproductive healthcare was predominant. They had a belief that supernatural forces caused diseases and thus they consulted Bamuni/Igu (local priest) for curative measures. But, with advent of time, they are changing their practices. The use of different reproductive healthcare practices is due to subsisting cultural beliefs. The tribals are not interested in sharing their knowledge with outsiders. After developing intimacy with some priests and experienced women of the community, some information on the reproductive healthcare practices could be collected and presented in this paper. The version of the villagers revealed that people are shifting towards the modern medical system. This is due to the effectiveness and quick action of the modern medical system. The present paper has highlighted the reproductive healthcare practices of the Idu Mishmi women.

From the conception to delivery of the child, the Idu Mishmis by and large do not have any idea of medical check-up in the earlier times. Women carry most of the household activities and they have less time to seek out healthcare services, making them disadvantaged. During pregnancy also, they do not get special care, which is necessary. They have to do all the works as they do normally.

During 2-5 months of conception, they perform a ritual called *Arrebbi* by the Bamuni (priest) for the safe delivery of mother and the child. The younger generation, along with the use of modern facilities, also performs this ritual.

All the expectant mothers of Idu Mishmi have to observe this taboo that she cannot touch the antlers hanging on the wall of their house.

From the Table 13.1, it is observed that there are some restricted food items and beliefs associated with their pregnancy. From the inception of pregnancy to its termination women consume no specific diet. It is same as the other members of the family. But, she is generally given whatever she wants to eat. On the other hand, some pregnant women reduce their intake of nutritious food to ensure that baby may remain small and the delivery may be easier. The version of some Idu Mishmi women revealed that there are some beliefs regarding some food items.

Table 13.1: Restricted food items and beliefs related to pregnancy

Sl.No.	*Food Items*	*Scientific Names*	*Beliefs related that*
1	Excess salt	Sodium Chloride	May cause miscarriage
2	Arum	Colocasia esculenta	Skin disease in child
3	Chilly	Capsicum annuum	Skin problem in child also the child may cry too much
4	Ginger	Zinger officinale	Skin problem in child also the child may cry too much
5	Fatty food items	-	May create problem during delivery

Table 13.2: Workload during pregnancy among the Idu Mishmi women

Type of Workload during pregnancy	*Number of women*	*Percentage*
Heavy workload	414	59.14
Light workload	286	40.86
Total	**700**	**100.00**

From Table 13.2, it is clear that the Idu Mishmi women take heavy workload and are to bear heavy reproductive role. It clearly highlights that out of 700 women, only 286 (40.86 per cent) women took care during their pregnancy i.e. they did not do any heavy workload during their pregnancy. But 414 (59.14 per cent) women did not take any care regarding their workload during pregnancy.

Table 13.3: Distribution of women according to the type of treatment utilised during pregnancy

Type of treatment	*No. of women*	*Per cent*
Indigenous method	257	36.71
Modern method	161	23.00
Both types	177	25.29
No treatment	105	15.00
Total	**700**	**100.00**

With regard to their awareness and receiving modern medical facilities, it has been found that the elderly people by and large are averse to modern medical treatment. This is, however, a ground reality that in certain areas, the facilities of modern medical treatment are not available in the neighbourhood of 15 to 20 km. But, even in the areas where these are available, it has been found that only the educated youths, particularly the girls, take more initiative to take the patients to the medical centres for treatment. The study (Table 13.3) reveals that out of 700 ever married women, 36.71 per cent (257) have utilised the indigenous method of treatment during pregnancy. It is followed by 25.29 per cent (177) of women who have utilised both the types of treatment, *i.e.*, indigenous and modern medical methods. Only 23 per cent (161) of women have utilised modern medical methods and 15 per cent (105) have not utilised any type of treatment during pregnancy.

Table 13.4: Number of conceptions immunised against TT

Vaccination	*Number of conceptions*	*Percentage*	*Number of live-births*	*Percentage*
Immunised against TT	1372	48.17	1320	96.21
Not immunised against TT	1476	51.83	1322	89.57
Total	**2848**	**100**	**2642**	**100**

From the Table 13.4, it is clear that maternal healthcare practices were found to be largely neglected in the Idu Mishmi community. Expectant mothers, to a large extent, are not inoculated against tetanus toxoid. It is also clear from the table that out of 2848 conceptions, only 1372 (48.17 per cent) were found to be immunised against tetanus toxoid and 1476 (51.83 per cent) were not immunised against tetanus toxoid. The table also reveals that 96.21 per cent (1320) of immunised conceptions were resulted into successful live births, whereas 89.57 per cent (1322) not immunised conceptions were resulted into successful outcome as live-births.

Table 13.5: Place of Delivery

Place of delivery	*Number of live-births*	*Percentage*
At Home / outside home	1693	64.08
At PHC/PVT. HOSP/DISTT. HOSP	949	35.92
Total	**2642**	**100**

The data shown in Table 13.5 reveal that out of 2642 live-births, only 949 (35.92 per cent) deliveries have been attended at PHC/Pvt. nursing home/district hospital, whereas, 1693 (64.08 per cent) deliveries were attended at home or outside home like agricultural field, etc. Actually, the Idu Mishmi women are very shy in nature, that is why, they like to deliver their child by themselves. There is no midwifery system present in the Idu Mishmi society. Earlier, the pregnant women nearby their delivery period, they used to carry blade or bamboo split and old clothes along with them wherever they go. When labour pain starts, they used to go to a lonely place where nobody could see them and perform all the delivery works like cutting the umbilical cord and washing the new born baby etc. by themselves. If the delivery becomes delayed/complicated at that time, only the pregnant woman is attended by the untrained but experienced female relatives or friends. But now the educated younger generation prefers to have their delivery under the supervision of trained personnel. After delivery, Iyu (local rice beer) is given to the mother of new-born baby to get relief and also to increase the milk production of the women.

The Idu Mishmi women, from the reproductive health perspective, are believed to be healthy if she has the ability of bearing healthy and normal children and if she can give birth consecutively as many as 3-10 children. Moreover, her hard work in the field and household activities should also be performed to the highest satisfaction of others.

With regard to their awareness and receiving modern medical facilities, it has been found that the elderly people, by and large, are averse to modern medical treatment. But, now the educated youths are taking initiative to utilise the modern medical treatment.

It may be generally noted that delivery generally does not take place in hospital or under the supervision of trained personnel for delivery. Only in the complicated cases of delivery, the expectant mother is helped by the untrained but experienced women of the village.

With regard to an ideal family size, it may be noted that the idea of family size goes against the traditional beliefs and values. They believe that the children are the gift of god. Also they are insecure about their population size. So, instead of decreasing their family size, they want to increase their family. Nevertheless, nowadays, most of the people realise that a small family with two or three children is better than a bigger one, so that they can bring them up in a better way. In practice also, most of the people have been found to take the contraceptive measures. The contraceptive measures are available free of cost at the healthcare centres.

On the whole, it seems that the members of the younger generation and the educated one, nowadays are realising the necessity of taking care of the reproductive health of the womenfolk. This awareness is reflected in their effort to plan the family size, reasonable inter-spacing of childbirth and arranging regular medical check-ups and providing nutritious diet during pregnancy by some Idu Mishmi families. The study further reveals that there has been a positive impact of various mass media programmes, in this regard, on the educated Idu Mishmis. As gender roles and relations within and between households vary from one material to another, social and cultural ideological context to another, decisions regarding matters of the healthcare become at once both complex and challenging to understand.

Table 13.6: Different medicare systems utilised during pregnancy related to morbidity scenario

Diseases	*No Treatment*		*Medical*		*Indigenous*		*Both*		*Total*	
	No.	*Per cent*	*No.*	*Per cent*	*No.*	*Per cent*	*No.*	*Per cent*	*No.*	*Per cent*
Gastritis	43	17.84	81	33.61	42	17.43	75	31.12	241	100.00
Back-pain	29	16.86	49	28.49	35	20.35	59	34.30	172	100.00
Joint-pain	21	22.34	11	11.70	51	54.26	11	11.70	94	100.00
Pressure	20	25.97	5	6.49	48	62.34	4	5.19	77	100.00
Sugar	7	17.07	2	4.88	26	63.41	6	14.63	41	100.00
Total	**120**	**19.20**	**148**	**23.68**	**202**	**32.32**	**155**	**24.80**	**625**	**100.00**

The most frequent general complaints of Idu Mishmi women are back-pain, joint-pain, gastritis, pressure and sugar. Table 13.6 reveals that maximum number of women, *i.e.*, 81 (33.61 per cent) who were suffering from gastritis had utilised the modern medical system during their pregnancy. Which is again followed by those women, *i.e.*, 75 (31.12 per cent) who had utilised both types of treatment during pregnancy. Again, in case of back-pain also, maximum number of women, *i.e.*, 59 (34.30 per cent) had utilised both types of treatment during their pregnancy. This is again followed by those women, *i.e.*, 49 (28.49 per cent) who had utilised modern medical treatment during their pregnancy. But in case of sugar and blood pressure, 63.41 per cent and 62.34 per cent of women, respectively, had utilised the traditional method of treatment during their pregnancy. Which is again followed by 54.26 per cent (51) of those women, who were suffering from joint pain, had utilised the traditional method of treatment during pregnancy. Thus, from the study, it is found that the type of treatment utilised during pregnancy and the type of diseases occur in the women in their later life period are closely related.

Conclusion

On the whole, it seems that the members of the younger generation and the educated ones, nowadays, are realising the necessity of taking care of the reproductive health of the womenfolk. This awareness is reflected in their effort to plan family size, reasonable inter-spacing of childbirth and arranging regular medical check-ups and providing nutritious diet during pregnancy by some of the families. The study reveals that, presently, very few elderly persons in the community practise traditional methods of reproductive healthcare. While the younger generations, due to modernisation, culture-contact and education, are changing themselves. Now they have become conscious about the reproductive health. So, they prefer to use medical service for reproductive health problems. Therefore, the younger generation of Idu Mishmi women enjoys better reproductive health condition than their older womenfolks.

References

Baruah, Tapan Kumar M. 1960. *The Idu Mishmis*. Advisor to the Governer of Assam. Shillong.

Goswami, Monali; Bijayalaxmi Dash, and N.C. Dash. 2011. "Traditional Method of Reproductive Healthcare Practices and Fertility Control among the Bhumija Tribe of Baleswar, Orissa", *Ethno Medicine* 5(1): 51-55.

Sharmeen, Shaila, and Taniya Sharmeen. 2005. "Traditional Health Practices of Munda Women: Continuity and Change", *Man and Life* 31(1-2):23-26.

Chapter - 14

Reproductive Factors and Risk of Cervical Cancer in *Manipur*–A Case-control Study

—Arundhati Devi Maibam and M. Shyamchand Meitei

Introduction

Cervical cancer is the fourth most common cancer affecting women worldwide, with 528,000 new cases every year. It is also the fourth most common cause of cancer deaths in women worldwide, with 266,000 deaths in 2012 (Cervical Cancer, 2012). Denny in Sreedevi *et al.* (2015) held it as the commonest cancer cause of death among women in developing countries. More than one-fifth of all new cases are diagnosed in India where 122,844 women are diagnosed with cervical cancer and 67,477 die from the disease every year. India also has the highest age standardised incidence of cervical cancer in South Asia at 22, compared to 19.2 in Bangladesh, 13 in Sri Lanka, and 2.8 in Iran (ICO Information Centre on HPV and Cancer, 2014).

Reproductive risk factors for invasive cervical cancer have been evaluated in many studies. Various studies have confirmed the link with sexual activity, multiparity, early marriage, multiple sexual partners, illiteracy, and low socio-economic status. Role of sexual and reproductive factors affecting the incidence of breast and cervical cancers has been well documented from the several epidemiological studies carried out in India as well as other parts of the world. Epidemiological data strongly implicate sexually transmitted agents in the etiology of cervical cancer.

The Population-based Cancer Registry, PBCR Report (2009-11), of Indian Council of Medical Research (ICMR) India (2013), had shown that Aizawl district of North-East India had the highest age adjusted incidence rates (AAR) of 24.3 for cervix uteri cancer among all the PBCRs.

The AARs of other North-eastern region PBCRs are as: Mizoram state (17.1), Kamrup urban (14.0), Nagaland (11.0), Cachar (10.9), Imphal West (10.6), Tripura state (10.1), East Khasi Hills (9.9), Manipur state (8.1) and Dibrugarh (5.6). Cervix uteri cancer features in the top five leading sites in North-East, viz. second in Cachar and Sikkim, third in Kamrup (urban), Manipur State, Imphal West District, Mizoram state and Aizwal and fifth in Dibrugarh District. According to the first report published by the registry in 2003-04, the incidence rate of cervical cancer in Imphal West District was 14.59 per cent, which increased to 15.09 per cent in 2005-06. The overall rate of incidence in the districts of Senapati, Tamenglong, Churachandpur, Bishnupur, Thoubal, Imphal West, Imphal East, Ukhrul, Chandel and others in 2005-06 was 14.33 per cent. According to the biennial report published by PBCR Imphal in 2007, the incidence rate in Imphal West District declined to 12.68 per cent in 2006-08. However, cervical cancer remains the second leading site of cancer among women in Manipur after lung cancer.

Methodology

This case-control study was designed to study the reproductive risk factors for cervical cancer among Manipuri women. Cases were diagnosed with histologically confirmed cervical cancer in RT Dept, RIMS (Regional Institute of Medical Sciences), Imphal, Manipur, India, during 2008-09. A total number of 64 incident cases were interviewed using a pretested schedule. Cases were interviewed only once at the OPD while they were waiting to be examined by the physician. For each case subject, four controls from the neighbourhood with an intact uterus were selected at random, matched by age.

Reproductive factors considered in this analysis include age at menarche, age at first child birth, total number of pregnancies, number of vaginal and caesarean section deliveries, number of abortions, miscarriages, still births, live births and contraceptive methods. Reproductive and menstrual history has been determined by combining age at menarche, age at menopause, parity, age at first pregnancy, nature of delivery, delivery done by trained or untrained personnel, menstrual hygiene and practices. The relationships between cervical cancer and possible reproductive risk factors have been measured using odds ratio (OR) and their 95 per cent confidence intervals (CI). Backward stepwise conditional logistic regression was also conducted to identify the most important factors associated with cervical cancer.

Results

Table 14.1: Reproductive History of Subjects

Variables	*Case (Per cent)*	*Control (Per cent)*	χ^2	*Crude-OR*	*P-value*	*95 Per cent CI for OR*
Age at menarche (yr)						
13	17(26.6)	58(22.3)		1.000		
13+	47(73.4)	198(77.7)	0.532	1.263	>0.05	0.674-2.366
Age at first pregnancy (yr)						
18	25(39.7)	60(23.9)		1.000		
18+	38(60.3)	191(76.1)	6.350	0.477	<0.05*	0.267-0.855
No. of pregnancies						
3	15(23.4)	81(31.6)		1.000		
3+	49(76.6)	175(68.4)	1.641	1.512	>0.05	0.801-2.855
No. of deliveries						
3	21(32.8)	105(41.0)		1.000		
3+	43(67.2)	151(59.0)	1.443	1.424	>0.05	0.799-2.538
No. of vaginal deliveries						
3	19(30.6)	94(38.4)		1.000		
3+	43(69.4)	151(61.6)	1.269	1.409	>0.05	0.775-2.562
No. of deliveries by trained personal						
0	43(67.2)	170(66.4)		1.000		
1+	21(32.8)	86(33.6)	0.014	0.965	>0.05	0.539-1.729
No. of deliveries by untrained personal						
0	14(21.9)	66(25.8)		1.000		
1+	50(78.1)	190(74.2)	0.417	1.241	>0.05	0.644-2.389
Last birth interval (mth.)						
<24	12(20.0)	42(18.5)		1.000		
24-36	23(38.3)	99(43.6)		0.813	>0.05	0.371-1.784
36+	25(41.7)	86(37.9)	0.543	1.017	>0.05	0.466-2.222
No. of live births						
0	2(3.1)	8(3.1)		1.000		
1-2	9(14.1)	55(21.5)		0.655	>0.05	0.119-3.591
3-4	28(43.8)	100(39.1)		1.120	>0.05	0.225-5.576
5-6	19(29.7)	71(27.7)		1.070	>0.05	0.210-5.464
7+	6(9.4)	22(8.6)	1.797	1.091	>0.05	0.182-6.555
No. of still births						
0	62(96.9)	247(96.5)		1.000		
1+	2(3.1)	9(3.5)	0.024	0.885	>0.05	0.187-4.201

(Contd...)

No. of abortions						
0	43(67.2)	217(84.8)		1.000		
1+	21(32.8)	39(15.2)	10.385	2.717	<0.01*	1.457-5.068
No. of miscariages						
0	58(90.6)	225(88.2)		1.000		
1+	6(9.4)	31(11.8)	0.292	0.776	>0.05	0.308-1.952

The influence of reproductive and menstrual factors is shown in Table 14.1. In the univariate analysis, age at menarche, numbers of deliveries, vaginal deliveries, pregnancies, deliveries by trained and untrained personnel, live births, still births, miscarriages and the last birth interval are not significantly different between cases and controls. The use of oral contraceptives (0 cases and 5 controls) and intra-uterine device (12 cases and 15 controls) are rare and unrelated to cervical cancer risk. Most of the women reported relying on 'safe period' or withdrawal method to avoid pregnancy in place of any form of modern contraceptives. No case or control woman reported a personal history of sexually transmitted disease, while HPV was unheard of till the time of investigation. However, the age at first pregnancy is found to be associated with cervical cancer (OR=0.477, P< 0.05). Women with first pregnancy at ≥18 years have more chances of developing cervical cancer than those with first pregnancy at 18+ years. Significant difference is also observed in the number of abortions undergone by the women under study. Women who reported one or more abortions (either induced or spontaneous or both) have a higher risk than those who had never gone for abortions (OR=2.717, P<0.01). Early age at first pregnancy and more number of abortions are responsible for causation of the disease in the present study.

Out of the twelve variables fitted in the stepwise multiple logistic regression (Backward Wald), two reproductive factors are found to have significant impact on incidence of cervical cancer. They are age at marriage (P<0.05) and number of abortions (P<0.05), as manifested in Tables 14.2 and 3.3. Considering the effects of eleven other variables, women with lower age at marriage (which is closely linked with early pregnancy) have statistically significant chance of having cervical cancer in the population under study. The finding indicates that a woman whose age at marriage reduces by one year has about 90 per cent chance of developing cervical cancer as evidenced by its OR value, 0.895 (with 95 per cent CI 0.819-0.977). This is to say that if a woman delays marriage by one year, the chance of early pregnancy, which helps in developing cervical cancer, may be reduced by 90 per cent while controlling the joint effects of eleven other factors under analysis. Further, the chance of developing the disease

Table 14.2: Odds Ratios of Variables on the Incidence of Cervical Cancer in Adjusted Logistic Regressions

Variable	*b*	*S. E*	*Wald*	*P-value*	*OR*	*95 Per cent CI for OR*	
						Lower	*Upper*
Age at marriage	-.111	.045	6.130	.013	.895	.819	.977
Age at menarche	-.154	.103	2.254	.133	.857	.701	1.048
Total no. of pregnancies	-.346	.369	.879	.348	.708	.344	1.458
No. of vaginal deliveries	.373	.369	1.016	.313	1.451	.704	2.994
No. of deliveries by trained personnel	.321	.368	.684	.408	1.379	.644	2.952
Age	.042	.021	4.241	.039	1.043	1.002	1.086
No. of abortions	.702	.396	4.001	.045	2.207	1.016	4.795
No. of miscarriages	.257	.444	.336	.562	1.293	.542	3.085
Period of abstinence	-1.439	.385	13.945	.000	.237	.111	.505
Educational level	.048	.039	1.530	.216	1.050	.972	1.133
Use of tobacco	-.187	.333	.316	.574	.829	.432	1.593
Duration of married life	-.008	.022	.142	.707	.992	.949	1.036
Constant	2.573	1.798	2.047	.153	13.099		

Table 14.3: Odds Ratios of Variables on the Incidence of Cervical Cancer in Stepwise Logistic Regressions

Step	*Variable*	*b*	*S.E.*	*Wald*	*P-value*	*OR*	*95 per cent CI for OR*	
							Lower	*Upper*
1.	Age at marriage	-.111	.045	6.130	.013	.895	.819	.977
	Age at menarche	-.154	.103	2.254	.133	.857	.701	1.048
	Total no. of pregnancies	-.346	.369	.897	.348	.708	.344	1.458
	No. of vaginal deliveries	.373	.369	1.016	.313	1.451	.704	2.994
	No. of deliveries by trained personnel	.321	.388	.684	.408	1.379	.644	2.952
	Age	.042	.021	4.241	.039	1.043	1.002	1.086
	No. of abortions	.792	.396	4.001	.045	2.207	1.016	4.795
	No. of miscarriages	.257	.444	.336	.562	1.293	.542	3.085

(Contd...)

	Period of abstinence	-1.439	.385	13.945	.000	.237	.111	.505
	Educational level	.048	.039	1.530	.216	1.050	.972	1.133
	Use of tobacco	-.187	.333	.316	.574	.829	.432	1.593
	Duration of married life	-.008	.022	.142	.707	.992	.949	1.036
	Constant	2.573	1.798	2.047	.153	13.099		
2.	Age at marriage	-.106	.043	6.066	.014	.899	.826	.978
	Age at menarche	-.153	.103	2.229	.135	.858	.702	1.049
	Total no. of pregnancies	-.356	.369	.931	.335	.701	.340	1.443
	No. of vaginal deliveries	.371	.371	1.000	.317	1.449	.701	2.996
	No. of deliveries by trained personnel	.323	.388	.691	.406	1.381	.645	2.954
	Age	.037	.016	5.453	.020	1.038	1.006	1.071
	No. of abortions	.804	.396	4.133	.042	2.235	1.029	4.852
	No. of miscarriages	.270	.442	.372	.542	1/309	.551	3.113
	Period of abstinence	-1.444	.385	14.070	.000	.236	.111	.502
	Educational level	.049	.039	1.568	.210	1.050	.973	1.134
	Use of tobacco	-.192	.333	.331	.565	.826	.430	1.586
	Constant	2.527	1.793	1.986	.159	12.518		
3.	Age at marriage	-.103	.043	5.82	.016	.902	.830	.981
	Age at menarche	-.155	.102	2.289	.130	.857	.701	1.047
	Total no. of pregnancies	-.371	.368	1.017	.313	.690	.336	1.419
	No. of vaginal deliveries	.387	.370	1.095	.295	1.472	.713	3.037
	No. of deliveries by trained personnel	.317	.388	.671	.413	1.374	.643	2.936
	Age	.038	.016	5.653‘	.017	1.039	1.007	1.072
	No. of abortions	.823	.395	4.349	.037	2.277	1.051	4.934
	No. of miscarriages	.282	.441	.409	.523	1.326	.559	3.145
	Period of abstinence	-1.411	.381	13.749	.000	.244	.116	.514
	Educational level	.050	.039	1.624	.203	1.051	.974	1.135
	Constant	2.317	1.746	1.761	.185	10.145		
4.	Age at marriage	-.103	.043	5.833	.016	.902	.830	.981
	Age at menarche	-.156	.102	2.315	.128	.856	.701	1.046
	Total no. of pregnancies	-.206	.248	.691	.406	.814	.500	1.323
	No. of vaginal deliveries	.228	.256	.794	.373	1.257	.760	2.076

(Contd...)

	No. of deliveries by trained personnel	.315	.387	.663	.416	1.371	.642	2.928
	Age	.038	.016	5.513	.019	1.038	1.006	1.071
	No. of abortions	.658	.286	5.311	.021	1.931	1.103	3.380
	Period of abstinence	-1.388	.378	13.504	.000	.250	.119	.523
	Educational level	.051	.039	1.722	.189	1.053	.975	1.136
	Constant	2.303	1.748	1.737	.188	10.007	.830	.981
	Age at marriage	-.103	.043	5.833	.016	.902		
5.	Age at marriage	-.102	.043	5.676	.017	.903	.830	.982
	Age at menarche	-.143	.100	2.044	.153	.867	.713	1.054
	Total no. of pregnancies	-.204	.246	.685	.408	.816	.503	1.322
	No. of vaginal deliveries	.216	.254	.719	.396	1.241	.754	2.041
	Age	.034	.015	4.952	.026	1.035	1.004	1.066
	No. of abortions	.656	.284	5.329	.021	1.928	1.104	3.366
	Period of abstinence	-1.381	.375	13.539	.000	.251	.120	.524
	Educational level	.057	.38	2.191	.139	1.058	.982	1.141
	Constant	2.402	1.735	1.917	.166	11.048		
6.	Age at marriage	-.104	.043	5.960	.015	.901	.829	.980
	Age at menarche	-.141	.100	1.984	.159	.869	.714	1.057
	No. of vaginal deliveries	.015	.076	.039	.843	1.015	.875	1.177
	Age	.034	.015	4.835	.028	1.034	1.004	1.066
	No. of abortions	.458	.151	9.249	.002	1.581	1.177	2.124
	Period of abstinence	-1.370	.374	13.429	.000	.254	.122	.529
	Educational level	.056	.038	2.127	.145	1.058	.981	1.140
	Constant	2.373	1.733	1.876	.171	10.733		
7.	Age at marriage	-.107	.040	7.279	.007	.898	.831	.971
	Age at menarche	-.140	.100	1.956	.162	.870	.715	1.058
	Age	.034	.015	5.162	.023	1.035	1.005	1.066
	No. of abortions	.458	.151	9.246	.002	1.580	1.177	2.123
	Period of	-1.367	.374	13.386	.000	.255	.123	.530
	Educational level	.055	.038	2.099	.147	1.057	.981	1.139
	Constant	2.455	1.685	2.123	.145	11.644		
8.	Age at marriage	-.115	.039	8,549	.003	.891	.825	.963
	Age	.036	.015	5.592	.018	1.036	1.006	1.067
	No. of abortions	.473	.150	10.004	.002	1.605	1.197	2.152
	Period of	-1.348	.374	12.995	.000	.260	.125	.541
	Educational level	.053	.038	1,980	.159	1.055	.979	1.136
	Constant	.606	1.030	.346	.556	1.833		

(Contd...)

9.	Age at marriage	-.088	.033	7.051	.008	.915	.858	.977
	Age	.030	.014	4.366	.037	1.031	1.002	1.060
	No. of abortions	.453	.150	9.108	.003	1.574	1.172	2.113
	Period of abstinence	-1.331	.370	12.911	.000	.264	.128	.546
	Constant	.625	1.023	.373	.541	1.868		

is also increased 2.21 times (OR: 2.207 with 95 per cent CI: 1.016-4.795) to each increment in the number of abortions undergone. The ill habit of abortion is reemphasised. A high risk of cervical cancer (P<0.01) can be quantified to be 57 per cent to each increment of abortion (OR=1.57 with 95 per cent CI: 1.17-2.11).

Discussion

In the univariate analysis conducted in the present study, age at first pregnancy and total number of abortions are found to be associated with cervical cancer. In the stepwise multiple logistic regression also, age at first marriage, which results in age at first pregnancy and number of abortions, are found to be statistically significant.

Boyd and Doll (1964) observed little evidence of link between risk of cervical cancer and age at menarche. In the present study, women attaining menarche before or after 13 years shows no significant risk to cervical cancer. Although a previous report suggested an inverse association between age at menarche and HPV infection, the finding of the present study is in agreement with the majority of the studies that did not report significant associations (Collins *et al.,* 2005:499).

According to Atalah *et al.,* Bjorge and Kravdal and Yoo *et al.* as cited in Reis (2011: 156), early age at first full-term pregnancy was associated with risk factors. In conformance with these findings, the results in this study show that early age at first pregnancy is a risk factor for cervical cancer. Cumulatively, 53.2 per cent of case women reported giving birth within the first year of age at first marriage. Among women with age at first marriage <18 years, 55.9 per cent were pregnant within the first year of marriage. However, Parazzini *et al.* (1989:807) could not find such a relationship. The mechanism by which the early experience of first pregnancy could influence the risk of cervical carcinogenesis may be explained by the steroid hormonal influence on HPV infection and on the host's immune response to HPV during pre-adolescence and adolescence. Biological immaturity during adolescence has also been proposed as an additional susceptibility factor (Singer and Monaghan, 2000:44). In their study, Dutta *et al.* (1990) also observed that the relative risk of acquiring the disease was six times more in case of women who had first parity before 18 years of age ($p<0.0001$) as compared to those who had the first parity after the age of 18 years. Lower age at first parity was found to be significantly associated with subsequent development of cancer cervix. This may be attributed to early sexual activities, hormonal changes during pregnancy or may be due to cervical trauma during delivery at a relatively younger age of mother.

Singer and Monaghan (2000:46) explained that the mechanism by which the early experience of first sexual intercourse and first pregnancy influence the risk of cervical carcinogenesis could be due to the steroid hormonal influence on HPV infection and on the host's immune response to HPV during pre-adolescence and adolescence. During adolescence and pregnancy, the cervix is exposed to augmented levels of hormonal changes in which oestrogen stimulation facilitates acidification of the vaginal cavity, a determinant of squamous metaplasia when the endocervical epithelial everts. When this oestrogen-stimulated metaplastic transformation occurs in the presence of HPV, the probability of cell transformation increases, resulting in neoplastic changes). This phenomenon is dependent primarily on parity, and is more likely to occur during the first pregnancy rather than subsequent pregnancies (Singer and Monaghan, 2000:48).

The Manipuri society expects newly married women to become pregnant soon after marriage. Women, therefore, never think of delaying pregnancy. Failure to bear a child immediately after or within one year of marriage puts a woman in an awkward position. In such situations, every available help is sought to avoid social stigma attached to barrenness. A feeling of insecurity develops within the woman and fears abandonment by the husband. So the general concept is: the sooner, the better; not realising the dangers and impediments to health due to early pregnancy and child birth.

Many studies have revealed that high parity women are at high risk for cervical cancer. The effect of parity in cervical cancer development seems to be mainly detectable in countries with high fertility rates and is rarely found in low parity countries. However, in this study, there is no significant association between risk of cervical cancer and total number of pregnancies. Most women had at least one pregnancy except for one case and four controls and a substantial number of women had more than three pregnancies (76.6 per cent of the cases and 68.4 per cent of the controls). There was no marked difference in relation to number of pregnancies among cases and controls. This may be due to non-adoption of contraceptive methods (both traditional and modern) due to lack of faith in the traditional methods and lack of easy access to the modern methods.

Several studies have suggested a positive association between induced abortion and cancer of the cervix (Parazini *et al.,* 1988: 202). This study also found number of abortions as an important factor. As most of the women depended on untrained personnel for abortion, infections might have occurred during the process which were left untreated. The care and attention with which the untrained personnel handled the cases is doubtful. Women in Manipur, despite being projected as important agents of social control, still remain subdued within the household. They do not enjoy the liberty to restrict pregnancies and avoid abortion. Decision on the number of children primarily rests with the husband and his mother (if any). Women have no choice but to abide by the decision of their husbands who do not understand the importance of checking the physical status of their wives in relation to pregnancy. Multiple pregnancies cause trauma to the cervix and leave it vulnerable to infections, which can lead to dysplasia and ultimately cancer. But, as the women do not have knowledge about it, they raise no objection for fear of being scorned by their husbands and family members. In most of the cases, the abortions were conducted without the knowledge of the husband. One major factor for abortion is non-adoption of effective modern birth control measures.

The use of oral contraceptive is a well-established risk factor for cervical cancer; analyses of case-control and cohort studies have confirmed that risk for both squamous cell and adenocarcinoma is directly related to the duration of use of oral contraceptives in all and in HPV-positive women (Moreno *et al.,* 2002: 3-5). The effect of oral contraceptives on cancer risk is strongest for current and recent use and decreases with time since last use. However, such association is not observed in this study as very few women reported use of contraceptive pills. This may be due to lack of awareness as 85.9 use of the cases and 83.2 use of the controls are either illiterate or under-educated. The most commonly practised method to avoid pregnancy is abstinence from coitus during the fertile period, which the women referred to as the 'safe period'.

The women barely used oral contraceptives. Other modern methods to avoid pregnancy were equally avoided due to the belief that they fail to be effective in most instances. As mentioned by Ghosh and Ghosh (1997:184), condoms reduce sexual pleasure and intimacy. Many women reported that their husbands were against the use of condoms while they reportedly experienced discomfort during intercourse. Owing to these reasons, the most commonly used method to control pregnancy by majority of the women is either withdrawal method or abstinence on certain days of the month. Such practice can undoubtedly control pregnancy to a certain extent, but not altogether. At the same time, the chance of infection remains high if genital hygiene is not maintained. The knowledge of safe sex is altogether absent as none of the women had knowledge of contracting infections from their husbands whose promiscuity, if any, remains unknown.

Conclusion

Cervical cancer is the third most common cancer in women, the most common in India and the second most common in Manipur. All women who are above 15 years of age have the risk of developing the disease. The reason for the high incidence and mortality rates can be lack of awareness of the risk factors, which cause the disease and non-attendance in organised screening. In India, it has been one of the most important cancers in women over the past two decades. The burden is enormous as it remains the most frequent cancer among women and number one cause of deaths in middle aged Indian women. In Manipur too, cervical cancer is a cause for alarm as it remains the second leading site of cancer among women after lung cancer. Cancer, in general, is related with cultural habits and cervical cancer is no exception.

Early marriage results in early pregnancy. The young cervix undergoes hormonal changes during pregnancy, which can lead to subsequent development of cervical cancer. Unwanted pregnancies are controlled not by contraceptives, but by abortion by a large number of women. Repeated abortions increase the risk due to chances of infection if proper care and precaution is not taken when the cervix is in a vulnerable state. Most often, abortions are performed in local dispensaries and health centres where adequate hygienic facilities are not available. There were reports of abortions having been performed by local *dais* (untrained personnel) who do not possess the skill to perform the task in a hygienic manner. Infections may occur on such occasions and they will undoubtedly remain untreated due to ignorance of both the performer and the patient in question.

The findings of the present study provide a significant contribution to public health research, in general, and cervical cancer, in particular. In developed countries, this preventable disease has attracted the attention of women who have started taking active participation in organised screenings due to which observable declines in rates of incidence and mortality have been reported. The scene is not the same in the developing countries where high rates of incidence and mortality are still reported. In India, despite the high incidence and mortality rates due to poverty, organised screening programmes are yet to gain momentum. In Manipur too, where cervical cancer ranks second after lung cancer, no organised screening programmes are conducted till date, except for the efforts put in by some private organisations working towards prevention of the disease. Since this disease is preventable if detected early, the burden can be reduced if organised screening programmes are introduced in the state on regular basis. Active participation by women, in general, and high risk groups, in particular, can be expected if awareness about the risk factors is given through the various media functioning in the state. Until and unless women receive the message and participate in screening programmes, the disease will continue to claim lives, which could have been saved with the effort of the health practitioners.

As cervical cancer is caused both by factors which can be changed and which cannot be changed, attention on the factors which can be changed is expected to bear fruitful results. Since early age at first pregnancy and abortions enhance risk of cervical cancer, use of recommended birth control measures needs to be made more pronounced. For situations, where abortion cannot be avoided, they need to have knowledge about the risks and dangers of undergoing it at places other than the recommended. Level of knowledge about Pap smear test which can ensure healthy status of the uterus by timely detection of cell abnormalities in the uterus is near to nil among the women population in the state. Therefore, it needs to be popularised and made affordable as it is more often women from low income families who are detected with the disease.

Young educated daughters with good awareness level of the risks need to break the barrier of 'sexual silence' to help their mothers from developing the disease. As women understand women's problems better, they can educate their illiterate mothers, especially those who belong to the high-risk group, about the risks and motivate them to go for regular screening for HPV and other infections.

Future similar studies, including status of HPV infection, should shed further light on the causation of the disease. More in-depth investigation on sexual behaviour of both male and female will strengthen the findings of the present study. The state is in dire need of data on risks of cervical cancer to attract the attention of health promoters and policy makers.

References

Boyd, J., and Doll, R. (1964). "A study of the aetiology of carcinoma of the cervix uteri", *Br J Cancer,* Vol. 18, 419-434.

Cervical cancer. Estimated incidence, mortality and prevalence worldwide in 2012. http://globocan.iarc.fr/Pages/fact_sheets_cancer.aspx (Accessed on March 18, 2015).

Collins, S.I., Mazloomzadeh, S., Winter, H., Rollason, T.P., Blomfield, P., Young, L.S., and Woodman, C.B. (2005). "Proximity of first intercourse to menarche and the risk of human papillomavirus infection: A longitudinal study", *Int J Cancer,* Vol. 114, 498–500.

Denny, L. (2012). "Cervical cancer: Prevention and treatment", *Discov Med, 14,* 125–131.

Dutta, P.K., Upadhyay, A., Dutta, M., Urmil, A.C., Thergaonkar, M.P., and Ganguly, S.S. (1990). "A case control study of cancer cervix patients attending Command Hospital, Pune", *Indian J Cancer,* Vol. 27, 101-108.

Ghosh, G.K., and Ghosh, S. (1997). *Women of Manipur*. Delhi: APH Publishing.

ICO Information Centre on HPV and Cancer. (2014). "Human Papillomavirus and Related Diseases in India", *Summary Report 2014.*

Moreno, V., Bosch, F.X., Muñoz, N., Meijer, C.J, Shah, K.V, Walboomers, J.M. Franceschi, S. (2002). "Effect of oral contraceptives on risk of cervical cancer in women with human papillomavirus infection:The IARC multicentric case–control study", *Lancet,* Vol. 359, 1085–1092.

Parazzini, F., LaVecchia, C., Negri, E., Fasoli, M., and Cecchetti, G. (1988). "Risk factors for adenocarcinoma of the cervix: A case-control study", *Br J Cancer*, Vol. 57, 201-204.

Parazzini, F., La Vecchia, C., Negri, E., Cecchetti, G., and Fedele, L. (1989). "Reproductive factors and the risk of invasive and intraepithelial cervical neoplasia", *Br J Cancer,* Vol. 59, 805–809.

Population Based Cancer Registry (ICMR). (2007). *Biennial Report 2005-2006.* RIMS, Imphal, Manipur.

Reis, N., Beji, N. K., and Kilic, D. (2011). "Risk Factors for Cervical Cancer: Results from a Hospital-Based Case-Control Study", *International Journal of Hematology and Oncology,* Vol. 21(3), 153-159.

Singer, A., and Monaghan, J. (2000). "Colcoscopy of the normal cervix: a prerequisite to establish the diagnosis of cervical precancer". In A. Singer &and J. Monaghan (Eds.), *Lower Genital Tract Precancer: Coloscopy, Pathology, and Treatment* (pp 43–70). Oxford, UK: Blackwell Sciences Ltd.

Sreedevi, A., Javed, R., and Dinesh, A. (2015). "Epidemiology of cervical cancer with special focus on India", *International Journal of Women's Health*, Vol. 7, 405-414.

Three-Year Report of Population Based Cancer Registries 2009-2011. (2013). *Incidence and Distribution of Cancer*. NCDIR-NCRP (ICMR), Bangalore.

Chapter - 15

Maternal Overweight and Obesity during Pregnancy and Birth Outcomes: An Overview

—Ak. Bojen Meetei and M. Monoranjan Singh

Introduction

The prevalence of overweight and obesity is increasing among women of childbearing age. Cogswell ME, *et al.* (2001) estimated 22 per cent of non-pregnant women of 18–49 years of age in the United States are considered overweight (body mass index (BMI) 25–29.9 kg/m^2) and an additional 22 per cent are classified as obese (BMI>29.9 kg/m^2). Observational studies show that obese women have up to a two-fold increased risk for a caesarean delivery compared with normal-weight women (Cogs well ME, *et al,* 2001; Baeten, JM, *et al.,* 2001; Kaiser PS, *et al.,* 2001; Bianco, AT, *et al.,* 1998; Shepard, MJ, *et al.,* 1998). The prevalence of obesity varies considerably between countries, and between regions within countries. It is estimated that more than half of adults, aged 35-65, living in Europe are either overweight or obese. Overweight is more common among men than among women, but obesity is more common among women. The prevalence of obesity in Europe is probably in the order of 10-20 per cent in men and 15-25 per cent in adult women. In most European countries, which have reliable data on time-trends, the prevalence of obesity seems to be increasing. In most European countries, obesity is usually inversely associated with socio-economic status, particularly among women. New classifications of overweight may be based on cut-off points for simple anthropometric measures which reflect both total adiposity as well as abdominal fatness.

The effect of maternal nutritional status prior to pregnancy on birth outcomes is of great public health importance. Epidemiological studies have shown a clear association between maternal pregravid weight and birth outcomes. As a marker of nutritional status, a woman's pregravid body mass index (BMI = kg/m^2), if low (<19.8 BMI), may reflect chronic nutritional deficiency, whereas a high BMI (>26.1 BMI) reflects an imbalance between energy intake and expenditure, and thus varying degrees of adiposity. The effects of each on birth outcomes differ, with low BMI being associated with intrauterine growth retardation (IUGR), preterm birth, and iron deficiency anaemia (Kramer M, *et al.,* 2000; Siega-Riz *et al.,* 1996). Whereas, BMI above the normal range of 19.8 to 26.1 (IOM 1990) is associated with a number of adverse reproductive health outcomes. For example, infertility (Zaadstra, BM *et al.,* 1993), gestational diabetes (Solomon, CG *et al.,*1997), pregnancy induced hypertension and pre-eclampsia (Thadhani, R *et al.,* 1999), birth defects (Anderson, JL *et al.,* 2005), large for gestational age (LGA) or macrosomia >4500 g (Larsen, CE, *et al.,*1990), caesarean sections (Cnattingius, S, 1998), prolonged labour (Vahratian A, *et al.,* 2004), and recently postpartum anaemia (Bodnar, LM, *et al.,* 2004) have all been associated with maternal overweight, yet the exact mechanisms have not been identified. The purpose of this paper is to provide an overview of the complications associated with maternal overweight and obesity; present updated information on the weight trends among women; and review prevention studies aimed at adolescents and women prior to pregnancy.

What is Obesity?

The most practical and commonly used definition of obesity is a body mass index (BMI) greater than 30 kg/m^2. Nonetheless, many experts believe that obesity represents the visible symptom of a complex medical entity referred to as the "metabolic syndrome," which incorporates associated conditions such as insulin resistance, dyslipidaemia, and diabetes mellitus. As shown in Figure 15.1, children of obese parents are at high risk of adulthood obesity; thus, the healthcare burden is anticipated to progressively increase in the future. In response to this challenge, a number of societies, including the American, Canadian, and British colleges of obstetricians and gynaecologists, have recently published guidelines for managing obese pregnant women (Davies, GA, 2010).

Despite anti-obesity drugs, dietary and exercise regimens, the only effective long-term means of controlling severe obesity remains bariatric or weight loss surgery. As most pregnancies are unplanned, there is often not enough time to implement effective dietary and exercise plans. Furthermore, anti-obesity drugs and bariatric surgery are not appropriate for the pregnant woman. Pregnancy is a unique time in a woman's life where she may feel especially motivated to adhere to strict weight gain guidelines. In 2009, the Institute of Medicine revised pregnancy weight guidelines such that obese women are advised to gain 11–20 pounds, in contrast to 25–35 pounds in the average weight pregnant population (Rasmussen, KM and Yaktine, AL, 2009). In some cases, a controlled or minimal weight gain during pregnancy may have a dramatic positive impact on pregnancy outcomes for both the mother and her baby.

However, past research has shown variable impacts of reproduction on energy reserves and nutritional status in humans. For example, in high income countries and among wealthy women in low-income countries, higher parity is associated with increased odds of being overweight (Davis *et al.,* 2009; Gunderson and Abrams, 1999; Kim *et al.,* 2006; Lopez-Arana *et al.,* 2013; Martinez *et al.,* 2012; Nenko and Jasienska, 2009; Winkvist *et al.,* 2003). In low- and middle-income settings, however, studies have variously shown that parity increases, decreases, or has no effect on maternal adiposity and nutritional status (Adair *et al.,* 1983; Adair and Popkin, 1992; Jelliffe and Maddocks, 1964; Kim *et al.,* 2007; Miller *et al.,* 1994; Tracer, 1991).

The regression analysis showed that pre-gestational weight was an important predictor of BMI in both the 1st and the 3rd month postpartum. A higher pre-gestational weight may be a factor that contributes to a higher BMI during the lactation period (Winkvist *et al.,* 2003). Women who have demonstrated difficulty in weight control (those who were overweight or obese before pregnancy or who gained excessive weight during pregnancy) should be identified as less likely to lose adequate weight postpartum, or at risk of gaining additional weight. Lactating women experience gradual weight loss during the first six months, varying within and across populations (Butte & Hopkinson, 1998); some undernourished populations gain weight (Hartmann *et al.,* 1998; Winkvist *et al.,* 2003). Ideally, nutrients stored antenatally, including fat stored energy, should be available during lactation (Butte & King, 2005).

Cigarette smoking during pregnancy appears to be the most important mediating factor for intrauterine growth restriction (IUGR), with low gestational weight gain and short stature also playing substantial roles. For preterm birth, socio-economic gradients in bacterial vaginosis and cigarette smoking appear to explain some of the socio-economic disparities; psychosocial factors may prove even more important, but their aetiological links with preterm birth require further clarification. Research that identifies and quantifies the causal pathways and mechanisms whereby social disadvantage leads to higher risks of IUGR and preterm birth may eventually help reduce current disparities and improve pregnancy outcome across the entire socio-economic spectrum.

Prevalence of overweight and obesity among women of childbearing age

Until recently, most studies on the topic of maternal pregravid weight focused on the lower end of the weight spectrum; however, with the shift in body weight that has occurred globally, more recent research has examined the effect of overweight and obesity on birth outcomes. Obesity worldwide (>30 BMI) now exists at a prevalence of 15–20 per cent and accounts for 2–7 per cent of the total healthcare costs (WHO, 2003). In the US, the latest NHANES survey (1999–2002) indicates that 26 per cent of non-pregnant women of 20–39 years of age are overweight at the range of 25–29.9 BMI, and 29 per cent are obese >29.9 BMI (Hedley AA, *et al,* 2004). On average, obesity among all women appears to have peaked at 33 per cent with no appreciable increase between 1999–2000 and 2003–2004 (Odgen, CL, *et al.,* 2006).

Determinants of overweight among women

A higher proportion of women of child bearing age are overweight or obese compared to men, and women of younger or older ages. In addition, upwards of 80 per cent of African-American women are either overweight or obese (Hedley, AA, *et al.,* 2004). Using 2003–2004 data from NHANES, non-Hispanic black women are twice as likely to be obese than their non-Hispanic white counterparts (Odgen, CL, *et al.,* 2006). Among individuals with less than high school education, the prevalence of obesity was roughly twice that of college graduates (Mokdad, AH, *et al.,* 1999). Paradoxically, low-income households appear to have a higher risk of obesity (Laitinen, J, *et al.,* 2001), although, at the same time, they are more likely to be at risk of food insecurity. Household food insecurity has been associated with increased BMI (Olson, CM., 1999) and an increased risk of overweight (Townsend, MS, *et al.,* 2001) in women, but not among men or children (Jones, SJ, *et al,* 2003).

Influences of adolescent overweight on reproductive health

Moreover, thirty per cent of non-pregnant adolescent girls of 12–19 years of age are considered overweight or at risk, based on a BMI for age at the 85th percentile or higher (Hedley, AA, 2004). Excessive weight gain at younger ages is associated with earlier menarche, especially among black and Hispanic girls. Younger and more severely obese girls reaching reproductive capacity perpetuate obesity if left untreated, directly through the influence of maternal weight on foetal origins and indirectly through maternal to child social and developmental interactions (Kral JG....).

Pregravid BMI is a predictor of gestational weight gain

Among women who become pregnant, the shift towards higher pregravid weight also appears evident (Yen, J; Shelton, JA., 2005). One study using a perinatal data base to ascertain weight before pregnancy for a 19 year period showed that the mean maternal weight of women at their first prenatal visit increased by 20 per cent between 1980 and 1999, and the percentage of women weighing >200 lbs at that visit increased from 7.3 to 24 and for those weighing >300 lbs the percentage increased from 2 to 11 (Lu GC, *et al.,* 2001). Another study, using a perinatal data system of all live births from 8 contiguous counties in New York, shows an 11 per cent increase in pregravid overweight and an 8 per cent increase in pregravid obesity between 1999 and 2003 (Yen, J, Shelton JA, 2005). Not only are more women beginning pregnancy at a higher BMI, but women are also gaining in excess of the 1990 Institute of Medicine recommendation for gestational weight gain (Institute of Medicine. Nutrition during Pregnancy, 1990). Specifically, overweight and obese women are more likely to gain excessive gestational weight and keep it on after delivery (Olson, CM, *et al.,* 2003; Carmichael, S, *et al.,* 1997; Keppel, KG and Taffel, SM., 1993). In affluent countries, women retain some weight with each successive pregnancy, gaining more weight than their non-pregnant counterparts (Winkvist, A, *et al.,* 2003). These observations beg the far larger and more important question of how and when to intervene in order to optimise reproductive and individual health?

Weight intervention studies

Many research studies of dietary and physical activity, and weight interventions focus on individuals who are already obese or experiencing co-morbidities such as heart disease, diabetes or cancer. In contrast, only a limited number of interventions have focused on weight loss and/or maintenance of optimal weight in the context of reproductive health. On the one end of the spectrum, surgical interventions such as gastric bypass and lap-band surgeries have been successful among obese women of child-bearing age with a decrease of reported rates of gestational diabetes, macrosomia, caesarean section while achieving adequate weight gain (Dixon, JB, *et al.,* 2001). Some interventions have been targeted to address obesity during adolescence, pregnancy, and the postpartum or inter-conceptional periods. These commonly have been school- or clinic-based in nature. School-based randomised intervention trails, such as the

Trial of Activity in Adolescent Girls (TAAG), are presently underway to determine if increased opportunities for moderate and vigorous activity may decelerate the age-related decline in physical activity (Stevens, J., *et al.*, 2005).

Clinic-based interventions

Clinic-based intervention usually begin with obesity management training for physicians because of the existence of a combination of a paucity of nutrition, physical and weight educational materials, lack of knowledge of how to counsel women, and lack of resources and personnel to assist with obesity management. For example, results from a survey of paediatricians found that only 12 per cent of paediatricians reported high self-efficacy in obesity management, although 39 per cent stated that physicians were important healthcare providers that could be effective with obesity management. Lack of non-MD staff reimbursement, of an on-site dietitian, and of patient educational materials were each highly associated with low self-efficacy in obesity management (Miller-Perrin, E, *et al.*, 2005).

Weight loss interventions

Tsai and Wadden (2005) conducted a systematic review of major commercial weight loss programmes undertaken to provide physicians with information on components, cost, and efficacy of these programmes. The review identified Weight Watchers as the least costly with maintenance of 3.2 per cent loss of initial weight at two years. Medically supervised very-low-calorie diet programmes had the greatest weight loss (approximately 15 to 25 per cent of initial weight), but were associated with high costs and high attrition rates. Finally, Internet (*i.e.*, eDiets.com) and organised self-help programmes (*i.e.*, Overeaters Anonymous) produced minimal weight loss. In a clinical intervention conducted among pregnant women, physicians were trained to chart and monitor gestational weight gain adequacy based on the Institute of Medicine weight gain recommendations. Women received five patient education newsletters by mail with action-oriented messages of how to gain adequate weight in pregnancy. Findings indicated that low-income women who received the intervention were less likely to gain excessive gestational weight. Overweight low-income women were at a reduced risk to retain more than 2.7 kg of weight at one year (Olson, CM, *et al.*, 2004). A hospital-based randomised control trail with an intensive stepped-care, behavioural intervention found that the intervention significantly decreased the percentage of normal weight women gaining in excess of the IOM recommendations (Polley, BA, *et al.,* 2002).

Significance of weight status during postpartum period

The postpartum period is hypothesised to significantly contribute to overweight and obesity through pregnancy weight retention. Olson *et al.* (2003) found that over 25 per cent of women participating in a cohort study experienced major weight gain, defined as 4.55 kg or more, at one year postpartum. Gestational weight gain, postpartum exercise frequency, and food intake were all significantly associated with weight change from early pregnancy to one year postpartum. Lower income women who gained more than the IOM recommendation were at increased risk for major weight gain at one year postpartum. In a randomised trial of 40 overweight postpartum women receiving either a 12 week structured or self-directed diet and physical activity intervention, the structured intervention group had significant weight loss (7.3 kg), decrease in per cent body fat (6 per cent) and no change in fat-free mass, whereas the self-directed group had no significant change at one year postpartum (O'Toole, ML, *et al.,* 2003). Randomized control trials are currently underway in low-income WIC populations receiving usual care or a multi-component intervention, including home visits, group classes and monthly telephone counselling (Peterson, KE, *et al.,* 2002).

Maternal Risks Associated With Obesity

Obesity is an independent risk factor for adverse maternal obstetrical outcome [9]. Consequences of maternal obesity in pregnancy are listed in Table 15.1 (Davies, GA, *et al.,* 2010; Robinson, HE, *et al.,* 2005). Many obese women have already faced significant health challenges before they arrive for the first ultrasound evaluation. These may include ovulatory infertility, increased foetal wastage, hypertension, diabetes, venous thromboembolism, cardiorespiratory disease, and obstructive sleep apnea. Maternal obesity is also associated with increased rates of complications in late pregnancy, including gestational diabetes, preeclampsia, non-progression of labour, shoulder dystocia, and caesarean section (Robinson, HE, *et al.,* 2005; Rosenberg, TJ, *et al.,* 2003; Catalano, PM., 2007).

Given the potential difficulties in performing an emergent caesarean section in the morbidly obese patient, a prescheduled procedure with preoperative consultations may be preferred. Difficulties in achieving intubation, line placement, and neuraxial anaesthesia may prolong and complicate the process, especially in the urgent setting. Despite the difficulties in placement of an epidural needle, general anaesthesia is generally avoided to reduce the difficulties of intubation and high ventilation pressures, which may result in barotrauma. During caesarean section, the abdominal pannus may need to be retracted or harnessed cephalad. In women, in the 350-pound range or more, the pannus may weigh as much as 100 pounds, and displacing this weight upward on the maternal abdomen may compromise the mother's breathing (Perlow, JH; Morgan, MA., 1994). Ultrasound guidance of neuraxial analgesia is being used to enhance the accuracy of needle placement (Halpern, SH, *et al.,* 2010). Pregnancy and the puerperium are well-established risk factors for venous thromboembolism, primarily on the basis of venous stasis, hypercoagulability, and vascular damage. The risk is greatest postpartum. Pulmonary embolism (PE) is a significant cause of maternal mortality (Chan, WS, and Ginsberg, JS, 2002). Both obesity and pregnancy are independent risk factors for the development of deep venous thrombosis and PE, with the risk for the obese pregnant patient (Sharma, S, and Monga, D., 2008; Robinson, HE, *et al.,* 2005).

Foetal Risks of Maternal Obesity

The increased risk of foetal structural anomalies remains independent of other maternal risk factors such as diabetes (Watkins, ML, *et al.,* 2003; Anderson, JL, *et al.,* 2005). The ultrasound diagnosis of a foetal anomaly presents a special challenge in the obese gravida for two main reasons: she is more likely to carry a foetus with a congenital anomaly, and the imaging of her foetus is technically more difficult. With regard to anomalies, the major anatomic areas of concern are the neural tube and heart. The two largest retrospective cohorts as well as a meta-analysis examining the relationship between maternal obesity and the risk of neural tube defects concluded that there is a direct correlation between maternal BMI and the risk of neural tube defects of 1.3–3-fold (Kallen, K., 1998; Rasmussen, SA, *et al.,* 2008). This risk persisted in obese women even after the widespread folic acid fortification in the 1990s (Ray, JG, *et al.,* 2005).

In a U.S. study of over 7,000 cases of congenital heart defects, the presence and severity of maternal obesity increased the risk of having a child born with the abnormality (Mills, JL, *et al.,* 2010). The most recent data from the U.S. National Birth Defects Prevention Study confirmed that the higher the BMI, the greater the risk of congenital heart disease (Gilboa, SM, *et al.,* 2010). Stothard and colleagues [Stothard, KJ, *et al.,* 2009] performed both a systematic review and meta-analysis of multiple studies involving maternal obesity and foetal anomalies and concluded that odds were greater for not only cardiac defects but also cleft lip and palate, anorectal atresia, hydrocephaly, and limb reduction anomalies.

Interestingly, the risk of gastroschisis was significantly lower in foetuses of obese women.

The risk of preterm delivery decreased with increasing BMI, with the highest risk among underweight women and the lowest risk among the overweight. The risk of pre-eclampsia was highest among overweight and obese women. Obese or overweight women did not have an increased risk of stillbirth in this study.

Diabetes and Obesity in Pregnancy

Obesity is an important risk factor for both pre-gestational and gestational diabetes (Yogev Y, and Visser GH, 2009). Maternal hyperglycaemia is a potent foetal cardiac teratogen (Allen VM, *et al.,* 2007). Measurement of the visceral fat by trans-abdominal ultrasound in the first trimester is positively correlated with abnormal glucose challenge testing in the third trimester (Martin AM, *et al.,* 2009). This ultrasound screening could be used to identify those women at greatest risk for gestational diabetes earlier and impact the onset of diagnostic testing and treatment.

Multiple Gestations

There are very limited data on multiple pregnancy outcomes in obese gravidas. Obesity does not appear to influence rates of prematurity, growth discordance, or birth weight less than 2,500 g, although increased risk of stillbirth and hypertensive disorders are documented (Lantz, ME, *et al.,* 1996). The estimation of EFW, in particular for Twin B, has been shown to be decreased in accuracy. This has potentially grave implications on the obstetrician choosing the safest mode of delivery (i.e., vaginal or operative route). Clearly, as our pregnant population becomes older, potentially more overweight and obese women will use artificial reproductive technology, and thus more multiple pregnancies are likely to be affected by obesity.

Maternal age, maternal smoking, parental socio-economic position, mode of delivery and its outcome

Maternal age, mode of delivery and infant size at birth had no significant impact on the risk of type 1 diabetes in the offspring in either cohort. A low level of parental socio-economic position was associated with a slightly increased risk of type 1 diabetes in the offspring. Consistent with previous studies (Dahlquist, G, and Kallen, B (1992); Robertson, L, Harrild, K (2010); Haynes, A, *et al.,* 2014), we found a reduced risk of type 1 diabetes in offspring of mothers who smoked in early pregnancy.

The mechanism behind the apparent protective effect of smoking for the development of diabetes in the offspring is unclear. Preeclampsia, more common in non-smokers (Duffus, GM and Mac Gillivray, I, 1968) has been associated with increased risk of type 1 diabetes in the offspring (Dahlquist, GG, *et al.,* 1999; McKinney, PA, *et al.,* 1999). Thus, the reduced risk of type 1 diabetes in offspring of smoking mothers could be due to immunological factors associated with preeclampsia (Dahlquist, G; Kallen, B (1992). Indeed, preeclampsia was more common among non-smokers than smokers in the present study. Mode of delivery has been associated with increased risk of type 1 diabetes in the offspring (Dahlquist, G, Kallen B, 1992). Maternal overweight and obesity are associated with increased insulin resistance and enhanced transfer of glucose and other nutrients across the placenta, stimulating foetal insulin secretion (Brandt, S, *et al.,* 2014). Offspring of overweight and obese mothers have significantly increased fat mass and signs of insulin resistance already at birth (Catalano, PM, *et al.,* 2009). Furthermore, maternal pre-pregnancy BMI is correlated with foetal insulin resistance and per cent body fat in the newborn (Catalano, PM, *et al.,* 2009). High maternal BMI is often associated with high BW in the offspring (Stamnes Koepp, UM, *et al.,* 2012), and high BW in turn is associated with increased risk of type 1 diabetes (Dahlquist, GG, *et al.,* 2005).

Short- and Long-Term Implications of Maternal Obesity on the Next Generation

Macrosomic infants have a nine-fold increased risk of adult obesity and development of the metabolic syndrome. Infants who had an accelerated foetal growth pattern are five-fold more likely to become obese adults (Gluckman, PD, *et al.,* 2005). In the U.S. Growing up Today Study, a cohort study of over 14,000 adolescents, a 1-kg increment in birth weight among full-term infants was associated with a 50 per cent increase in the risk of overweight at ages 9–14 years (Oken, E, *et al.,* 2008). It is speculated that maternal obesity, hyperglycaemia, and the metabolic syndrome may result in a vicious cycle leading to foetal hyperinsulinemia, which, in turn, may reset the CNS appetite regulation centres leading to future hyperphagia (overeating) with impaired glucose tolerance. This, in turn, leads to a hypothalamic form of insulin resistance with alterations in neurotransmitter production for satiety promoting obesity and the metabolic syndrome in the child of an obese mother. Thus, macrosomic infants and children of obese mothers are at significantly increased risk to become obese adults and develop the metabolic syndrome.

Conclusion

Obesity is a major health challenge for our society. The estimated annual healthcare cost due to obesity is estimated to approach \$39–100 billion. Obesity in pregnancy will have an increasingly significant impact on healthcare resources in the future. Urgent action is needed to help diagnose and treat the complications of this epidemic to make pregnancy management and childbirth safer for our mothers and infants. From a public health perspective, obesity is an important modifiable risk factor for adverse maternal and foetal outcome, beginning in the womb with lifelong and even multigenerational impact. Important issues that require further investigation include the optimisation of foetal scanning and prenatal screening, estimation of foetal weight, and the potential role of MRI in both maternal and foetal diagnosis. Given that the costs associated with treating obesity are so high and their limited success rates, the best strategy is to prevent obesity from occurring in the first place. However, prevention first requires a clear understanding of its aetiology. Obesity is a chronic disease thought to be developed from a complex interaction of genotype and environmental factors. Our knowledge of how and why this disease develops is far from complete, but currently funded research projects are targeting the integration of social, behavioural, cultural, and biological factors. In addition, best practices at obesity prevention, treatment and optimal weight maintenance must be identified to provide practitioners with an array of strategies to help curb the ensuing epidemic. Most women in this good-outcome sample would have been suspected of being at increased risk for poor outcome on the basis of their weight gain. This confirms the IOM recommendation that evaluation of the underlying causes of excessively high or low weight gain during pregnancy is necessary before appropriate interventions can be applied. Overweight and obese women have an increased risk for pre-eclampsia, while underweight women have an increased risk for preterm delivery. Pre-pregnancy body mass index and gestational weight gain are risk factors for preeclampsia and transient hypertension. Obesity appears to be a strong risk factor for transient hypertension and a milder risk factor for preeclampsia. High gestational weight gain was associated with increased risk of transient hypertension but not pre-eclampsia. The effects of gestational weight gain on pregnancy outcome depend on the woman's pre-pregnancy BMI. Pregnancy weight gains of 6.7-11.2 kg (15-25 lb) in overweight and obese women, and less than 6.7 kg (15 lb) in morbidly obese women, are associated with a reduction in the risk of adverse outcome.

References

Anderson, JL, Waller, DK, Canfield, MA, Shaw, GM, Watkins, ML, Werler, MM. "Maternal obesity, gestational diabetes, and central nervous system birth defects", *Epidemiology,* 2005; 16:87–92.

Baeten, JM, Bukusi, EA, Lambe, M. "Pregnancy complications and outcomes among overweight and obese nulliparous women", *Am J Public Health,* 2001; 91:436–40.

Bianco, AT, Smilen, SW, Davis, Y, Lopez, S, Lapinski, R, Lockwood, CJ. "Pregnancy outcome and weight gain recommendations for the morbidly obese woman", *Obstet Gynecol*, 1998; 91:97–102.

Bodnar, LM, Siega-Riz, AM, Miller, WC, Cogswell, ME, McDonald, T. "Who should be screened for postpartum anemia? An evaluation of current recommendations", *Am J Epidemioly,* 2002; 156:903–12.

Butte, NF and Hopkinson, JM (1998). "Body composition changes during lactation are highly variable among women", *J. Nutr.,* 128, 381S–385S.

Cnattingius, S, Bergstrom, R, Lipworth, L, Kramer, MS. "Prepregnancy weight and the risk of adverse pregnancy outcomes", *N Engl J Med,* 1998; 338:147–52.

Cogswell, ME, Perry, GS, Schieve, LA, Dietz, WH. "Obesity in women of childbearing age: risks, prevention, and treatment", *Prim Care Update Ob Gyns,* 2001; 8:89 –105.

Davies, GA, Maxwell, C, McLeod, L, *et al.* "Obesity in pregnancy", *Int J Gynaecol Obstet* 2010; 110: 167–173.

Gunderson EP, Abrams, B: "Epidemiology of gestational weight gain and body weight changes after pregnancy", *Epidemiol Rev,* 2000, 22:261-274.

Hedley, AA, Ogden, CL, Johnson, CL, Carroll, MD, Curtin, LR, Flegal, KM. "Prevalence of overweight and obesity among US children, adolescents, and adults, 1999–2002", *JAMA* 2004; 291:2847-50.

Jones, SJ, Jahns, L, Laraia, BA, Haughton, B. "School-aged food insecure children who participate in food assistance are less likely to be at risk of overweight: Results from the PSID-CDS", *Arch Pediatr Adolesc Med,* 2003; 157:780–4.

Kaiser, PS, Kirby, RS. "Obesity as a risk factor for caesarean in a low risk population", *Obstet Gynecol*, 2001; 97:39–43.

Keppel, KG, Taffel, SM. "Pregnancy-related weight gain and retention: implication of the 1990 Institute of Medicine guidelines", *Am J Public Health,* 1993; 83:1100-3.

Kramer, M, Seguin, L, Lydon, J, Goulet, L. "Socio-economic disparities in pregnancy outcome: Why do the poor fare so poorly?" *Paediatric and Perin Epi,* 2000; 14:194–210.

Kramer, MS, Platt, R, Yang, H, McNamara, H, Usher, RH. "Are all growth-restricted newborns created equal(ly)?" *Pediatrics*, 1999; 103:599–602.

Laitinen, J, Power, C, Jarvelin, MR. "Family social class, maternal body mass index, childhood body mass index, and age at menarche as predictors of adult obesity", *Am J Clin Nutr,* 2001; 74:287–94.

Larsen, CE, Serdula, MK, Sullivan, KM. "Macrosomia: influence of maternal overweight among a low-income population", *Am J Obstet Gynecol,* 1990; 162:490–94.

Martínez, H, Allen, LH, Lung'aho, M, Chávez, A and Pelto, G (1994). "Maternal fatness in Mexican women predicts body composition changes in pregnancy and lactation." In: *Nutrient Regulation during Pregnancy, Lactation and Infant Growth*, ed. L Allen, J King and B Lönnerdal, pp. 99–107, New York: Plenum Press.

Miller-Perrin, E, Flower, KB, Garrett, J, Ammerman, AS. "Preventing and treating obesity:Pediatricians' self-efficacy, barriers, resources, and advocacy", *Ambul Pediatr*, 2005; 5:150–6.

Mokdad, AH, Serdula, MK, Dietz, WH, Bowman, BA, Marks, JS, Koplan, JP. "The spread of the obesity epidemic in the United States, 1991–1998", *JAMA*, 1999; 282:1519–22.

Odgen, CL, Carroll, MD, Curtin, LR, McDowell, MA, Tabak, CJ, Flegal, KM. "Prevalence of overweight and obesity in the United States, 1999–2004", *JAMA*, 2006; 295:1549–55.

Olson, CM, Strawderman MS, Hinton, PS, Pearson, TA. "Gestational weight gain and postpartum behaviors associated with weight change from early pregnancy to 1 y postpartum", *Int J Obes*, 2003; 27:117–27.

Olson, CM, Strawderman, MS, Reed, RG. "Efficacy of an intervention to prevent excessive gestational weight gain", *Am J Obstet Gyn,* 2004; 191:530–6.

Olson, CM. "Nutrition and health outcomes associated with food insecurity and hunger", *J Nutr*, 1999; 129:512S–24S.

Rasmussen, KM, Yaktine, AL. Institute of Medicine. *Committee to Re-examine IOM Pregnancy Weight Guidelines: Weight Gain during Pregnancy— Re-examining the Guidelines.* Washington, DC: National Academies Press, 2009.

Shepard, MJ, Saftlas, AF, Leo-Summers, L, Bracken, MB. "Maternal anthropometric factors and risk of primary caesarean delivery", *Am J Public Health,* 1998; 88:1534–8.

Siega-Riz, AM, Adair, LS, Hobel, CJ. "Maternal underweight status and inadequate rate of weight gain in the third trimester of pregnancy increases the risk of preterm delivery", *J Nutr*, 1996; 126:146-53.

Siega-Riz, AM, Adair, LS, Hobel, CJ. Institute of Medicine maternal weight gain recommendations and pregnancy outcome in a predominately Hispanic population", *Obstet Gynecol,* 1994; 84:565–73.

Solomon, CG, Willett, WC, Carey, VJ, Rich-Edwards, J, Hunter, DJ, Colditz, GA, Stampfer, MJ, Speizer, FE, Spiegelman, D, Manson, JE. "A prospective study of pregravid determinants of gestational diabetes mellitus", *JAMA,* 1997; 278:1078–83.

Stevens, J, Murray, DM, Catellier, DJ, Hannan, PJ, Lytele, LA, Elder, JP, Young, DR, Simons-Morton, DG, Webber, LS. "Design of the Trail of Activity in Adolescent Girls (TAAG)", *Contemp Clin Trials,* 2005; 26:223–33.

Thadhani, R, Stampfer, MJ, Hunter, DJ, Manson, JE, Solomon, CG, Curhan, GC. "High body mass index and hypercholesterolemia: risk of hypertensive disorders of pregnancy", *Obstet Gynecol*, 1999; 94:543–50.

Townsend, MS, Peerson, J, Love, B, Achterberg, C, Murphy, SP. "Food insecurity is positively related to overweight in women", *J Nutr*, 2001; 131:1738–45.

Tsai, AG, Wadden, TA. "Systematic review: An evaluation of major commercial weight loss programs in the United States", *Ann Intern Med,* 2005; 142:56–66.

Winkvist, A, Rasmussen, KM, Lissner, L. "Associations between reproduction and maternal body weight: examining the component parts of a full reproductive cycle", *Eur J Clin Nutr,* 2003; 57:114–27.

Winkvist, A, Habicht, J-P and Rasmussen, KM (1998). "Linking maternal and infant benefit of a nutritional supplement during pregnancy and lactation", *Am. J. Clin. Nutr.*, 68, 656–661.

Winkvist, A, Jalil, F, Habicht, J-P and Rasmussen, KM (1994). "Maternal energy depletion is buffered among malnourished women in Punjab, Pakistan", *J. Nutr.*, 124, 2376–2385.

Winkvist, A, Nurdiati, DS, Stenlund, H and Hakimi, M (2000). "Predicting under- and overnutrition among women of reproductive age: a population-based study in central Java, Indonesia", *Publ. Hlth. Nutr.*, 3, 193–200.

Winkvist, A, Stenlund, H, Hakimi, M, Nurdiati, DS and Dibley, M (2002). "Weight gain patterns from pre-pregnancy until delivery among women in Central Java, Indonesia", *Am. J. Clin. Nutr.*, (in press).

World Health Organisation. Obesity and overweight. Geneva, Switzerland: World Health Organisation, 2010. Available at www.who.int/mediacentre/factsheets/fs311/en/index.html

Yen, J, Shelton, JA. "Increasing prepregnancy body mass index: Analysis of trends and contributing variables", *Obestet Gynecol,* 2005; 193:1994–8.

Zaadstra, BM, Seidell, JC, Van Noord, PA, te Velde, ER, Habbema, JD, Vrieswijk, B, Karbaat, J. "Fat and female fecundity: prospective study of effect of body fat distribution on conception rates", *BMJ,* 1993; 306: 484–7.

PART - III

ETHNO MEDICINE AND HEALTH CARE PRACTICES

Chapter - 16

Ethno-medicinal Practices of the *Sonowal Kacharis of Lakhimpur District, Assam,* with Special Reference to Childcare

—Ritamoni Konch, R and Ajit K Tamuli

Introduction

Ethno-medicine deals with the study of healthcare medical systems practised by ethnic groups around the world. Often considered synonymous with traditional medicine (TM), "Ethno-medicine refers to the study of traditional medical practice, which is concerned with the cultural interpretation of health, diseases and illness and also addresses the healthcare seeking process and healing practices" (Krippner, 2003: 11). "The practice of ethno-medicine is a complex multi-disciplinary system constituting the use of plants, spirituality and the natural environment and has been the source of healing for people for millennia" (Lowe *et al.,* 2000: 170). The World Health Organisation (WHO) refers TM to health practices, approaches, knowledge and beliefs incorporating plant, animal and mineral based medicines, spiritual therapies, manual techniques and exercises, applied singularly or in combination to treat, diagnose and prevent illness or maintain well-being. "Countries in Africa, Asia and Latin America use TM to help meet some of their primary health needs. In Africa, up to 80 per cent of the population uses TM for their primary healthcare. The use of plants in traditional medicine is well known in rural areas as well as among urban population" (WHO, 2003: 1). Indigenous people dwelling in forests and the fringe areas around the world depend on ethno-medicine for treatment and management of scores of ailments or diseases. Their healing practices comprise rituals based on folk beliefs, herbs, animals and also minerals. "Several local and indigenous populations meet their ends from the practice of traditional medicines even in the present-day scenario" (Kuru *et al.,* 2012: 47). "Herbal medicines are found to be safer to a large extent and provide in the treatment of various health problems" (Mitalaya *et al.,* 2003: 389). According to Anonymous (1994), nearly 8000 plant species are found of ethno-medicinal importance. Pushpagandan (1995) reported, over 2000 ethno-medicines are newly identified as drug yielding plants and also about 7500 plants are used in traditional health practices mostly in rural and tribal dominating villages of India. "About 85 per cent of traditional medicine involves the use of plant extracts" (Farnsworth, 1988: 91). "In India, it is reported that approximately 8000 of 17209 different plants have medicinal values in a range of communicable and non-communicable diseases" (Basu, 1994: 137).

The Sonowal Kacharis is one of the major ethnic groups of Assam. Like other cultures, Sonowal Kacharis depend on their traditional knowledge for subsistence activities and utilisation of natural resources. Ethno-botanical reports of the Sonowals are scattered (Kalita and Deb, 2004; Ahmed Das and Bora, 2008; Barua and Sonowal, 2011; Sonowal, 2013, 2014; Talukdar, 2014; Kalita and Bora, 2008), but healthcare practices and ethno-medicines of Sonowal Kacharis of Lakhimpur district have been hardly studied. They rely on ethno-medicines as a source of remedy for myriad of ailments. Their ethno-medicines include herbals, animals and even minerals, besides ritual healing practices. Use of ethno-medicinal plants is more prevalent among the people over other systems of healing, such as allopathic, homeopathic and Ayurvedic medicines. For many resource poor families, ethno-medicine is the only source of solace for health well-being. Ethno-medicines of the Sonowal Kacharis have a system for disease diagnosis, treatment and management using locally available herbs. Their cultural health practices also involve rituals, taboos and avoidances. Ethno-medicinal plants of the Sonowal Kacharis of Lakhimpur district have been barely studied. Ethno-medical practices and medicinal plants for childcare among the Sonowal Kachari tribe of Lakhimpur district, Assam, are the main objectives of the present study. This study is expected to document general healthcare practices and the use of medicinal plants by the Sonowal Kacharis in their healing system, particularly childcare and their local wisdom of ethno-medicinal knowledge. Such study can help in identifying valued medicinal plants for further phytochemical and pharmacological investigations.

Sonowal Kacharis and their Culture

The Sonowal Kachari is one of the scheduled tribes of Assam. Ethnically, they are Mongoloid in origin and form a branch of Bodo Kachari group (Bordoloi and Sharma, 1988). It may be mentioned that there were at least two migrations from north and northeast into Brahmaputra valley. One entered into Bengal and Assam through the valley of Tista, Dharla and Sonkosh, and the other taking its way through Suwansiri, Dibang and Dihong into upper Assam. The Sonowal Kacharis are possibly from the second group of migration. It is said that during the reign of the Axom King, some of the Kacharis were engaged in washing gold particles from the sands of river and therefore the prefix "Sonowal" was added to signify them. The Sonowal Kacharis believe that they were the descendants of great *Bhaskar Barma, Norakasur, Ban, Bhagadutta, Hirimba, Ghototkas, Bhim, Prahlad* and *Bali.* Although it is not definitely known about their origin, yet it can be assumed that their ancestors were king *Manik* and his grandson *Mukuta*.

Kacharis have many clans like *Bodowsa*, *Dhyan* or *Dehan*, *Lathowsa*, *Thawthensa*, *Hafalongsa* and *Hammusa*. The Sonowal Kacharis are said to be descendants of the *Hammusa* clan. According to the folk song *Haidang Geet*, the family tree of the Sonowal Kacharis includes seven major clans or *Khels,* which are divided into fourteen sub-clans or *Bongshas* and the *Bongshas* are further sub-divided into 108 *Hons* or *Pariyals*. The *Khels* are *Ujani Kusia, Namoni Kusia, Amorabomia, Tipomia, Dhulial Siripuria* and *Balikhitiari*. The fourteen Bongshas are *Madanial, Manikial, Hogral, Muktal, Ezmal (Ehmal), Formal, Horu Hazual, Bor Hazual, Lothial, Chotial, Kumral, Bormal (Athuwal), Dongral* and *Dingial*. Since, the *Bongshas* and the *Honses* are blood relatives, marriage among the same *Bongshas* and *Honses* is strictly prohibited. Monogamy is the most popular form of marriage, but acquiring more than one wife is permissible if the first wife gives her consent to it. The practice of inter-caste marriage is not rare.

Sonowal Kacharis are Hindus by religion. But nowadays, some Sonowals have embraced Christianity for a change of faith. They follow traditional animistic religion that includes concepts of a supreme creator and immorality of souls after death. Nature is seen to be abode of invisible forces, minor deities, and spirits with which priests and medicine men mediate. Ancestral spirits remain in the family and their propitiation is believed to help the family members in agriculture and protection of the members. Prior to the advent of the *Satra Sanghati* (a religious institution), the Sonowal Kacharis believed in ancestor worship. In the seventeenth century, the *Satradhikaries* (the designated head of the *Satra* institution) introduced *Vaishnavism* and most Sonowal Kacharis accepted this new faith. Every Sonowal Kachari village has a *Namghor* (religious place) that follows strict religious rituals and customs. Though *Vaishnavism* is completely against the worship of any other God or Goddess, with or without sacrifice, many Sonowal Kacharis still continue to hold sacrificial worship to their traditional deities. They offer animals, birds, fruits and plants to these deities for the welfare of the society. There are two forms of worship—community worship and household worship. Household deities are worshipped for maintenance of peace in their family and community worship for the welfare of the society. *Baitho Puja, Baghdeo Puja, Gatigiri Sabah, Gojai Bhoj, Sorogdeo Puja, Gokalika Puja, Jolkhai Puja, Kula Samon Puja, Ronga Samon Puja, Lokhimi Tola Sobah* and *Bhur Utua Sobah* are some of the forms of community worship of the Sonowal Kacharis. Important household worships are *Khin Bhonga, Chaul Khowa, Morak Diya, Piri Diya, Lokhimi mota, Ai-mota, Apeswari Sobah, Batoruwa Sokam, Chumoni Puja, Dangoriya Puj*a, etc. *Bihu* is their main festival.

The food habits reflect the unique cultural traits and traditional legacy of the Sonowal people. They love to add a few spices and chilies in their daily diet, but do not prefer too much spicy foods. They also have habit of taking various light *Jalpans* (repast) like *Kumol Chaul, Chira, Pitha, Chewa Diya Bora Bhat, Chungat Diya Bhat* and other recipes. People prepare *mod* (rice beer) by fermenting rice with locally prepared yeast starter cakes that has rice and plants as ingredients. Men often prefer to wear colourful outfits with *Dhuti-Kurta* and decorated *Phulam-Gamusa*. Weaving is major occupation of women, the tradition being handed down through generations among the Sonowal Kacharis. Warm and colourful embroidered hand-woven cloth, such as *Eri-Sadar, Muga-Sadar, Borkapur, Mugar-Mekhela, Kopahi-Mekhela, Kopahi-Sadar, Riha, Dhuti, Gamusa, Ekathia,* and *Seleng Kapur,* make magnificent souvenirs. The majority of the Sonowal Kachari population is engaged in ericulture for producing *Muga* silk. Women are very fond of traditional ornaments like *Gam-kharu, Keru, Thuria, Zangphai, Biri, Kongkon, dugdugi* and *latumoni*.

At present, the Sonowal Kacharis are predominant in Dibrugarh, Dhemaji, Lakhimpur and Tinsukia districts of Assam; scattered settlements can also be found in the districts of Sivsagar, Jorhat and Golaghat. Unlike most of the other communities, the Sonowal Kacharis do not have their own dialect; they speak the Assamese language.

Materials and Methods

Study Site

The present study was carried out during the period from October, 2014 to December, 2015 in eight Sonowal Kachari dominated villages of

Telahi and Boginadi area (Bhorti Sonowal gaon, Majgaon, Sonardheki, Natabari, No. 1 Singaramari, Tinikhuti, Kutuhaguri and Tariyani Rajgarh Sonowal gaon) in Lakhimpur district, Assam (Figure 16.1). All villages are far from urban settlements. Modern healthcare facilities are not adequate in these villages. There is one medical sub-centre in both Telahi and Boginadi areas for primary healthcare. In case of any serious health problem, the people have to move to North Lakhimpur Government Civil Hospital, which is about 14 km from Telahi and 10 km from Boginadi. Agriculture is the main occupation of the inhabitants; other occupations include cattle rearing, poultry and fishery. Farmers cultivate rice, mustard, legumes, sesame, aroids and other vegetables in agriculture fields and kitchen gardens for their daily food supplement. Nowadays, farmers use mechanised tools such as tractor for cultivation.

Data Collection

Information on ethno-medicines for child health was collected from 200 informants, out of whom 170 (85 per cent) were women elders. Semi-structured interview method was adopted for collection of data. Traditional healers and birth attendants (women) were interviewed as key informants. Increasing number of women informants was based on societal beliefs that childcare is mainly the domain of women. Informants were asked about etiology, healthcare delivery systems and herbal prescriptions for child health problems. All information was recorded on datasheet and then tabulated. The medicinal plants were collected with the participation of key informants and identified with the help of floras (Balakrishnan, 1983; Kanjilal and Bor, 1934-40).

Results and Discussion

Use of ethno-medicines is vibrant in Sonowal Kachari society and they form the primary source of healthcare. Herbs, animals and minerals are used for treatment of various ailments of adults and as well as children. Rituals, charms, taboos and avoidance are also important part of Sonowal Kachari healing system. This study documented thirty seven medicinal plants (Table 16.1) and some animals (fish, leech and dragonfly) used to cure seven health problems of children, namely excessive crying, regurgitation, diarrhoea, cough, delayed growth, fever and oral thrush. Ethno-medicines are prescribed as oral therapy, *tabij* (amulets), local application, massage and bath. As a social practice, childcare is considered as the primary responsibility of women, hence, such ethno-medicinal knowledge is mainly transmitted through women. But, men are not ignorant about child health and equally contribute to the well-being of children.

Both healers and birth attendants are considered more knowledgeable about child health than others in the Sonowal society.

Sonowal Kachari Healing Practices

Sonowal Kachari ethno-medicines share the three common elements prevalent in other traditional medical traditions (Cox, 1993:8): (i) a cosmological foundation, (ii) a repertoire of medicinal plants or other pharmacologically active substances, and (iii) a healthcare delivery system. According informants, they believe in evil spirits, ancestral spirits, evil eyes, curses of deities, and consider these forces as the causes of diseases in both adults and children. The people have a deep trust in God. When someone suffers from disease, the family members of the patient pray to God at home or in *Namghor* for recovery. Sometimes, the family offers *prashad* (religious offering) in *Namghor*. This traditional practice is called *Xarai diya*. Besides, the family members pray to ancestral spirits wishing for blessings and quick recovery of the patient. This practice is called *Tupula bondha*. After that, they organise *Nam-Kirtton* (religious pray) at home led by priests for blessings. Healing practices of the Sonowal Kacharis include both rituals and medicines for management of diseases or health conditions. Therefore, various *pujas* or rituals are performed to appease the spirits and deities for good health and blessings. Healthcare delivery system in Sonowal Kacharis' ethno-medicine is briefly enumerated below.

Amulet** or **charms is the most common practice of administration of ethno-medicine. The medicine man takes plant/animal/mineral and chants sacred verses (known only to him), said to be related to a deity. The sanctified medicine is then stuffed in a small brass container or other objects. This container stuffed with medicinal ingredients is called *tabij* which is worn on arm, waist and neck. Along with plant and animal parts, ingredients such as broom, fishing net and fishing hook are also included in *tabij*. To prevent the ingredients from escaping, mouth of the *tabij* is usually sealed with candle wax. Sometimes, the medicinal ingredients are made into beads and worn around the neck; this is called *mala*. When a baby constantly suffers from fever, curse of goddess of water is considered as the cause of the problem. So, the mother takes bath in the nearby stream in early morning and releases flowers of *Tabermontana divaricata* to nullify curse of the goddess.

Oral therapy is another prevalent form of healthcare; the medicines (with or without charms) are taken orally as advised by the medicine man. Both oral therapy and charms are used in Sonowal society to negate evil eyes and effects of evil eyes.

Topical or local application involves local application of medicines in the form of solution or paste for health problems, such as wound, sprains, skin diseases, animal bites and bee sting. Cast of earthworm is applied on forehead of baby as a mark to save the child from evil eyes of people.

Bathing patients with plant-treated water is generally practised for diseases such as small pox. Bath is also given with leaves of *tulsi* (*Ocimum tenuiflorum*) with the belief that the soul will be purified and will be able to resist evil spirits. Water from crab's hole is used for bath in case of delayed growth.

Aroma therapy is mostly practised for infants and children and in certain cases for adults also. Plants or animal parts are tied to the body or made into beads and tied around neck. This is done to prevent possession by evil spirits and evil eyes. In cases of diarrhea and jaundice, aroma therapy is the most practised ethno-medicine.

Ethno-medicines for Childcare

Thirty seven medicinal plants (Table 16.1) and animals (fish, leech and dragonfly) or their products, used in treatment and management of ailments of children, have been documented. Healing practice is not uniform; the same plant is used for more than one ailments with different methods of administration. Seven health problems of children have been reported, namely excessive crying, regurgitation, diarrhoea, cough, delayed growth, fever and oral thrush. Ethno-medicines for these problems are described below.

Excessive crying: This is a common health problem of children in the study area. According to informants, evil eyes of people and evil spirits are said to be the causes of excessive crying. The child suddenly starts crying extremely without any provocation.

- Roots of *Mimosa pudica* and rhizomes of *Thunbergia grandiflora* are put in an Eri cocoon, tied with black threads and then put around the neck of the baby as a *tabij* on Tuesday or Saturday. Charms are used during the administration of this *tabij*.
- Three small pieces of roots (from eastern direction of the plant) of *Mimosa pudica*, three thorns of *Ziziphus mauritiana*, three thorns of *Anthocephalus cadamba*, some seeds of *Brassica campestris*, three pieces of broom and a piece of fishing net are put into a *tabij*. The mouth of the *tabij* is closed with candle wax and tied with thread. The *tabij* is put around the baby's neck in

one breath in the morning on Tuesday or Saturday. The mother is prohibited from touching the baby before putting the *tabij*.

- Roots of *kauri-moni* (*Coix lacryma-jobi*) and a fish *Rasbora rasbora* are stuffed in Eri cocoon and tied with white-black-red threads to make *tabij* for the baby.
- Inner portion of fruits of *Trapa natans* is put into an empty Eri silk cocoon or wrapped with polyethylene and tied with black threads to make amulet.
- Rhizomes of *Acarus calamus* and bulbs of *Allium sativum* are sewed with black threads to make garland for the baby.
- Leaves of *Murrya koenigii* and *Acarus calamus* are kept under the mattress of child; this is said to prevent the child from evil spirit.

***Regurgitation*:** The child vomits the milk after feeding, which occurs many times in a day. Sometimes, the child becomes weak, feels fatigue because of this health problem. Evil eye is said to be the cause of regurgitation.

- Leaves of *Stephania hernandifolia* are crushed and applied on baby's scalp. The stem is also put around the baby's neck as a garland.
- Shoots and leaves of the fish *borali bokuwa* (*Pouzolzia zeylanica*) are crushed and applied on baby's scalp.
- Mother milk is put into a flower of *Catharanthus roseus* and buried in the ground near threshold.
- Flowers of *jati lau* (*Lagenaria siceraria*), shoots of *Eclipta prostrata*, stems of *kariya bijol* (*Impatiens tripetala*) and shoots of *Stephania hernandifolia* are crushed and the paste is applied on baby's scalp.
- Dry pericarp of fruit of *dhunduli* (*Trichosanthes cucumerina*) is mixed with water and a little salt; one or two tea spoonful is given orally to the baby.
- The vomited milk of the child is put into the stem of *ronga era* (*Ricinus communis*) and the opening is closed with the leaves and buried in the ground near threshold.
- Shoots of *Cynodon dactylon* are crushed and mixed with rice flour and applied on baby's scalp. Sometimes, a little salt is added to the juice and 1 or 2 ml is given orally to the baby.

- Bark of *Alstonia scholaris* is crushed and mixed with mother milk and applied on baby's scalp.
- Leaves of *jatipaan* (*Piper betel*) and 1 or 2 bulbs of garlic are grinded and the juice is given orally to the baby.
- Stem of *Opuntia* species is crushed and applied on baby's scalp.
- Stem of *Euphorbia neriifolia* is crushed and applied on baby's scalp.

***Diarrhoea*:** Evil eyes of people and contaminated foods are the causes of abnormal cramps, frequent passing of loose watery faces, nausea and vomiting. The child becomes weak when suffers from diarrhoea.

- Roots of *maalbhug kol* (*Musa paradisiaca* AAB) are grinded with little salt and the juice is given orally to the baby. For 1-2 years old baby, one black peeper is mixed with this dosage.

***Cough*:** Cold and foreign substances in the body are the causes of the disease. It usually begins with a sore throat, sneezing, fatigue, runny nose.

- Shoots of *Ocimum tenuiflorum*, shoots of *Citrus jambhiri* and one-fourth parts of fruit of *letaguti* (*Caesalpinia bonduc*) are grinded. One tea spoon honey is mixed with the juice and given orally to the baby.

Delayed Growth: Sonowal Kachari people believe that evil eyes and curses of deities are the causes of this child health problem. Due to interruption of growth, the child looks abnormally young and may have trouble gaining weight. Sometimes, the face of the child becomes hideous for delayed growth.

- Shoots of *modhuri* (*Psidium guajava*) and *bogori* (*Ziziphus mauritiana*) are crushed and mixed with water. The mixture is given as bath to the baby on Tuesday or Saturday. But oral therapy is prescribed by healer. On the third day of bathing, a *tabij* is made for the baby by putting one dried leech and any species of dragonfly into Eri cocoon.

- Middle portion of leaves of *bo-kanari* (*Crinum* sp.) and roots (from southern direction) of *athiya kol* (*Musa balbisiana*) are cut into small pieces, tied one by one with white-black-red thread to make garland for the baby. In the morning of Tuesday and Saturday, the baby is seated on threshold and then the healer uses charms and puts the garland around the neck. On the second day, the garland is taken out with the feet and disposed.

- Roots (from eastern direction) of *chengmara* (*Lasia spinosa*) are cut into small pieces and tied with white-black-red threads to make garland for the baby.
- Flowers of *bhetphool* (*Nymphaea pubescens*) are grinded and about 125 ml fresh goat milk is mixed with the juice and given orally in empty stomach.

Fever: Excessive sweating, chills, body aches, weakness, fatigue, cough, sore throat, etc are the symptoms of this disease. Ill health of mother and curse of deities are said to be attributed to fever.

- Leaves of *kariya bijol* (*Impatiens tripetala*) and egg shell of chicken are grinded and the mixture is applied on baby's scalp.

Oral Thrush: A white patch occurs on the tongue of the baby. According to informants, continuous feeding is the cause of this common health problem.

- Tongue of the baby is cleaned with leaves of *jetuli poka* (*Rubus moluccanus*).
- Leaves and stems of *laijabori* (*Drymaria cordata*) are crushed and used to clean tongue of the baby.
- Whole plants of *soru manimuni* (*Hydrocotyle sibthorpioides*), *Centella asiatica*, *bonjaluk* (*Oldenlandia corymbosa*) and shoots of *Cynodon dactylon* are grinded and the juice is given orally to the baby.

Transmission of Ethno-medicinal Knowledge

Ethno-medicines or traditional medicines are prevalent for primary healthcare among the Sonowal Kacharis. It is passed-on local wisdom, orally transmitted from parents to children through generations. It is more than healing system, but has implications for transmission of their culture as well. This factor has been a key driver for continuation of local healing practices. Though ethno-medicinal knowledge is chiefly concentrated to healers and birth attendants, common ethno-medicines are known to all. But, ethno-medicinal knowledge, based on women reproductive health and childcare, is mainly the domain of women because of societal structure. Charms or incantations of some ethno-medicinal practices have been written and used as *puthi* or source book of ethno-medicine by healers.

Despite access to modern medicines, some educated groups still prefer ethno-medicines for transmission of their culture through generations. But, with socio-economic changes and acculturation, particularly among youths, ethno-medicinal knowledge is gradually declining. This situation presents a case for urgent documentation of available ethnomedicines and traditional knowledge of the Sonowal Kacharis and explores for conservation of their ethno-medicinal plants.

Conclusion

The present study reveals that ethno-medicines are indispensable for childcare in Sonowal Kachari society. Access to biomedicines, socio-economic changes and acculturation have shown signs of decline in ethno-medical system. But, this invaluable knowledge, nurtured for generations and contributed to healthcare and culture, needs further exploration and documentation of the ethno-medicinal practices and medicinal plants. Besides, due to continued collection and economic value, numerous local medicinal plants are threatened with extinction. There is scope for chemical screening of bioactive compounds in medicinal plants and also ecological studies for their conservation. Folk medicines need to be promoted through standard validation processes for the benefit of mankind at large. Among others, this study will contribute towards documentation of ethno-medicines and traditional knowledge of the Sonowal Kacharis and provide ready reference for future ethno-biological research on the tribe.

Acknowledgements

The authors are grateful to all informants and other members of Telahi and Boginadi for their cooperation and support. We specially thank

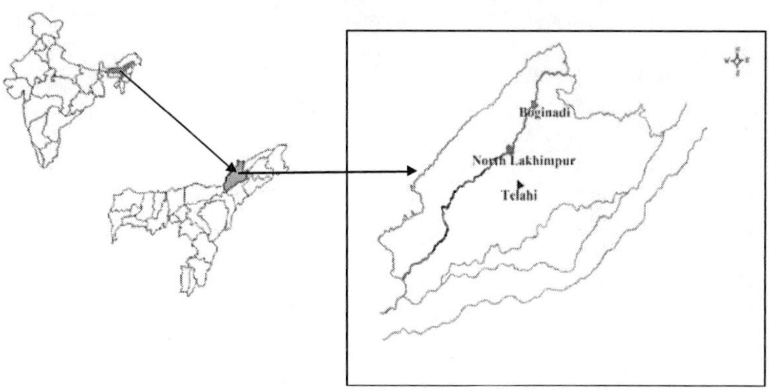

Figure 16.1: Map of Lakhimpur district, Assam, where field study was undertaken.

Mr Boloram Sonowal (the gaonbura of Bhorti Sonowal gaon), Mrs. Kumari Sonowal (Gagaldubi Baligaon) and Mrs. Ghanakanti Saikia (Dhakuakhana) for their assistance during the field survey. We thank the Institutional Biotech Hub (sponsored by Department of Biotechnology, Government of India), Department of Life Science and Bioinformatics for infrastructural support.

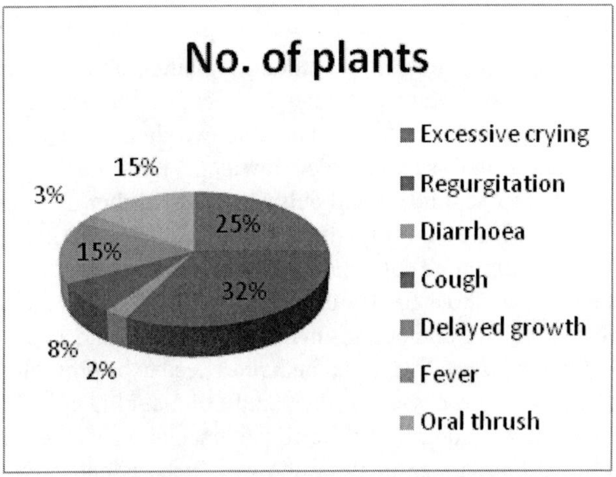

Figure 16.2: Percentage composition of medicinal plants used in seven health problems of children.

Table 16.1: Ethno-medicinal plants used by the Sonowal Kacharis for child healthcare

Medicinal plants	*Family*	*Local name*	*Parts used*	*Child health problems*
Acorus calamus L.	Acoraceae	*Bach*	Rhizomes, leaves	Excessive crying
Allium sativum L.	Liliaceae	*Naharu*	Bulbs	Excessive crying
Alstonia scholaris (L.) R. Br.	Apocynaceae	*Chtiyana*	Bark	Regurgitation
Anthocephalus cadamba (Roxb.) Miq.	Rubiaceae	*Kadam*	Thorns	Excessive crying
Brassica campestris L.	Brassicaceae	*Shariyah*	Seeds	Excessive crying
Caesalpinia bonduc (L.) Roxb.	Caesalpiniaceae	*Letaguti*	Fruits	Cough

(Contd...)

Catharanthus roseus (L.) G.Don	Apocynaceae	*Nayantara*	Flowers	Regurgitation
Centella asiatica (L.) Urban	Apiaceae	*Bor manimuni*	Whole plant	Oral thrush
Citrus jambhiri Lush.	Rutaceae	*Gul nemu*	Shoots	Cough
Coix lacryma-jobi L.	Poaceae	*Kauri moni*	Roots	Excessive crying
Crinum sp.	Amary-llidaceae	*Bo-kanari*	Middle portion of leaves	Delayed growth
Cynodon dactylon (L.) Pers.	Poaceae	*Dubori bon*	Shoots	Regurgitation, Oral thrush
Drymaria cordata Willd.	Caryophy-llaceae	*Laijabori*	Leaves, stems	Oral thrush
Eclipta prostrata (L.) L.	Asteraceae	*Keheraaj bon*	Shoots	Regurgitation
Euphorbia neriifolia L.	Euphorbiaceae	*Hiju*	Stems	Regurgitation
Hydrocotyle sibthorpioides Lam.	Apiaceae	*Soru manimuni*	Whole plant	Oral thrush
Impatiens tripetala Roxb. ex DC.	Balsaminaceae	*Kariya bijol*	Stems	Fever, Regurgitation
Lagenaria siceraria (Molina) Standl.	Cucurbitaceae	*Jatilau*	Flowers	Regurgitation
Lasia spinosa (L.) Thwaites	Araceae	*Chengmara*	Roots	Delayed growth
Mimosa pudica L.	Fabaceae	*Nilaji bon*	Roots	Excessive crying
Murrya koenigii (L.) Spreng.	Rutaceae	*Noroshingho*	Leaves	Excessive crying
Musa balbisiana Colla.	Musaceae	*Aathiya kal*	Roots	Delayed growth
Musa paradisiaca AAB	Musaceae	*Maalbhug kal*	Roots	Diarrhoea
Nymphaea pubescens Willd.	Nymphaeaceae	*Bhet phool*	Flowers	Delayed growth
Ocimum tenuiflorum L.	Lamiaceae	*Koliya tulashi*	Shoots, leaves	Cough
Oldenlandia corymbosa L.	Rubiaceae	*Bonjaluk*	Whole plant	Oral thrush
Opuntia sp.	Cactaceae	*Cactus*	Stems	Regurgitation
Piper betel Blanco	Piperaceae	*Jatipaan*	Leaves	Regurgitation
Pouzolzia zeylanica (L.) Benn.	Urticaceae	*Borali bokuwa*	Shoots, Leaves	Regurgitation
Psidium guajava L.	Myrtaceae	*Modhuri*	Shoots	Delayed growth

(Contd...)

Ricinus communis L.	Euphorbiaceae	*Ronga era*	Stems, leaves	Regurgitation
Rubus moluccanus L.	Rosaceae	*Jetuli poka*	Leaves	Oral thrush
Stephania hernandiifolia (Willd.) Walp.	Menisper-maceae	*Tubuki lata*	Leaves	Regurgitation
Thunbergia grandiflora (Roxb. ex Rottl.) Roxb.	Acanthaceae	*Kauri lata*	Rhizomes	Excessive crying
Trapa natans L.	Lythraceae	*Pani singari*	Fruits	Excessive crying
Trichosanthes cucumerina L.	Cucurbitaceae	*Dhunduli*	Dry pericarp	Regurgitation
Ziziphus mauritiana Lam.	Rhamnaceae	*Bogori*	Thorns	Excessive crying, Delayed growth

References

Ahmed Das F. and I. Bora (2008): 'Ethno-medicinal Practices: A case study among the Sonowal Kacharis of Dibrugarh, Assam', *Ethno-Med.*, Vol. 2(1): 33-37.

Anonymous (1994): *Ethnobiology in India: a status report of All India Co-ordinate Research Project on Ethnobiology*. Ministry of Environment and Forest, Government of India, New Delhi.

Balakrishnan N.P. (1983): 'Flora of Jowai', *Botanical Survey of India,* Howrah. Vol. 2: 343-344.

Barua, I. and R. Sonowal (2011): 'Indigenous herbal medicine among the Sonowal Kachari tribe: A study in a forest village in Dibrugarh, Assam, India', *Nebio.* Vol. 2(4): 31-35.

Basu, S.K. (1994): "Health problems and health care of the tribal population of India", *In: Tribal Economy, Health and Wasteland Development*. Ed. N. Mahanti, Inter-India Publications, New Delhi. 137.

Bordoloi, B.N. and G.C. Thakur Sharma (1988): *Tribes of Assam (Part-II)*. Tribal Research Institute, Assam, India.

Cox, P.A. (1993): 'Ethno-pharmacology and the search for new drugs', *Collegium Aesculapium.* Vol. 11(1): 5-10.

Farnsworth, N.R. (1988): "Screening Plants for New Medicines". In: Wilson E.O. (Eds.), Biodiversity National Academy Press, Washington, D.C. 83-97.

Kalita, D. and B. Deb (2004): 'Some folk medicines used by the Sonowal Kachari tribe of the Brahmaputra valley, Assam', *Natural Product Radiance.* Vol. 3(4): 240-246.

Kalita, D. and R.L. Bora (2008): 'Some folk medicines from Lakhimpur district, Assam', *Indian Journal of Traditional Knowledge.* Vol. 7(3): 414-416.

Kanjilal, U.C.; A. Das; P.C. Kanjilal and R.N. De (1934-1940): *Flora of Assam.* Govt. of Assam, Shillong.

Krippner, S. (2003): 'Models of Ethnomedicinal Healing', Paper presented at the Ethnomedicine Conference, Munich, Germany. April 26-27 and October 11-12.

Kuru, S.; G. Viji Senthilmurugan; S. Pandiselvam and S. Karuppuraja (2012): 'Ethnomedicinal Plants used by the Rural people in Thiruppachethi village of Sivagangai District, Tamil Nadu, India', *J. Biosci. Res*, Vol. 3(1): 47-51.

Lowe, H.; A. Payne-Jackson; S.M. Beckstrom-Sternberg and J.A. Duke (2000): *Jamaica's Ethnomedicine: Its potential in the healthcare system.* Canoe Press; University of the West Indies, Kingston, Jamaica. 170.

Mitalaya, K.D.; D.C. Bhatt; N.K. Patel and S.K. Didia (2003): 'Herbal medicines used for hair disorders by tribals and rural folk in Gujarat', *Indian Journal of Traditional Knowledge*. 389-392.

Pushpagandan, P. (1995): "Ethnopharmacology of Trichopus zeylanicus- The ginseng of Kerala- A review". In: P. Pushpagandan, Uff Nyman and V George (Eds.), *Proceeding of the first National Conference on Ethnopharmacology*. Visual Security Printing Enterprises Pvt. Ltd., New Delhi (India).

Sonowal, R. (2013): 'Indigenous Knowledge on the Utilisation of Medicinal Plants by the Sonowal Kachari Tribe of Dibrugarh District in Assam, North-East India', *International Research Journal of Biological Science*, Vol. 2(4): 44-50.

Sonowal, R. (2014): 'Some Folklore Medicines of the Sonowal Kachari Tribe of Upper Assam, North East India', *Scholars Academic Journal of Biosciences*, Vol. 2(8): 541-543.

Talukdar, M. (2014): 'Ethnomedicinal Plants used by the Sonowal Kacharis of Bhekulajan Village in Dibrugarh District, Assam, NE India', *International Research Journal of Environment Sciences*, Vol. 3(8): 54-57.

World Health Organisation (2003): 'WHO Fact Sheet No.134: Traditional Medicine'. https://en.wikipedia.org/wiki/Sonowal Kacharis (Retrieved on 31.05.16).

Chapter - 17

Ethno-medicinal Practices among the Mishings of Assam: An Anthropological Study

—Somnath Sonowal and Afsana Shabnam

Introduction

People have used various plant resources suitable for their purposes and usually more by the healers of different ethnic communities from time immemorial. It is true that use of medicinal plants for curing disease in human society is as old as existence itself. The earliest mention of use of medicinal plants is found in "Rigveda", the holy Hindu epic, which happens to be the oldest Indian scripture. Traditional healthcare practices constitute a major element in every culture. The medical system prevalent in a society is a combination of traditions, beliefs, techniques, ecological adaptation, etc. This system is an integral part of the society and provides the means to the members of the society for maintaining health and preventing and curing diseases (Medhi, 1995). Ethno-medicine refers to the study of traditional medicinal practice, which is concerned with the cultural interpretation of health, diseases and illness and also addresses the healthcare-seeking process and healing practices. Ethno-medicine has been recognised as an important field of anthropological research today. It has been defined as those beliefs and practices relating to disease which are the products of indigenous cultural development and are not explicitly derived from the conceptual framework of modern medicine (Pool and Geissler, 2005). World Health Organisation (WHO) estimated that nowadays as many as 80 per cent of the world's population rely predominantly on plants and plant-extracts for health care.

Today, most of the tribal people use plants as a source of medicine in their own medical lore. The Mishing tribe of Assam has also been practising the use of medicinal plants available locally for curing some common illness. Utilisation of this traditional knowledge of medicinal plants is not only useful for conservation of cultural traditions and biodiversity, but also for community healthcare and drug development.

Material and Method

The Study Area

The community among whom the present study was carried out are the Mishings living in Majuli of Jorhat districrt of Assam. The estimated population of the Mishings-living in the village as per our survey was about 518, out of which 156 are males and 139 are females. Majuli or Majoli is a large river island in the Brahmaputra River in the Indian state of Assam. Majuli is the largest river island in the world. It is situated at 26°-25' and 27°-12' North latitude and 93°-39' and 94°-35' East longitude and 85 m above the sea level. Majuli, which spreads over 924.6 square kilometres with a population of about 150,000. The island, threatened with constant erosion by the mighty and unstable Brahmaputra River, had been the principal place of pilgrimage of Vaishnavites since the age of the Ahom rulers. A river made island, Majuli is the largest of its kind over the world; and it is also the place of numerous Vaishnava monasteries of Assam called Satra that include the most well-known ones of the state. Several Sattras (monasteries) resembling those of medieval times are headed by Satradhikars teaching Vaishnavism, which was introduced by Srimanta Sankardeva (1449-1568).

Methodology

The study was carried out in the year 2015. The eldest person who possessed folk medicinal knowledge and practices was interviewed in order to collect the information regarding their traditional system of treatment. Interview and detailed personal discussions were conducted with the traditional healers to know about the medicinal use of plants. The discussion contains the details of plants, their parts used, medicinal uses, and the mode of preparation. Samples of plant species were collected from forest and their own kitchen gardens and photographs were taken using digital camera.

Result and Discussion

The study reveals different plant species used for curing various diseases found in the locality by the Mishings of Naganchuk village of Majuli. The plants are usually collected from the jungle and also from their kitchen gardens. Despite the improvement of medical facilities in the form of modern medicines and improved equipments, the villagers still rely mainly on the local medicine men. The people believe that these medicine men have special powers for curing diseases. Most of them attribute diseases and premature deaths to evil spirits, magic or breach of taboos. Sometimes, both traditional and modern treatments are taken simultaneously. Usually, they go to hospital when the traditional treatment fails. The medicines are prepared by herbal specialists, *i.e.*, medicine men of the village, who has considerable knowledge about the herbs and its medicinal use. They are found to be specialised in one or more diseases and extend their services both inside and outside the village. None of them, however, takes this profession as their primary source of earning. All of them consider this expertise as a gift of the Almighty as well as their forefathers. As such, they undertake the treatment of the ailments more as a service than as a source of income. Of course, it has also been observed that the medicines for a few common ailments are also known to the general people who use the same in their day-to-day life.

In Naganchuk, the villagers use herbal medicines also for treatment of diseases. As found in the study, herbal medicine or indigenous medicine is their first preference for treatment, which is obtained through local people or from the jungle. It was observed that s tribal people use tulsi leaves, turmeric powder in case of fevers and injuries. They use the juice of tulsi leaves with ginger for cough, etc. In the village, use of both allopathic and ethno-medicine is also found. When a patient is very weak and cannot go for treatment, he/ she will take ethno-medicine. After a few days of treatment, there may be some relief in his/ her condition. Then he/she will go to a hospital for treatment. Thus, the tribal people select the type of medicine according to their need and pressure of circumstances.

However, the influence of modern medicine has shaken the base of their age-old concept of disease and its treatment. It has also been observed that because of faster change among the Mishings, they are now relatively more modern in this respect.

Table 17.1. Medicinal Plants Used by the Mishings of Naganchuk

Sl. No.	*Local Name*	*Scientific Name*	*Parts Used*	*Ailments*
1.	*Tulasi*	*Ocymum santum*	Leaf	Cold and Cough
2.	*Ada*	*Zinziber officinale*	Rhizome	Cold and Cough
3.	*Haladhi*	*Curcuma longa*	Rhizome	Gastric
4.	*Jaluk*	*Piper nigram*	Seeds	Pneumonia
5.	*Gol nemu*	*Citrus aurantifolia*	Leaf and Fruit	Dysentery, Pneumonia

(Contd...)

6.	*Dupar tenga*	*Bryophyllum pinnatum*	Leaf	Urinary trouble
7.	*Kuhiyar*	*Saccharum officiarum*	Stem	Jaundice
8.	*Paan*	*Piper betle*	Leaf	Pneumonia
9.	*Naharu*	*Allium sativum*	Bulb	Menstrual pain
10.	*Nilakantha*	*Ajuga bracteosa*	Leaf	Pneumonia
11.	*Sirata*	*Andrographis paniculata*	Leaf	Pneumonia
12.	*Bormanimuni*	*Centella asiatica*	Whole plant	Jaundice, Toothache
13.	*Doron bon*	*Leucas linifolia*	Leaf	Sinusitis, Toothache, Stomach ache and indigestion, eye infection
14.	*Tubuki lota*	*Stephania elegans*	Leaf	Menstrual pain
15.	*Shilikha*	*Terminalia chebula*	Fruit	Constipation
16.	*Keheraj*	*Eclipta prostata*	Leaf	Eye injuries
17.	*Bhedailata*	*Paederia foetida*	Leaf	Dysentery
18.	*Leta guti*	*Caesalpinia bonducella*	Fruits	Cold and cough, Pneumonia
19.	*Matikothal*	*Annanas comosus*	Leaf	Pneumonia
20.	*Bhimkal*	*Musa balbisiana*	Fruits	Jaundice
21.	*Sarumanimuni*	*Hydrocotyle sibthrorpioides*	Leaf	Dysentery, Pneumonia, Sinusitis
22.	*Gorukhis*	*Duchesenea indica*	Leaf	Jaundice
23.	*Konaihimola*	*Commelina diffusa*	Stem	Jaundice, white discharge, Urinary trouble
24.	*Bos*	*Acorus calamus*	Rhizome	Pneumonia
25.	*Madhuriaam*	*Psidium guajava*	Twigs	Pneumonia
26.	*Urium*	*Bischofia javanica*	Leaf	Pneumonia
27.	*Helosh*	*Antidesma ghaesembilla*	Leaf	Pneumonia
28.	*Bikholyakoroni*	*Heliotropium indicum*	Leaf	Septic
29.	*Dimoru*	*Ficus glomerata*	Gum	Fracture
30.	*Modhuhuleng*	*Polygonum chinense*	Leaf	Toothache
31.	*Tubuki lota*	*Stephania lernandifolia*	Leaf	Menstrual Pain
33.	*Pipoli*	*Piper longum*	Leaf	Pneumonia
34.	*Keya bon*		Seeds	Pneumonia
35.	*Tarua* kadam	*Acacia nilotica*	Bark	Tonsillitis

Table 17.2. Diagnosis of Ailments and their Therapeutic Use

Sl. No.	*Name of Diseases*	*Diagnosis of Disease by the Villagers*	*Content of Medicine*	*Therapeutic Use*
1.	Cold and Cough	It is diagnosed from the symptoms which includes coughing, sore throat, runny nose, sneezing and fever	1 piece of Ginger about 1 inch, 10-15 leaf of sweet basil and about 2-3 tblspn of honey	Juice of ginger (*Zinziber officinale*) and leaf of sweet basil (*Ocymum santum*) mixed with a little amount of honey and taken orally twice a day until cure.
			1-2 Leta guti and about 2-3 tblspn of honey	The fruit of *Leta Guti* (*Caesalpinia bonducella*) is grinded to powder mixed with honey and administered orally.
2.	Dysentery	Pain in the abdomen, loose motion and blood in the feces.	*Saru manimuni* and honey	The juice of *Saru manimuni* (*Hydrocotyle sibthrorpioides*) mixed with honey and taken orally for fifteen days to get rid of dysentery.
			Bhedailata	Paste made from the leaves of *bhedailata* (*Echiles fructescene*) is also a good medicine for dysentery.
3.	Gastric	Often diagnosis is made based on the patient's description such as upper central abdominal pain around to the back.	*Haldhi* and Milk	Rhizome Juice of *Haldhi* (*Curcuma longa*) mixed with milk (about 1 glass) is taken in empty stomach for two weeks to cure acidity.
4.	Stomach ache	Pain in the abdomen	*Durun bon*	A kind of wild herb known as *durunbon* (*Leucas aspera*) is taken as vegetables.
5.	Septic	Infection, sometimes accompanied by high fever, swelling, flushed skin.	The milky white substance obtained from cactus and *Bikholyakoroni*	The milky white substance obtained from cactus plant is mixed with the paste of *Bikho-lyakoroni* leaves (Heliotropium indicum) and then applied to the infected area.
6.	Pneumonia	Pneumonia is typically diagnosed based on a combination of physical signs such as cough, fatigue, fever, chest pain.	*leta guti* (2), *jaluk* (5-6) and a pinch of salt	The powder obtained by grinding *leta guti* (*Caesalpinia bonducella*) and *jaluk* (*Piper nigrum*) is mixed with a glass of luke warm water along with a pinch of salt and administered orally in empty stomach till cure.
			Bos 1 piece (1 inch) and 1 tblspn of water	The decoction of the rhizome of *bos* (*Acorus calamus*) mixed with a tablespoon of water and taken orally for two days also cures pneumonia.
			Young leaves of *matikothal* (3), twigs of *madhuri-*	The juice extracted from the young leaves of *matikothal* (*Ananas comosus*), twigs of madhuriaam

(Contd...)

			aam (3), twigs of *Urium* (3), leaves *gul nemu* (9), *jaluk* (21), *paan* (3), a bunch of *sarumanimuni*, 5-6 leaves of *barmanimuni*, water and a pinch of salt	(*Psidium guajava*), twigs of *urium* (*Bischofia javanica*), *gul nemu* leaves (*Citrus aurantifolia*), *jaluk* (*Piper nigrum*), *paan* (*Piper betle*), a bunch of *sarumanimuni* (*Hydrocotyle sibthrorpioides*), and leaves of *barmanimuni* (Centella asiatica) are heated in a bowl of water and administered orally for two days.
			Bark of *helosh gosh* (*Antidesma ghaesembilla*), *3 keya bon guti,* 1 *sirata paat*, 1 *nilakantha paat*, 3 *latu guti* ( ), 3 *jaluk*, 5-6 *gul neemu paat* and a pinch of salt.	The decoction obtained by boiling the bark of helosh gosh *(Antidesma ghaesembilla)*, keya bon guti sirata paat *(Andrographis paniculata)*, nilakantha paat *(Ajunga bracteosa)*, latu guti, jaluk *(Piper nigrum)*, gul neemu paat *(Citrus aurantifolia)* and a pinch of salt is taken in empty stomach for three days (1 table spoon for adult and ½ tablespoon for small children).
7.	Jaundice	Yellow discoloration of the white part of the eyes (sclera) and of the skin.	*Konaihimola* stem, *missiri* (10 gm), *tukhmaah* (about 10 gm) and 1 *bhim kol*	The juice extracted from the stem of *konaihimolu* (*Commelina diffusa*) is mixed with *missiri*, *tukhmaah* (a kind of small gram) and *poka bhim kol* (*Centella asiatica*) and taken in empty stomach until cure is another medicine for jaundice.
			Twigs of elephant apple, *bormani-muni* and *gorukhis*	The extract obtained by squeezing the twigs of elephant apple, *bormanimuni* (*Centella asiatica*) and *gorukhis* (*Duchesnea indica*) in a glass of water is taken orally once daily for three days in empty stomach.
8.	Fracture	Broken bone or bone break are common colloquia-lism for a bone fracture. A bone fracture is usually diagnosed based on the history given by the patient.	Gum of *Dimoru gosh* and bandage	The gum obtained from *Dimoru gosh* (*Ficus glomerata*) is applied as a thick layer over the fractured area and then a bandage it tied over it for four.
9.	White discharge in women		*Konaihimola*, *missiri* and *tungmaah*, 1 local hen egg	The juice extracted from the stem of *konaihimola* (*Commelina diffusa*), is mixed with *missiri*, and *tungmaah* (*a kind of small gram*) and kept overnight. The juice is then taken in empty stomach the next day and after 1 hour of con sumption 1 local hen egg is consumed raw.

(Contd...)

10.	Toothache	It is generally diagnosed from the cavity developed and is characterised by pain.	3 twigs each of *durunbon* and *madhuhuleng* and 3-5 leaves of *barmanimuni*	Twigs of *durunbon* (*Leucas aspera*) and *madhuhuleng* (*Polygonum chinense*) and *barmanimuni* leaves (*Centella asiatica*) are all squeezed together and then applied to the affected teeth overnight.
11.	Sinus	Headache often accompanied by thick nasal discharge (blood).	*Durunbon, sarumanimuni*	The juice extract of *durunbon* (*Leucas aspera*) and *sarumanimuni* (*Hydrocotyle sibthrorpioides*) applied to the nostril in case of sinus is found to be very effective.
12.	Spot on the eye ball	It is diagnosed from the spot developed in the white part of the eyes (sclera) as a result of injury.	*Sarumanimuni* and *keheraj*	The decoction of *sarumanimuni* (*Hydrocotyle sibthrorpioides*) and *keheraj* (*Hydrocotyle sibthror-pioides*) when applied to the eye for a few days seems to reduce the spot.
13.	Urinary Trouble	It is mainly diagnosed from its symptoms like burning sensation at the time of urination, pain during urination.	*konaihimola* stem, *missiri* and cow's milk	1 glass extract of *konaihimola* stem (*Commelina diffusa*) is mixed with *missiri* and kept over night. In the morning the same is mixed with a glass of cow's milk and taken orally in empty stomach
14.	Tonsillitis	It is diagnosed from its characteristics like sour throat, fever, tonsils pain, coughing, headache, difficulty in ingesting and swallowing meal and liquid intake	Bark of *Tarua* kadam	Bark extract of *Tarua* kadam (*Aca cia nilotica*) mixed with lukewarm water is gargled twice daily until cure.

Table 17.3. The Perception of Mishings Regarding Diseases

Sl. No.	*English Equivalent*	*Name of the Disease*
1.	Ant bites	*Merangtetou*
2.	Alcoholic intoxication	*Tuidura*
3.	Bee bites	*Mullangtetuo*
4.	Barrenness	*Baji*
5.	Blind	*Miglu*
6.	Blister	*Abukbu*
7.	Burns	*Amegunam*
8.	Cough	*Sagresagdune*
9.	Cut	*Patone*
10.	Constipation	*Piripparare*
11.	Death	*Sikang*

(Contd...)

12.	Dog bite	*Ikirekto*
13.	Ear disease	*Yerungkinam*
14.	Eye disease	*Amigkinam*
15.	Epilepsy	*Aomuria*
16.	Fever	*Ramnam*
17.	Finger disease	*Lekekinam*
18.	Fox bite	*Mensurangrekto*
19.	Headache	*Mittubkidag*
20.	Heart attack	*Angkengkidag*
21.	Itches	*Tarug*
22.	Leg fracture	*Ale dirkane*
23.	Measles	*Ai abuk*
24.	Mumps	*Robnam*
25.	Nose bleeding	*Yabong-e-lennam*
26.	Piles	*kesumuria*
27.	Retarded growth in children	*Singkinmang*
28.	Stomach ache	*Aki kidung*
29.	Sprain	*Kitagkiagdang*
30.	Sty on eye lid	*Asina*
31.	Throat problem	*Lipongkinam*
32.	Tiger bite	*Sumyourekto*
33.	Vomiting	*Badnam*

Conclusion

On the basis of the forgoing discussion, it may be stated that there are a number of traditional medicines being used by the villagers in their day-to-day life. People of the village preferred traditional medicine because of culture-rooted faith on the indigenous healer; their easy accessibility, low cost, and cultural acceptability, elaborate patient-healer relation, long-term family association, friendly attitude of the healers and so on. People first prefer their traditional system for curing disease by taking herbal medicine because they have deep faith in herbal treatment as they are very friendly and familiar with the natural resources present around them. They use many herbal medicines for the treatment of the various diseases such as pneumonia, jaundice, cough, dysentery, gastric, stomach ache, etc. Extensive research is required to find out the scientific basis of traditional medicines so that proper suggestive measures can be recommended for the upliftment of their health status. It is quite clear that they are hardly utilising modern healthcare facilities provided by the government under the circumstances. It is highly desirable to formulate a need-based healthcare policy with education and awareness among the people of Naganchuk to uplift their health standards.

References

A Committee of Royal Anthropological Institute of Great Britain and Ireland, 1954 (Reprint), *Notes and Queries on Anthropology*, Routledge and Kegan Paul Ltd., London.

Acherknecht, Erwin, 1942. "Problem of Primitive Medicine", *Bulletin of the History of Medicine*, Vol. 11: 503-521.

Ali, A.N.M. Irshad and Indranosee Das, 2002. "A Note on Ethnomedicinal Specialist Among the Karbis of Goria Ghuli of Sonapur Area, Assam, *Bulletin of the Department of Anthropology*, Dibrugarh University, Vol. 30; 47-49.

Basu, Amitabha, 1990. *Anthropological Approach to Tribal Health in Tribal Demography and Development in N.E India,* New Delhi, B.B. Publishing Corporation: 131-142.

Beals, Rlph L, Harry Hoijer and Alan R. Beals, 1977. *An Introduction to Anthropology (Fifth Edition)*, Macmillan Publishing Co. Ltd., New York.

Bhat, K.H., 1986. "Concept of Health and Disease among the Pnars of Meghalaya", in *Tribal Health: Socio-cultural Dimensions*, in B. Choudhury (Ed.) New Delhi, Inter India Publications: 275-272.

Bhattacharya, S and S.K. Sengupta, 1986. "The Concept of Disease and Its Treatment among the Birhors of Purulia", in *Tribal Health: Socio-cultural Dimensions*, B. Choudhury (Ed.) New Delhi, Inter India Publications: 201-208.

Biswas, P.C., 1934. "Concept of Disease among the primitive people of India", in *Journal of the Department of Culture*, Calcutta, University of Calcutta, 25: 1-26.

Bordoloi, B.N., 1982. *Chomangkan: The Death Ceremony Performed by the Karbis*, Tribal Research Institute, Guwahati.

Bordoloi, B.N., 1984. *Death, in the Dimasa Kacharis of Assam*, Tribal Research Institute, Guwahati: 61-65.

Bordoloi, B.N., G.C. Sahrma Thakur and M.C. Saikia, 1987. "The Miris (Mishings)", in *Tribes of Assam: Part–I*, Tribal Research Institute, Guwahati: 107-126.

Bordoloi, B.N., G.C. Sahrma Thakur and M.C. Saikia, 1988. *Tribes of Assam:* Part II, Guwahati Tribal Institute.

Dube, S.I., 1958. 'Herbal Medicine around Oria' in *Bulletin of Tribal Institute*, Chinduare, 1: 87-95.

Elwin Verrier, 1953. *Tribal Medicine in India*, Calcutta.

Ember, Carol R., M. Ember and P.N.Peregrine, 2003 (Reprint). *Anthropology* (10th Edition), Pearson Education (Singapore) Pvt. Ltd., Delhi.

Medhi, B.K., Mahaswetta Saikia, And Arifur Zaman, 2005. "Use of Medicinal Plants in the Assamese Society", in the *Bulletin of the Department of Folklore Research*, Guwahati, Guahati University, Vol.8, No. 6: 118-130.

Pegu, N.C., 1981. *The Mishings of Brahmaputra Valley*, Milan Nagar, Dibrugarh.

Young, P.V. 1960. *Scientific Social Survey and Research* (3rd Ed.), New Delhi. Prentice-Hall of India.

Zaman, A., 2009. "Continuity of Traditional Health Care System among the Rural Tiwas of Assam", in the *Journal of Politics*, Dibrugarh University, Vol. 14: 95-102.

Chapter - 18

Ethnomedicine and Primary Healthcare Practices among the Karbis of Assam

—Kh. Narendra Singh

Introduction

World Health Organisation has defined traditional medicine as the sum total of knowledge, skills, and practices based on the theories, beliefs, and experiences indigenous to different cultures, whether explicable or not, used in the maintenance of health as well as in the prevention, diagnosis, improvement or treatment of physical and mental illness (WHO, 2001). World Health Organisation (WHO) estimated that about 80 per cent of the world's population depends on traditional medicine for their primary healthcare needs. In his book WHR Rivers *Medicine, Magic and Religion,* argued that indigenous medical practices, which might seem irrational to Westerners, were rational when placed in the wider context of local beliefs and culture.

Anthropological studies of health and medicine as a social institution have shown that every known human society has developed, according to premises implicit in its own culture, a system of values regarding health and disease, as also methods of coping with them. Studies in ethnomedicine are the pioneer natural attempts to combat human problem. Their history itself witnesses how they paved their way to classic medicine. Through the ages, the knowledge, practices and innovations of worldwide ethnic communities, has been turned into traditions, whether written or oral. Medicine is one such manifestation of traditions.

The knowledge and practice of ethnomedicine have been orally transmitted over centuries. It includes both magico-religious and herbal remedies for treatment of various diseases and illness. The ethno-medical system has two universal categories of disease etiology-natural and supernatural causes. Ethnomedicines form the major source of healing among the tribal communities. Tribal communities often depend on local available ethnomedicinal plants and animal products. The traditional knowledge practitioners or ethnomedicinal practitioners often serve as their healthcare service providers.

Early studies on indigenous medical systems were mostly limited in focus on witchcraft and illness caused by super-natural forces, and on specialists such as folk healers, and shamans (Evans-Pritchard, 1937; Turner, 1967; Fabrega and Silver, 1973). During this period, the emphasis was on the meaning of the illnesses and on the symbolism of the curing rituals performed by the folk healers with the result that scholars mostly overlooked empirical aspects of indigenous medical cultures (Waldstein and Adams, 2006).

Ethnomedicine is still plays a vital role in the healthcare among the tribes of northeast India including the Karbis of Karbi Anglong. Practice of ethnomedicine is not only a source of healing, but the practice is also an important part of their culture. Scientific approach for their exploration, utilisation, conservation and value addition may be the key points for development by exploiting the traditional technology knowledge.

Objectives

To study the use of ethnomedicine as healthcare practice among the Karbi tribe of Assam, northeast India.

Methods

Field survey was conducted in the selected villages of Lumbajong area of Karbi Anglong district of northeast India. Information was collected following both unstructured interview methods and group discussions. Secondary data were collected from research journals, edited volumes and reports.

Field study was undertaken during the period from March 2015 to June 2015. A total of 75 informants were selected from five villages and the selection was based on their recognition as knowledgeable relating to healthcare practices.

About the Karbis

Karbis represents one of the prominent indigenous tribes of Northeast India. Racially, Karbis belong to the Mongoloid group and linguistically belong to the Tibeto-Burman group particularly the Kuki-Chin subgroup of languages. Karbis follow patrilineal system of family and socially divided into five major *Kur* or clans *viz., Lijang, Hanjang, Ejang, Kronjang* and *Tungjang*. Clans are further divided into many sub-clans.

Findings

Northeast India is the homeland of many precious medicinal plants and most of the communities rely on ethno-medicine for their healthcare practices. The local people utilise different parts of plants to cure disease and illness. Most of the traditional medicines are prepared from fresh leaves which are used both for topical application of wound healing, skin diseases etc, and oral administration for health problems like stomach disorder, diarrhoea, fever etc.

There is an increasing focus on the importance of medicinal plants and traditional health systems to solve the healthcare problems of the world. Northeast India represents an extremely unique eco-system rich in medicinal plant wealth associated with folk medicine. The medicinal plants also have traditionally engaged an important position in the socio-cultural, spiritual and medicinal arena of the people in the region. Medicinal plants play an important role in supporting rural healthcare system.

Ethnomedicine and primary healthcare practices among the Karbis

Ethnomedicine is an indispensable part of primary healthcare among the Karbis. Treatment involves various practices such as therapies, charms and rituals. Therapies or prescription prepared from plants, animals or minerals are also used; for a few ailments, therapies may be accompanied with charms before being given to the patient. For certain ailments ritual involving blood-sacrifice is done for recovery of the patient. Among the Karbis traditional medicine is not only source of healing, but also an important part of culture.

Traditional knowledge considered as a body of information and set of skills developed by a group of people over time, which is based upon their necessity, observation; and in a constant state of change. The information about folk medicine of northeast India are still not gathered in systemic way or not documented in old literature, these are generally passed over generation vocally. In order to consider the "preservation" of traditional knowledge, perhaps it need documentation of those old and useful literature and to explore the nature of this system, how it evolves over time, and identify some of the forces involved in its destruction. The documentation of traditional knowledge is useful to address the intellectual property right issues and for evidence based research work. Multidisciplinary research and development work using the traditional folk medicinal plants based upon their traditional knowledge can provide deep motivation for identification of new pharmacophores. Multidisciplinary approach in combination with established traditional health principles may be useful in understanding health culture behaviour as well as improving community health. Fish is also used for curing mental depression-like symptoms is still prevalent. Traditional healthcare practices of the Karbis are based on religious beliefs and therefore, are an important driver for continuation of their culture.

The Karbis have rich tradition regarding medicinal uses of plants and are quite knowledgeable about locally available medicinal plants and depends on the ethno-medicinal plants naturally grown in the forest for treatment of most of their common ailments and diseases. They also consume some wild varieties of plants both as vegetables and medicine on a regular basis. The knowledge medicinal uses of plants have been passed from generation to generation through the oral tradition. A large number of medicinal plants have been reported from this region and the Karbis still follow the tradition of indigenous healthcare. Many medicinal plants in the region are becoming endangered due to over-exploitation. However, attention is being paid to preserve and expand the locally available medicinal plants that may also help in providing primary healthcare to the local community. The safety and effectiveness of natural medicines and the regulatory environment should accompany the incorporation of the traditional systems of healthcare into the national healthcare (Bodekar, 1994).

The local cultivation and production as well as utilisation of such medicinal plants need to be addressed scientifically. The Bio-diversity-cum-Recreation Park at Diphu (Karbi Anglong) managed by the Department of Environment and Forest, Karbi Anglong Autonomus Council, Diphu harbor varieties of medicinal plants endemic to the region and about 560 species of medicinal plants are available.

The following table provides list some medicinal plants and its usage.

Table 18.1: Medicinal plants used by the Karbis

Sl.No.	*Local name*	*Botanical name*	*Used for the treatment*
1	Chuselok	*Abrus precatorius* Linn.	Cough
2	Bapchuki	*Acmella paniculata*	Stomachache
3	Jok–an-kelok	*Adhatoda zeylanica*	Dysentery
4	Phrikangnek	*Alpinia galanga*	Bronchitis

(Contd...)

5	Raeaba	*Alternanthera sessilis*	Skin disease
6	Hen saiku	*Amorphophalus bulbifer*	Piles
7	Ingchum	*Antidesma acidum*	Appetizer
8	Chamua	*Arisaema tortuosum*	Piles
9	Bengali dido	*Beta vulgaris*	Jaundice
10	Pri	*Calamus rotang*	Vitality
11	Bapduli	*Cassia tora*	Jaundice
12	Churu	*Chenopodium album*	Dysentery
13	Repichingthun	*Cissus quandragularis*	Joint pain
14	Phelang-riho	*Clerodendrum serratum*	Wound
15	Kurveng	*Commelina benghalensis*	Earache
16	Tharmit tharve	*Curcuma amada*	Gastritis
17	Or -oh	*Cycas pectinata*	Gastritis
18	Kur-vengso	*Drymaria cordata*	Sinusitis
19	Ok hi atehang	*Homalomena aromatica*	Joint pain
20	Lopong brik	*Lippia geminata*	Conjunctivitis
21	Hewali	*Nyctanthes arbor-tristis*	Malaria
22	Nopak ban	*Oroxylum indicum*	Intestinal worm
23	Pharchingki	*Solanum nigrum*	Intestinal worm
24	Thebongkang	*Physalis peruviana*	Stomach pain
25	Rikang menthu	*Paederia foetida*	Gastritis
26	Vorke abap	*Vitex negundo*	Malaria
27	Parok hanthor	*Xanthium strumarium*	High blood pressure
28	Phrilangdung	*Zingiber zerumbet*	Blood dysentery

Source: Field study 2015.

The understanding of indigenous knowledge and practices in relation to natural resource utilisation and management is one of the key issues for achieving sustainable development communities of the region. There is a need to strengthen the forest conservation measures based on the traditional knowledge and value system.

Observations indicated an interesting and intricate pattern of health behaviour and health communication among the Karbis. It is evident that the communication skills of the tribal healers are excellent and their trust, credibility and accessibility can go a long way in co-opting them as 'agents' of change for health practices.

Conclusion

Healthcare behaviour is an integral part of culture and understanding of the ethnomedical practices of the various communities is of great importance to promote the health status of a community. Tribes of northeast

India possess a vast traditional knowledge on effective ethnomedicines, which was acquired through the experience, are usually passed on by oral traditions. Thus, the potentialities of ethnomedicinal studies in northeast India should be given the importance as it can provide us a lead to discover of more and potential useful chemical compounds. A detailed scientific study is required to document all those rare species of medicinal plants and protection of such traditional knowledge and their practices will be significant important for future research.

Rapid changes in traditional lifestyles and cultural practices due to modernisation, globalisation and reliance on modern medical care have put this age-old traditional knowledge under threat. This calls for preservation of the knowledge and conservation of the plant and animal biodiversity of medicinal value.

Traditional medical system still plays an important role in healthcare behaviour among the Karbis. In most cases, causes of an illness and healing system are found to be associated with the magico-religious beliefs. Along with herbal treatment, magico-religious practices are still occupying a significant position in their indigenous methods of treatment. The analysis reveal that factors like age, sex, education of the patient, types of illness, severity of diseases, healthcare facility, beliefs regarding the cause of diseases and previous experiences effect selection of different ways of treatment.

The use of traditional healing practices seems to have an influence on their healthcare-seeking behaviour and treatment of illness. The link between the tribal healers and the Karbis is strong and well-established, since healers are, to a large extent, the only source of advice on good health and provision for treatment and cure. Modern medicine and state health service making in-roads into these remote and far flung villages have been a rather recent phenomenon. In order to be effective in the implementation of any health programme, effective communication among health providers, health seekers, and traditional healers is essential. For effective implementation of any health programme, effective communication among health providers, health seekers, and traditional healers is vital.

A comprehensive research studies needs to be carried out to identify, document and study ethnomedicinal plants for planning of sustainable resource management of the northeast region of India. Undertaking research studies on such ethnomedicinal plants would be helpful for conservation of rare plant species as well as environment.

References

Baruah, S., S.K. Borthakur, P. Gogoi and M. Ahmed, 2013. Ethnomedicinal plants used by Adi-Miniyong tribe of Arunachal Pradesh, Eastern Himalaya, *Indian Journal of Natural Products and Resources*, 4(3), 278-282.

Bhattacharjee, T. Sociology of the Karbis. Delhi: B.R. Publishing Corporation; 1986.

Phangcho, PC. Karbi anglong and north cachar hills: A study of geography and culture. Diphu: Printwell; 2001.

Evans-Pritchard, EE. 1937. Witchcraft, oracles, and magic among the Azande. Clarendon Press, Oxford.

Fabrega, H, Silver, D. 1973. Illness and shamanistic curing in Zinacantan: an ethnomedical analysis. University Press, Stanford.

Foster, G. 1976. Medical Anthropology and international health planning. Medical Anthropology Newsletter 7(3):12-18.

Kleinman, A. 1980. Patients and healers in the context of culture. University of California Press, Berkeley.

Rivers, WHR, 1924. *Medicine, Magic and Religion.* London: Routledge.

Ronghang, R, Teron, R, Tamuli, AK, Rajkhowa, RC. Traditional zootherapy practiced among the Karbis of Assam (India) The Ecoscan. 2011;1:161–6.

Singh, Narendra and B.C. Agrawal 2009. "Role of Magico-Religious Healers in Community Health: A Study of the Tribal Communities of Chhattisgarh". In Binod C. Agrawal (ed.), *Media for Health Planning, programmes and Practice.* New Delhi Concept Publishing Company.

Shankar, R., G.S. Lavekar, S. Deb and B.K. Sharma, 2012. Traditional healing practice and folk medicines used by Mishing community of North East India, *J Ayurveda Integr Med.*, 3, 124-9.

Traditional Medicine. Geneva, Switzerland: 2008. World Health Organisation Fact Sheet No. 134 (December 2008).

Waldstein, A, Adams C. 2006. The interface between medical anthropology and medical ethnobiology. Journal of Royal Anthropological Institute N.S.:95-118.

Warren, D.M. 1990. Indigenous Knowledge and Development. Background paper for seminar session on Sociology, natural resources management and agri-development.

Winkelman M., 2009 *Culture and Health,* San Francisco, John Wiley and Sons.

World Health Organisation, 1999. *Fifty years of WHO in South East Asia* 1948–1998.

Chapter - 19

A Study on Ethno-medicinal use for Pre- and Post-natal care among the *Kaibartas of Assam*

—*Jyoti Hazarika and S. Sengupta*

Introduction

Ethno-medicine encompasses the whole gamut of traditional medical system, which is concerned with the cultural interpretation of health, diseases, and illness and also addresses the health-seeking process and healing practices. It is a complex multi-disciplinary system, comprising the use of plants and animals, spirituality and the natural environment. The traditional knowledge of ethno-medicine has been used for centuries by the indigenous communities for the treatment of various types of health problems.

Prenatal and postnatal cares are two important aspects of health seeking behaviour. The health of a mother and child depends upon the kind of maternal healthcare, both at prenatal and postnatal periods. For healthy childbirth, proper prenatal care is utmost necessary. It can be considered as an essential safety net for healthy motherhood and childbirth, where the well-being of both the prospective mother and her offspring can be monitored (United Nations, 2008).

Postnatal, on the other hand, is the period required by a woman to recover from the effects of childbirth. Neglect during this period results in aggravation of multiple health problems, such as anaemia, malnutrition, chronic backaches and other conditions that affect the overall well-being of women. Instead of having proper medical facilities, approximately one-half million women die each year during pregnancy and childbirth; and 99 per cent of these are from developing countries (Zahr *et al.,* 1996).

Despite of giving much attention on antenatal care for preventing maternal mortality, four-fifths of all maternal deaths occur during delivery and in postnatal period (Li *et al.,* 1996). Thus, it is a matter of concern, especially in rural Indian villages.

It has been estimated by World Health Organisation that 80 per cent of the world's population relies on traditional medicine to meet their daily health requirements. Even though modern medical systems are available, ethno-medicine has still maintained its popularity in all regions of the developing world. Moreover, allopathic doctors and clinics are not affordable in many rural communities of the world, and such communities still depend on traditional medical systems as their first tier of primary healthcare (Goleniowski *et al.,* 2006). The uses of various plants and their products have been reported for healthcare by Blackwell (1990) and for post-delivery care by Kaur (1999) and many others.

Every culture, irrespective of its simplicity and complexity, has its own beliefs and practices concerning diseases (Chowdhury, 1967). Kaibartas under study also have their own conception towards the understanding of health, disease, healthcare and healing practices and developed their individual ethno-medicinal practices to cure various illnesses by using different kinds of plants available in their surrounding environment. The present study aims to document the magnitude of existing system of traditional knowledge among the Kaibartas of Assam, especially for healthy child birth and easy recovery of mother's health after delivery.

Kaibatras are one of the aboriginal caste populations of Assam who have been living in Assam since time immemorial. Traditionally, Kaibarta was a socio-economically backward fishing community. Among them, literacy rate is relatively lower in comparison with other neighbouring communities. However, in the present-day situation, the people of Kaibarta community are actively engaged with cultivation and also in various government services.

Material and Method

Data for the present study has been collected from two villages, namely "Sonapur Village Number 2" and "Deodubi Village" of Bordoloni Block of Dhemaji District, Assam. Information on different ethno-medicinal plants and animal products that are used for pre- and postnatal ailments was collected and documented. Married women having at least one child, besides few traditional healers and aged persons from the two aforesaid villages having profound knowledge about ethno-medicinal practices, have been selected for in-depth interview.

Result and Discussion

It has been observed that the Kaibarta population under study was well acquainted with the indigenous ethno-medicinal knowledge. Among them, there is an existing belief that during prenatal and postnatal periods, allopathic medicine should be avoided as far as possible because there may have some ill-effects on the baby if it used during these periods. Thus, the Kaibarta women under study prefer to treat ailments like abdominal pain and over bleeding after delivery, inflammation of hands and foots during pregnancy, augmentation of lactation, etc., with the help of locally available medicinal plants. In this paper, information on medicinal plants applied for the treatment of different ailments that crop up before and after delivery has been documented. The plants are enumerated along with the local name, English equivalent, parts used, dosages and the mode of preparations. A brief description about pre- and postnatal care has been given below:

Panchamrit Rituals

For the satisfactory growth and development of the foetus, proper dietary habit is very essential. During the fifth month of pregnancy, "*Panchamrit*" (*i.e.*, a kind of rice pudding made from five sweet products such as cow's milk, curd, ghee, honey and sugar) is given to a pregnant woman for the better growth of baby. Kaibarta women under study believed that *Panchamrit* is a very prized food item for a pregnant woman during her first pregnancy, which can help in better growth of brain and one should not keep away from it.

Some Kaibarta women under study used to drink a cup of milk with the extracted juice of *Centella asiatica* (Asiatic pennywort) or locally called *Bormanimuni* and *Hydrocotyle sibthorpioides* (dwarf pennywort) or *Sorumanimuni* in the morning. They believed that it would endow with better growth of brain and proper health of the foetus. However, the women who used to drink this type of juice are very few in number.

Inflammation of Hands and Foots during Pregnancy

(i) *Spilanthes acmella Murr* (pellitary) or locally called *Maichang,* a kind of herb easily available in all rural Kaibarta villages, has a vital role to cure inflammation of body during pregnancy. Some young head leaves of *Maichang* are cooked without oil with little amount of salt and is given the pregnant women two times a day to get ride from this problem.

(ii) The meat of *Xenopus laevis* (water frog) *Patbang* is considered as an important source of medicines, which have been used by the Kaibata women to treat inflammation of hands and foots during pregnancy. Flesh of *Patbang* is boiled with water without chilly and onion and is given to the affected women to eat with rice for a minimum period of three days.

Stomach Problems

(i) Young head leaves of *Alternanthera sessilis* (dwarf copper leaf sessile joy weed), locally called *Matikaduri*, entire plants of *Hydrocotyle sibthorpioides* (dwarf pennywort) or *Sorumanimuni* and young head leaves of *Spilanthes acmella Murr* (pellitary) or *Maichang* in Assamese are cooked with *Trigonella foenumgraecum* Linn or locally called *Methiguti* in a little amount of mustard oil and is given to eat with rice for stomach problems such as constipation, lack of appetite, etc.

(ii) Entire plant of fresh *Houttuynia cordata* or locally called *Machunduri* is steamed with a little amount of salt and is given to eat in empty stomach two times a day for three consecutive days to get relief from loose motion and indigestion during pregnancy.

For Easy Delivery

(i) Roots of the plant called *Cissampelos pareira* (chaste creeper) or locally called *Tupuki lata* are collected and washed properly, and then these are crushed and applied over vagina for a brief period during the time of delivery for easy and smooth delivery of baby.

(ii) A little amount of water given by the father-in-law of the pregnant woman, which is locally called as *Bhoridhuwa Pani* (water that used to wash foot), is given to the expectant woman to get relief from the pain and easy child birth.

Fifty gms. of urine from any related person of the mother is given to drink to clear placenta and any other waste materials after the birth of baby. It should be given very secretly without knowing any other person, except the men/ women who arrange it.

After delivery, the mother should avoid spicy and liquid food and prefer to eat locally available medicinal plant to cure stomach pain, to dry naval chord, over bleeding after delivery, augmentation of lactation, etc., which are given below:

To stop bleeding after delivery

Twenty-five gms of *Pepper nigrum* (black pepper) or locally called *Jaluk*, with *Allium sativum* (garlic green) or *Boga nohoru* in Assamese, have to grind and roast (*puri diya*). This medicine is given to the mother to consume with rice in the first three days to stop bleeding after delivery.

Stomach pain after delivery

(i) *Pogostemon benghalensis* (*patchouli*) or *Sukloti* in Assamese is cooked with black pepper and given to the mother to reduce stomach pain after delivery.

(ii) A cup of extracted juice from whole plants of *Hydrocotyle sibthorpioides* (dwarf pennywort) or *Sorumanimuni*, *Centella asiatica* (Asiatic pennywort) or locally called *Bormanimuni* and 21 *pepper nigrum* (black pepper) or *jaluk* in Assamese with little amount of salt is given to mother to consume in empty stomach for three to five days to cure stomach pain after delivery.

(iii) Young head leafs of *Leucus aspera spreng* (thumbe) or locally called *Durunbon*, *Vitex negundo* or *Pochotiya aagh* in Assamese, entire plants along with the roots of *Oldenlandia corymbosa* or *Bonjaluk* in Assamese, *Hydrocotyle sibthorpioides* (dwarf pennywort) or *Sorumanimuni* with adequate amount of *Pepper nigrum* (black pepper) locally called *Jaluk* and *Allium sativum* (garlic green) - *Boga nohoru* in Assamese are cooked with a very little amount of mustard oil. Kaibarta women under study consider it a very effective and essential medicine to cure stomach pain and bleeding after delivery and used to eat for five to seven days with rice.

For Naval chord

(i) Seven to 21 *Pepper nigrum* (black pepper) or locally called *Jaluk* are fried without oil and then have to grind and mixed with coconut oil. This paste is given to apply over naval chord to get it dry soon.

(ii) Young leafs of *Paederia scandens* (Sewer Vines) or locally called *Vedai lata,Murraya Koenigi* (curry plant)-*Norosingha* in Assamese, *Pogostemon benghalensis* (Patchouli) or *Sukloti* in Assamese and whole plants of *Hydrocotyle sibthorpioides* (dwarf pennywort) or *Sorumanimuni* along with some *Pepper nigrum* (black pepper) locally called *Jaluk* are grinded and cooked without oil and given to the mother to eat with rice in the morning consecutively for five days.

The Kaibarta people believe that a mother loses her strength and vigour after giving birth to a baby and thus she requires proper nutritious diet to regain her energy. But, she should not consume all kinds of foods. She has to avoid all kinds of citrus fruits (like lemon, olive, mango etc.,), meat, eggs, bottle gourd, pumpkin, and oily and spicy food till one month. After three days of birth, a special kind of food item called "*Jaalor Vaat*" is prepared, especially for the mother, to reduce pain and get energy.

A curry prepared with young stems of *Colocasia esculentus* or locally called *Kola Kochu* and fish like *Canna punctatus* (*Goroimass* in Assamese) with adequate amount of black pepper and *Allium sativum* (garlic green)-*Boga nohoru* in Assamese is offered to the mother to eat with rice.

Another curry, which is given along with *Jaalor vaat,* is that the meat of local varieties of chicken and *Carica papayer* or locally called *omita* along with adequate amount of *Pepper nigrum* (black pepper) or locally called *Jaluk* and *Allium sativum* (garlic green)-*Boga nohoru* is cooked in a very little amount of mustard oil and is given to the mother to eat with rice to get energy and reduce pain.

Augmentation of lactation

(i) *Lens culinaris* (Lentil) or locally called *Mochur dail* and *Carica papayer* or *Omita* in Assamese are boiled with 21 pieces of *Pepper nigrum* (black pepper) or locally called *Jaluk* and are given to the mother to eat for three consecutive days to increase breast milk.

(ii) A cup of juice extracted from the root of *Thunbergia coccinea wall* (scarlet thunbergia) or *Nilokontha* in Assamese and *Mimosa pudica* (sensitive plant) locally called *Lajukilata* with 21 numbers of *Pepper nigrum* (black pepper) or locally called *Jaluk* and little amount of salt is given to eat in empty stomach for three consecutive days for augmentation of lactation.

Conclusion

From the above discussion, it is observed that among the Kaibarta population under study, indigenous ethno-medicinal system is widely practised in a variety of problems associated with pre- and post-natal periods, even though the accessibility of the modern medicine for various types of diseases is not totally out of their reach. There is no well established health centre within the villages and government hospital is also far away from both the villages. Moreover, the people are not economically sound also, that's why, the people primarily depend upon the locally available ethno-medicines for maintaining their health, but, in case of diseases with serious nature, they prefer to go to government hospitals for better treatment. Therefore, healthcare infrastructure in government sector should be improved and made easily accessible.

References

Blackwell, H.W. 1990. *Poisonous and Medicinal Plants*. New Jersey: Prentice Hall Inc.

Chowdhury, B. 1967. "Magic vs. Medicine in a Tribal Village", *Adivasi*, 9 (1): 3-9.

Goleniowski, M.E., G.A. Bongiovanni, L. Bongiovanni, C.O. Palacio, and J.J Cantero, 2006. "Medicinal Plants from the Sierra de Comechingones, Argentina", *J. Ethno Pharmacology*, 107: 324-341.

Kaur, T. 1999. *Scientific Validation of Indigenous Homestead Practices for Use by Rural Home Makers*. Ph.D. Dissertation, (Unpublished). Ludhiana: Punjab Agricultural University.

Li, X. F., J. A. Fortney, M. Kotelchuck, and L. H. Glover. 1996. "The Postpartum Period: The Key to Maternal Mortality", *International Journal of Obstetrics and Gynaecology*, 54: 1-10.

United Nations, 2008. *The Millennium Development Goals Report*. New York: United Nations.

Zahr, A., C., T. Wardlaw, C. Stanton, and K. Hill. 1996. "Maternal Mortality", *World Health Statistics Quarterly*, 49 (2): 77-78.

Chapter - 20

Traditional Healthcare Practices in *Nongpok Sekmai, Manipur*

—*Keisham Ingocha Singh and*
Mayanglambam Manibabu Singh

Introduction

The pottery community of Nongpok Sekmai has the beliefs and practices concerning health and diseases as most of the communities have. The people of this community from the early times are found to have a firm and well developed traditional healthcare system. In all human groups, no matter how small or technologically 'primitive', there exists a body of beliefs about the nature of disease, its causation and cure, its therapeutic and preventive practices, and its relations in other aspects of group life (Chakrabarti, S.B. and Sarkar, B.N., 1998). Korn, L.E. (2013) rightly says, "In response to challenges well beyond their control, different peoples developed through cultural practice various ways of coping, healing, and responding to disease, poisons, and both accidental as well as intentional violence enabling them to survive productively in spite of the threats to life." This is proved by their belief in super-natural and socio-cultural adaptive strategies that have adapted in their medical system, to culturally based behaviour and belief forms that advent in response to the threats posed by disease among the people of Nongpok Sekmai. The traditional healthcare of this community involves a body of concepts and beliefs as well as practices related to the state of health, the nature of disease, causation and cure, therapeutic and preventive practices.

The people take leafs, flowers, fruits, roots, tubers, etc. grown in the nature and also animals, birds, and fish as a part of ensuring good health. The concept of good and bad food, preferred food and food taboo, special food during illness, pregnancy and lactation and ceremonial are marked and practised as their cultural code. For many ages, all civilisations and cultures used plants and took advantage of herbs to cure diseases and ease sufferings. So, all societies develop their own traditional medicine system to ease their sufferings. According to the World Health Organisation (WHO), "Traditional medicine is the sum total of knowledge, skills and practices based on the theories, beliefs and experiences indigenous to different cultures that are used to maintain health, as well as to prevent, diagnose, improve or treat physical and mental illnesses."

In the community of Nongpok Sekmai, traditional medical system is a combination of real practices, superstitions, magic and religion. The ethno-medical practices are based upon religion, magic, massage and administering of plant and animal products, externally or internally (Devarapali, J. and Kumar, R.K., 1998, p.74). Traditional health practitioners each with different specialisations of indigenous methods are evident for diagnosis as well as treatment of diseases. This perhaps indicates the close relationship between culture aspect, disease and treatment. For many communities, traditional healers are an inherent component of their societal culture, and seeking traditional healers can be a natural extension of their worldview (Amal, Adnan and Aasim, 2011).

The area of ethno-medicine has remained neglected and overlooked with the advent of modernisation. But, in rural areas, the traditional system is still surviving and retains its roots in their culture. There are some sporadic studies conducted on the Traditional Healthcare Practices among some communities. Nobody has so far conducted study on this topic to a particular community, who are traditionally engaged in pottery craft from medical anthropological perspective. Therefore, an attempt is made in this paper to focus upon the concept of health and disease, profile of ethno-medical specialists who involved in different cases and the utilisation of various biological products, both plants and animals, and the mode of their application with reference to various ailments in the ethno-medical practices of Nongpok Sekmai.

Study Area

Nongpok Sekmai is a pottery village in Manipur, which is situated at a distance of 35 km. east of Imphal in Thoubal District of Manipur. The village is bounded on the east by Shikhong, on the north and west by Gwarok Maring village and on the south by Ukhongshang and Salungpham. This village enjoys a climate similar to the valley areas of Manipur. According to the Census of India (1991: 9), the Sikhong-Sekmai area, which is an extension of the Eastern Hill system, belongs to the Barail Series and Simsang formation (Garo Hills). One can reach the village from Imphal via Yairipok or Charangpat. The Sekmai River flows down towards the northwestern side and joins the Thoubal River at Chandrakhong. Sikhong bazar, the most immediate market place at Nongpok Sekmai, is the primary outlet of their products—the earthen pots. Most of their products are transported to the nearby markets by various means. At present, Imphal-bound buses and other public conveyances transport earthen pots to the main market in Imphal town. As the village falls under the "notified areas" of the Government of Manipur, it has a local self-government in the form of Sikhong Sekmai Nagar Panchayat, which is divided into nine wards and pottery making is confined to only three wards, *i.e.*, Ward Nos. 2, 3 and 4.

This pottery community belongs to the *Chakpas*[1] people who are regarded as the guardian of the tradition of the development of pottery through the handling of clay in the state of Manipur. The society consists of seven *yeks*[2] in different proportions—Khuman (71 households), Mangang (49 households), Angom (48 households), Luwang (42 households), Moirang (20 households) and Kha-Nganba (19 households). The presence of all the seven clans of the Meitei (the largest community in Manipur) is a clear indication of the self-contained nature of the village. The society being patrilineal and patriarchal, men play important roles in various social activities and engage in major economic pursuits. Marriage within the village has been a regular practice although inter-village marriages are on the rise these days.

Distinctiveness of Nongpok Sekmai, in terms of religious beliefs and practices, is discernible by the presence of three local deities (*umang lais*[3]), called Nongpok Ningthou, Ikop Ningthou and Sawang Ningthou. The people of Shikhong areas worship Nongpok Ningthou, while the people of Lilakambong, Makha Leikai and Mayai Leikai (three localities in the settlement area) worship Ikop Ningthou. Sawang Ningthou is worshipped by the people of Awang Leikai.

The village is no more an isolated as the modern means of transportation and communication have reached the village. Movement of people from one place to another for various purposes is increasing due to the emerging transport facilities. Apart from this, communication keeps them informed about the world's events and trends thus bringing in positive changes in the life of the people of Nongpok Sekmai by enhancing job and education facilities. The ultimate result is the improvement of their socio-economic conditions.

Objectives

Keeping in view the traditional healthcare practices in the pottery village, the present study aims:

- To understand the concept of health and diseases under the ambit of their culture.
- To find out the people's beliefs associated with the causes of diseases and illness.
- To search the profiles of ethno-medical specialists in the village.
- To investigate traditional method of treatments for various diseases and illnesses.
- To investigate the ethno-pharmacological knowledge of the people.

Significance of the Study

Some studies of ethno-medicines in Manipur have been attempted from different perspectives, like botany, history and sociology. However, no anthropological study addressing traditional healthcare practices in a pottery village has been undertaken. This study is an attempt to explore the age-old traditional medical system of a pottery village from anthropological perspective. Such a study may provide a body of knowledge that can add new information to the existing body of knowledge on the topic. This study may help in conserving the traditional wisdom of the healthcare practices and also in paving the way of protecting the tradition amidst the modernised bio-medical world.

Methodology

Primary data were collected directly from the field using three research tools such as semi-structured interview, focused interview and observation. Semi-structured interview schedule was prepared to collect information on traditional medicine preparation, application, utilised part and form. The semi-structured interview schedules were pre-tested before administering in the field. The interviewees were given a uniform instruction highlighting the purpose and objectives of conducting the interview.

Focused interviews were also conducted with traditional medicine practitioners. In focused interview, data on specific information like the method of treatment for a particular illness or the process of driving out the evil spirits in case of magico-religious practitioners were conducted. A checklist was used to guide the focused interview. Apart from this, case studies were also conducted from the specialists to find out the in-depth data on specific cases encountered by specialists. Both qualitative and quantitative methods have been used to collect the data. Recorded data were sorted and analysed with simple statistical method.

Findings

A. Concept of Health and Diseases

A village elder man said, "For me, the term 'health' means, 'proper functioning of the body' and disease means 'a change in a person's state of being, which is seen as discontinuous with his everyday state of being'. "Healthy persons are those who get up early in the morning, worship God, doing exercises, able to work in agricultural works or pottery work and alike, can take heavy food and have a sound physical body", he added. When inquired about the meaning of illness, an old man said, "An ill person is recognised when a person stops eating, does not perform his work or is unable to carry out his responsibilities as a member of a family and society to which he belongs." Another woman said, "For us, illness is conceived primarily in terms of not feeling well."

They believe that a healthy person must be able to work for long hours in the field without any physical constrain. They also believe that good health is the outcome of pious life and illness is the punishment meted out by spirits. They also believe that their sufferings have genesis in the deeds of their past life. The healthy person is the one who has adhered to the norms and codes of the village and pleased the God. They think that individual life is controlled by the will of God.

Inquiring about the community's perception on woman's health, a traditional medical specialist said, "Women is considered healthy when she is able to give birth to children, should be able to work in the pottery occupation, weaving for long hours and agricultural activities like weeding and sowing and also should be able to carry out all the household chores."

B. Causes of Illness as Belief by the Villagers

Every culture has its own beliefs and practices related to health and diseases, which are products of indigenous cultural development. The community has a peculiar way of looking into the phenomenon of sickness and diseases, depending on various situations. When enquired about the causes of disease and illness, one male specialist said, "*laiok tinoknaba* and *tinmu laimu changba* (encountering spirits), *hingchabi changba*[4], *potsem-jadu,*[5] breach of taboo, wrath of god and *mahousagi oiba* (natural causes) are the factors that cause various diseases and illness."

They believe that a number of evil spirits are found in the village. As belief by them, *helloi*[6], *apumbi soren*,[7] ancestral spirits, and insatiated souls of unnatural death are the spirits roamed around the village. These spirits can cause disease and illness through the mental disturbance to individuals. Regarding about *hingchbi changba,* it is believed that some people have the power to cause on others by just looking at them. These people possess some supernatural power and this power, in the form of spirits, enters into the victims causing mental disturbance and body imbalances. *Potsem-jadu* is done with a purpose to harm or control an individual due to personal animosity or gain, which causes illnesses. It is done by means of spells and charms or by placing some objects in the house of a person. Cases of casting powers to food items regarding jealousy among members of the society and also avoiding extra-marital affairs among the partners are prevalent in the village. Another cause of disease and illness, as believed by the villagers, is the breach of taboo. Among these people, they practise clan exogamy. If members of the same clan marry, there is a belief that the couple will have disfigured and handicapped children with diseases. They also have clan food taboo. If one happens to have food taboos, then it is believed that one's teeth will have infections and also will have incurable diseases like leprosy.

The causes of diseases and illness are also described in naturalistic terms by the people of Nongpok Sekmai. This may be the change of weather leading to cold and fever. Excessive work leading to headache and fever, unclean body giving rise to boils and dryness of skin and overeating or intoxicants causing stomach pain and intestinal disorders are also in the category of *mahousagi oiba* (natural causes), as believed by the people.

C. Ethno-medical Specialist

The cosmology of Nongpok Sekmai society revolves around the tradition of *Maibas* (male practitioners) and *Maibis* (female practitioners), in case socio-religious, health and illness are considered. The *maiba* and *maibi* are the generic terms, which indicate different groups of practitioners rooted in either socio-religious, magico-religious and traditional medicine. Some *maibas* and *maibis* are, respectively, priests and priestesses, which play a major role in the society, while others are possessed by spirits. The details of *maibas* and *maibis* are given below:

The *maiba*

There are three types of *maibas* in the village as (i) the *maiba* who performs religious rituals, (ii) the *maiba* who practises both medicine, prayer and spell, and (iii) the *maiba* who practises only medicine.

(i) The *maiba* who performs religious rituals

He is recognised as the ritual specialist in the society. Being the traditional priest in the society, he performs rituals in most of the religious functions. He is the specialist in the *Lai Haraoba*[8] ceremony. At the time of natural calamities, like draught, flood and unnatural events, he performs rituals. The *maiba* learns his profession through apprenticeship.

(ii) The *maiba* who practises both medicine and prayer and spell

He is treated as a megico-religious specialist and specialises to treat and cure diseases with the help of offerings, spells, rituals, and exorcism. In other words, he is the *Shaman* in the society. Some of the magico-religious specialists is masseur (*pukli suba maibas*) who is very expert in reading the pulses of the body, the nerves and body parts. He is endowed with skills to determine health complications under the spell of magic or witchcraft through *'mihun'* (pulse beat). Through *mihul* reading, the *maiba* can predict and diagnose whether the patient is possessed by an evil spirit, deity or of super-natural forces and, accordingly, he will prescribe the medicines and perform rituals like *khayom lakpa, chaban thaba, iratpa, ushin shinba,* and *yenling thaba,* which need to be conducted.

(iii) The *maiba* who practises only herbal medicine

Besides the magico-religious treatment of the diseases, treatment by only plants is very much popular among the people of Nongpok Sekmai for curing various diseases. There is one medicine man (*mana mashingna laiyengba maiba*) in the village. He prepares and prescribes various herbal medicines for all sorts of common diseases. The medicine man goes to the client's house when he gets a request call from the concerned person. The medicine he prescribes is neither religious nor magic, but with his knowledge of healing with natural resources available in his surroundings.

The maibi

There are two types of *maibis* in the village. They are (i) the *maibi* who performs religious rituals and (ii) the *maibi* who is trained as midwife for assisting child delivery and other related activities.

(i) The *maibi* who performs religious rituals

She is a priestess and spiritist, who is a ritual specialist, and plays a major role in religious life. She performs rituals in most of the religious functions. She is the specialist in the *Lai Haraoba* ceremony. Becoming *maibi* is to be selected by the *lai* (god), which means that she has been possessed by *lai*. A woman can become *maibi* at any age. She has common symptoms like abnormal behaviour and of being constantly weak, restless and anxiety. It even affects her speech, language and can witness strange events happening in her life. If she possesses such symptoms, she is sent to a senior *maibi* for determining whether she is under the possession of a *lai*. If she is found to be possessed by *lai*, she becomes a *maibi* under the guidance of a senior. A *maibi* is the intermediate person between the *lai* and the human being through whom the god transmits his massages. The path of a *maibi* is generally traversed by a female. But there are some cases when a man becomes possessed by the *lai* and he wears clothes of the female *maibi,* and is termed as male *maibi*.

Besides officiating religious rituals, a *maibi* gets into trance and has connection with god and acts as diviners, delivered oracles and performs propitiating rites for their clients. When a client asks for a *senmit* (requesting for prediction), the *maibi* asks the person to place some coins (fees) on a piece of plantain leaf. She chants the language of god, mediates for a while and when she becomes possessed by the *lai*, the *maibi* predicts the details of the person. The words of the possessed *maibi* are believed to be the words of the god and are obeyed with greatest reverence and sincerity. She has the capabilities to give ritual treatments or use of ritual or offering in treating the patients.

(ii) The *maibi* who assists child delivery and other related activities

If a female assists in child delivery in the village with the traditional knowledge, she is also referred to as *maibi*. There is one *maibi* who assists child delivery and other related activities in the village. She is not possessed by *lai,* but acquires knowledge from her mother and grandmother. She acts as a traditional midwife (ethno-gynaecologist) in the village. The traditional midwife is one who is well-versed and trained within their own culture and uses indigenous systems of treatment.

D. Treatment of Disease and Illness

The traditional methods of treatment of diseases, which are still evident in Nongpok Sekmai village, can be grouped into three categories:

(i) Magico-religious treatment,

(ii) *Pukli suba* or *Hakchang noiduna Laiyengba* (masseur), and

(iii) Natural folk medicine treatment.

(i) Magico-religious treatment

When gods and goddesses are not given due recognition and reverence, they get angry and this wrath causes diseases and illness to them. They are appeased or propitiated with appropriate offerings and, therefore, sacrifices are made with due methods. This includes the ways of treatment for possession by *hingchabi,* a malevolent spirit, infliction of evil eye and black art. At first, the *maiba* diagnoses the ailment by feeling *mihun* of the client and then prescribes which method of treatment is to be followed. The different types of appeasement rituals are described below. Spells remain an indispensable part of these rituals.

Iratpa

This is one of the methods of worshipping the deity in one's residence for curing illness and also for obtaining a prosperous happy life among the family members. Offerings such as fruits, flowers, and puffed rice are to be made daily along with agarbati and lighted candle or lantern.

Chaban Thaba

This is also another method of appeasement and consists of offering of cooked vegetables or meat or rice cakes, burnt chillies, depending on the kind of illness. This is mainly done when a person is possessed by a malevolent deity or when a dead person appears in one's dream.

Khayom Lakpa

It is an offering method to deities consisting of a cultic packet by layers of banana leaves in which rice, *langthrei,* flowers and eggs are put in. The offering is to be made in the river water or pond and is mainly conducted for general weakness such as nausea, vomiting and giddiness.

Ushil Touba

In this method, representation of the ill person is made with the help of any other living being such as hen, pigeon, duck, cow, *ngamu* (channa oriental's) or leaves of trees. Offerings are made representing the illness by any of the above animals or trees, to take its place and carry away the ailment.

Yenlling Thaba

It is another method of *ushil* type of ritual. The replacement is mainly done taking the help of a domestic hen, in which the living being is allowed to move in wherever it likes independently.

(ii) *Pukli suba* or *Hakchang noiduna Laiyengba* (masseur)

He is the expert who also reads the pulse of the body, knows well of the nerves, bodily parts and who massages well. By feeling the pulses, he

Table 20.1: List of plants documented along with their family, local name, part used and ethno-medicinal use

Sl. No.	*Botanical Name*	*Family*	*Local Name(Manipuri)*	*Part Used*	*Remedy*
1.	Achyranthus aspera L.	Amarantheceae	Khujumpere	Leaf, root and seed	Irregular menstruation, piles, gum complaints.
2.	Acorus calamus L.	Araceae	Ok hidak	Rhizomes	Asthma
3.	Adhatoda vasica Nees.	Acanthaceae	Nongmangkha angouba	Leaves	Muscular pain, common cold, jaundice.
4.	Aegle marmelos Linn.	Rutaceae	Harikhagok	Leaves	Dysentery, diarrhea, constipation.
5.	Ageratum conyzoides	Asteraceae	Khongjai napi	Leaves	Dysentery, diarrhea, constipation.
6.	Alliumhookerli	Liliaceae	Maroinapakpi	Leaves	Blood pressure, stomach ulcers.
7.	Allium sativum Linn.	Liliceae	Chanam	Bulb	Bronchitis, asthma.
8.	Aloe vera	Liliceae	Dhrita kumar	Leaves	Ulcer, Irregular menstruation.
9.	Alpinia galangal wild.	zingiberaceae	Kanghoo	Rhizome	Ring worm, skin diseases
10.	Alternanthera sessilis.	Amaranthaceae	Phakchet	Leaf, stem	Snake bite.
11.	Amaranthus spinosus Linn.	Amaranthaceae	chengkruk	Shoot	Snake bite, skin sores
12.	Argemone mexicana L.	papaveraceae	Khomthokpi	Leaves, seeds	Jaundice, snake bite.
13.	Aryngium foetidum.		Awa phadigom.	Leaves.	Jaundice.
14.	Bambusa tulda Roxb.	Gramineae.	Ootang.	Leaves and shoots.	Chicken pox and dog bite.
15.	Basella alba Linn.	Basellaceae.	Uroksumbal.	Leaves.	Boils and constipation.
16.	Bixa orellana Linn.	Bixaceae.	Ureirom.	Leaves.	Snake bites and jaundice.
17.	Calotropis procera (Ait) R. Br.	Asclepiadaceae.	Angkot.	Leaves.	Leprosy and other skin diseases.
18.	Cannabis sativa Linn.	Cannabinaceae.	Ganja.	Leaves and flower.	Diarrhea and dysentery.

(Contd...)

19.	Centella asiatica (Linn) Urban.	Umbelliferae.	Peruk.	Leaves and runners.	Stomach ulcer and urinary troubles.
20.	Cissus javana Roxb.	Vitaceae.	Kongngouyen laba.	Leaves.	Removing stone from kidney.
21.	Cynodon dactylon Pers.	Gramineae.	Tingthou.	Leaves.	Excessive bleeding in urine.
22.	Datura stramonium Linn.	Solanaceae.	Sangoi hidak.	Leaves.	Asthma.
23.	Eclipta prostata Linn.	Asteraceae.	Uchi sumbal.	Leaves.	Liver enlargement, cough and fever.
24.	Eupatorium birmani cum DC.	Asteraceae.	Langthrei.	Leaves.	Stomach ulcer.
25.	Euphorbia hirta Linn.	Euphorbiaceae.	Pakhangba-maton.	Whole plant.	Dysentery and asthma.
26.	Ficus hispida	Moraceae.	Ashi-heibong.	Bark, fruit, leaves.	Promoting secretion of milk and ring worm.
27.	Garcinia peduculata Roxb.	Guttiferae.	Heibung.	Fruits.	Dysentery and jaundice.
28.	Gynura cusimba D.Don.	Asteraceae.	Terapaibi.	Stem and leaves.	Stop bleeding (wounds).
29.	Houttuynia cordata.	Saururaceae.	Toning-khok.	Leaves.	Measles, dysentery, gonorrhea.
30.	Hireola auricular.	Auriculeriaceae.	Uchina.	Whole parts.	Stomach ulcer.
31.	Impatiens balsamina Linn.	Balsaminaceae.	Khujang.	Leaves.	Nail injury.
32.	Ipomea aquatic Forsk.	Convolvulaceae.	Kolamni.	Leaves.	Relieve pain on insect's bite.
33.	Menthe arvensis Linn.	Lamiaceae.	Nungshi-hidak.	Shoots and leaves.	Diarrhea, irregular menstruation.
34.	Meriandra bengalensis Benth.	Lamiaceae.	Kanghuman.	Leaves.	Reduce high blood pressure.
35.	Meyna laxiflora Robyns.	Rubiaceae.	Heibi.	Leaves and dry fruits.	Blood purifier, boils and dysentery.
36.	Mimosa pudica Linn.	Mimosaceae.	Kangphal ikaithabi.	Leaves and seeds	Urinary problems, sores and piles.
37.	Nelumbo nucifera Gaerta.	Nymphaeaceae.	Thambal.	Roots, flower and seeds.	Diarrhea, cholera, piles and dysentery.
38.	Nyctanthes arbortristis Lnn.	Oleaceae.	Singgarei.	Leaves.	Fever and liver disorder.

(*Contd...*)

39.	Ocimum sanctum Linn.	Lamiaceae.	Tulsi. .	Leaves.	Fever, cough, and congestion of lungs.
40.	Piper betle Linn. P	Piperaceae.	Panamana.	Leaves.	Healing wounds and cough.
41.	Plantago erosa Wall	Plantaginaceae.	Yempat.	Leaves and seeds.	Boils, fresh injuries, dysentery.
42.	Pogo stemon sp.	Labiatae.	Shangbrei.	Leaves.	Insect repellant and hair lotion.
43.	Portulaca quadrifida Linn.	Portulacaceae.	Leipak kundo.	Leaves and stems.	Asthma, cough, ulcer.
44.	Ricinus commenis L.	Euphorbiaceae.	Kege.	Leaves.	Cure bleeding pile.
45.	Schizophyllum commune.	Agaricaceae.	Kanglayen.	Whole plant.	Asthma and tonsillitis.
46.	Sesamum indicum.	Pedaliaceae.	Thoiding amuba.	Seeds.	Burns and piles.
47.	Solanum nigrum Linn.	Solanaceae.	Leipung khangkha.	Leaves and fruits.	Stomach ache, fever, diarrhea.
48.	Sochus wightianus DC.	Asteraceae.	Khomthokpi.	Root.	Jaundice.
49.	Syzygium cumini		Gulamchat.	Leaves.	Tonsillitis.
50.	Vitex trifolia Linn.	Verbenaceae.	Urikshibi.	Leaves and flowers.	Fever and skin diseases.
51.	Xanthium strumarium Linn.	Asteraceae.	Hameng sampakpi.	Leaves.	Fever and cough.
52.	Zingiber officinale.	Zingiberaceae.	Sing.	Rhizome.	Asthma, cough, rheumatic pain.

Table 20.2: Medicinal animals, birds and fishes

Sl. No.	*Scientific Name*	*Family*	*Local Name (Manipuri)*	*Remedy*
1.	Amauronis phoenix curus pennant.	Ralliadae.	Ureng konthou.	The boiled flesh along with cissus adnanta (kongouyen) is given as a medicine in urinary problems due to stone formation.
2.	Apis indica fabricius.	Apidae.	Hayingkhoi.	Honey extracted from this insect is applied in eye diseases, fever, cough and small pox.
3.	Bolostomaindica lep, et. Sev.	Belostomatidae.	Naoshek.	The roasted insect is prescribed in piles. The poison of this insect is an antidote to snake bite.
4.	Cannonys badius hodgsom.	Muridae.	Shabi.	The boiled extract is prescribed in general weakness.
5.	Capra sibirica pallas.	Bovidae.	Hameng.	Liver boiled with salt is prescribed in night blindness and dried liver is recommended in tuberculosis.
6.	Clarias batrachus linnacus.	Claridae.	Ngakra.	The fresh blood mixed with the juice of garlic is prescribed in bleeding piles. Also fresh blood mixed with warmed milk is prescribed in debility.
7.	Dytiscus indicus italics.	Dticidae.	Tharaikokpi.	The insect is roasted and prescribed in piles.
8.	Gallus gallus murghi.	Phasianidae.	Yen.	The yolk mixed along with raw raisin (mekruk) is prescribed for dysentery. The soup of the flesh and bone is useful in general weakness.
9.	Gyps bengalensis gmelin.	Accipitridae.	Langja.	The smoke of the feather is prescribed in epilepsy.
10.	Hirudinaria gramulosa.	Hirudidae.	Tinpha.	The powder of the dried body along with the mineral oil is rubbed on the scalp for grey hair.
11.	Homo sapiens L.	Flaninidae.	Taibang mee.	The urine is applied on the body to relieve muscular pains. Nursing mother's milk is prescribed for eye infection. Saliva is used as an antidote to insect's bite.
12.	Leptoptilosdubius Gmelin	Ciconidae	Laishagol.	The crest

(Contd...)

13.	Melanis scabra	Melanidae	Laitharoi.	The paste is used externally in small pox, chicken pox and boils by the local people.
14.	Monapterus albus Zuiew	Symbranchidae.	Ngaprum.	The cooked fish or the fresh blood along with the boiled milk is prescribed for the infant to cure general weakness.
15.	Osteobrama cotion Ham.	Cyprinidae.	Ngasheksha.	The cooked flesh along with achyranthe aspera (khujumpere) is prescribed in cough, tuberculosis and heart diseases.
16.	Pigeon Columba livia.	Columbidae.	Khunu.	The fresh blood along with milk is prescribed in tuberculosis. The boiled flesh is given in paralysis and to reduce heart beat.
17.	Puntius chola hamiltons	cyprinidae	Phabounga.	The fermented fish locally termed as 'ngari' is recommended to cure plague disease.
18.	Prentius phutunio hamilton	Cyprinidae.	Ngakha.	The ash of the fish along with hair oil is applied externally to cure mouth ulcer.
19.	Rhinoceros unicornis Linnaeus	Rhino cerotidae.	Samuganda.	The paste of the horn is applied on the pimples, boils and blisters.
20.	Sympeturme strialatum.	Agrionidae.	Charang.	The fresh body is crushed and applied on the injury of the nail.
21.	Vivipara oxytropis.	Pilidae.	Tharoi ningkhabi.	The juice for the apex of the snail is useful in small pox and chicken pox. It is also used in fever, piles and dysentery.
22.	Wallago attu.	Siluridae.	Sharing.	The liver of the fish is used in night blindness.

can predict well, whether the patient has been possessed by an evil spirit, deity or supernatural forces. Exorcism to drive away evil spirits, performance of the appeasement method, is rarely practised by this type of *maiba*. But chanting mantras is associated with him.

(iii) Natural Folk Medicine Treatment

Besides the magico-religious treatment of diseases and illness, treatment by natural folk medicine is also popular among the people of Nongpok Sekmai for curing various diseases. The treatment consists of medicines prepared out of medicinal plants, birds, animals and fish. The medicines are prepared by *maiba* (medicine man) on certain auspicious days.

E. Ethno-pharmacological Knowledge of the People

The people of Nongpok Sekmai have been using different plants and animals for treating different types of ailments since the time immemorial. The practitioner gave the medicinal plant names in the regional language. Very rarely the medicinal data like identification, dosage, description, guidelines and techniques are provided. Only in few instances, they have mentioned about how the process of the medicines is used. There are many constrains on the part of the researcher in getting all information but whatever information gathered is shared below.

Discussion

The people of Nongpok Sekmai have a strong faith in their own beliefs, customs, rituals, patterns of behaviour and ways of doing things. In every culture, a substantial and integral set of beliefs, knowledge, techniques and practices are related to the major life experiences of health and diseases (Indira, B. and Roopa, P., 1998, p.352). The people of Nongpok Sekmai also have their own beliefs and practices related to health and diseases, which are products of indigenous cultural development. The concept of health, as believed by them, is free from diseases, able to work in agricultural works, can take heavy food and have a sound physical body. The same concept is witnessed in a study conducted by Nilanjan among the Hill Korwa as 'the proper functioning of the body'. This is also found among the people of Thanga, a *loi*[9] community in Manipur, showing in a study conducted by Mangang, P.B. (2012) as, "Those, who can do manual work, can take normal food and can do domestic work, are considered to be healthy". Healthy persons are those who are able to work hard and can take heavy food (Nilanjan, K. n.d. p. 52). The recognition of illness or disease for this pottery community is a matter of cultural prescription.

Explanation of illness and its preventive, curative measures reflect the knowledge, cultural values and traditions of the society. The people are so emotionally attached to these beliefs that despite of the inroads made by the modern medical system, they cannot abandon their early beliefs and practices. Traditions, which have been rooted in their culture since generations, are hard to die.

There are two broad categories of diseases or illnesses recognised by the people of Nongpok Sekmai. The first group is related to illness caused by spirits, black magic, sorcery, and supernatural powers. The other group of diseases or illnesses is associated with common ailments caused by physical imbalanced induced by some factors. Therefore, they again recognise two categories of treatments as magico-religious and herbal medicines. Diagnosis of illness and its etiological determination are conjointly resorted to while dealing with both the natural and supernatural approaches (Singh, N.N., 2015). Magico-religious treatment is associated with beliefs of which the spirits should be appeased to relieve from the pain. The role of the spirits and deities in the life of the people in the causation and treatment of the disease is so important that the local people have to seek the help of traditional practitioners for appeasing, controlling or driving away the disease causing agents. The common beliefs, customs, practices and complex interplay of socio-cultural factors linked with the health and diseases have been found intimately connected with the treatment of the disease in their society. The Sonowal Kacharis are also superstitious and they firmly believe that most of the diseases or natural calamities are caused by the wrath or displeasure of deity or ancestral spirit (Indira, B. and Roopa, P., 1998, p. 352). Thus, the people of Nongpok Sekmai take the task of driving away the evil spirits and unknown supernatural powers through *maiba*.

The ethno-medical specialists (practitioners) have different reasons for initiating into folk herbal and medico-religious medicine. Among the *maibas,* either priest or masseurs or medicine man learns the profession through apprenticeship, while among the maibis, some are possessed by *lai* in case of priestess and others are through apprenticeship in case of ethno-gynaecologist. It is also observed that the practitioners who are not possessed by any respective *lai* more often initiated into this profession as a matter of choice and being groomed by environment. They got training informally from early years and soon with decades of experiences and individual efforts, they have become truly professionals. The ethno-gynaecologist (midwife) is also trained informally. Their knowledge of healthcare practices comes from experiences rather than formal training.

The *maiba* has magical and mystical insights and these things cannot be revealed to everybody. The *maiba* who specialised as magico-religious specialist tries to observe the cause of a person's illness through *mihun* reading of which he can diagnose the cause of the illness as either supernatural power or spirits or psychological disorders. This is the belief system underlying the concepts of soul, spirits and also incantations recited to cure ailments in a person. His understanding of the causes of health and illness reflects both a rational, physiological basis as well as a supernatural one (John, R., 2014, p. 5).

They are the staunch believers in the natural theory of diseases. According to them, human life is governed by the sun, rain, wind, and other elements of nature and when man falls out of the harmony with nature, he becomes susceptible to disease and accidents. The first step to restore harmony with nature is usually done through rituals by the practitioner. The above-mentioned categories regarding the practitioner have made the nature of treatment varied as well as more ritual-oriented. Therefore, a close nexus of herbal medicine and rituals is vividly seen in the traditional healthcare system.

As far as the ethno-pharmacological knowledge is considered, the people of Nongpok Sekmai use different parts of plants like leaves, buds, flowers, fruits, stem, bark, seeds, secretions, tubers, roots, and bulb. They know which part of the medicinal plant to be used, as medicinal value or active ingredients are either concentrated in one part or in many parts of the plant. It clearly indicates that the people have a well-understood knowledge on traditional medicine. Some of the leaves are used while a lot many of the plants are used together by mixing with different ingredients, which however is not revealed by the practitioner. It is made clear that most of the medicinal plants become more effective when mixed with others and the way and process of how such medicines are made is hardly shared by the practitioner. It is because of the belief of the practitioner that the value and utility of the medicine reduces when told or shared to others. The underlying assumption is that it (ethno-medicine knowledge) should strictly remain to the practitioner.

Conclusion

The present study gives an insight into the richness of traditional knowledge on the healthcare practices among the people of Nongpok Sekmai, Manipur. The study shows the people's perceptions of health and diseases that are defined in their culture as free from diseases, can take heavy food and have a sound physical body; and those who cannot perform such things and have physical disabilities due to some factors are termed as diseases.

The presence of multitude systems of curative practices, like supernatural treatment and ethno-pharmacological medicines, is evident in the village. Ailments like possession by a deity, a supernatural power, evil spirit, and sorcery are considered to be curable by the super-natural healers, *i.e.*, the *maiba* (*shaman*) and the *maibi* (spiritist). The study also shows that various diseases and illnesses can be treated by using the plant and animal species. They consider that herbal medicine is a good remedy for many ailments without any side effects. This would be helpful for further research on exploring their medical efficacy, value addition and use in curing for various old and new diseases.

The lack of credibility of the use of traditional medical practices is also evident among the people of Nongpok Sekmai, though the system has been well-rooted into their culture. It may be because of the fast popularity of the modern allopathic medicine, the value and knowledge of the traditional system, more particularly among the new generation, is almost virtually on the verge of extinct. It may be due to the conflicts and challenges presented by development and the changes in the traditional medical system. Development, however, will cause the loss of those resources if they go unrecognised and unprotected (Korn, L. E., 2013). So, there is a strong need to sensitise the local people not only on the importance of traditional medicine, but also in helping them out to formulate feasible strategy to preserve and manage the traditional medicinal knowledge system on the development sustainability.

The study findings provide a valuable insight into the potential utilisation and production of species and such information may be used to identify particular species worthy of further investigation, while contributing towards the local and national sustainable exploitation of biodiversity database, particularly medicinal herbs and food plants (Thokchom, S., *et al.,* 2015).

Notes

1. Naorem, S.(2005). *Manipur, Past and Present: The Heritage and Ordeals of a Civilization,* Vol. 4, New Delhi: Mittal Publications, p. 425.
2. Hodson, T. C. (2006). *The Meitheis-A Study of the Tribe of the Brahmaputra Valley,* India: Obscure Press pub., p. 85.
3. Lisham, K. (2011). *Encyclopedia of Manipur* (3 Vol.), New Delhi, Gyan Publishing House, p. 338.
4. Devi, L.S. (2003). "Ethnomedical Practice in Manipur: A Case of Evil Eye", *Anthropologist*, 5 (1): p. 27, Kamla-Raj.

5. Devi, O. H. (2006). *Dynamics of Health and Ecology- a study of indigenous medicine among the Karang fisherman of Manipur in Cultural Ecology and Sustainable Development*, Mittal Publications, p.147.
6. Devi, S.U. (2014). "Religious Beliefs and Practices among the Meitei in Manipur", *International Research Journal of Human Resources and Social Sciences,* Volume-1, Issue-5, p. 52.
7. Devi, O. H. (2006). *Dynamics of Health and Ecology- a study of indigenous medicine among the Karang fisherman of Manipur in Cultural Ecology and Sustainable Development*, Mittal Publications, p.147.
8. Chanu, N. (2014). "Ritual Festival for Appeasing Ancestral Gods: A Study of Kanglei Lai-haraoba Festival of Manipur", *Journal of North East India Studies* (JNEIS).
9. Devi, L.B., (2002). *Lois of Manipur*, Mittal Publications, New Delhi.

References

Amit, P., Rajashree, G. M., and Garg, J.K. "Revitalizing Traditional Health Care Practices by Exploring Medicinal Plants: A Case Study of Jorhat, Assam", *India. Bull. Env. Pharmacol. Life Sci.,* Vol. 3 (1), pp. 282-288, 2013.

Chakrabarti, S.B. and Sarkar, B.N. "Anthropology and Medicine: An Overview", *The Jounal of the Anthropological Survey of India,* Vol. 47, No. 3, 1998.

Chanu, N. "Ritual Festival for Appeasing Ancestral Gods: A Study of Kanglei Lai-haraoba Festival of Manipur", *Journal of North East India Studies (JNEIS),* 2014.

Devi, L.B. *Lois of Manipur.* Mittal Publications, New Delhi, 2002.

Devi, L.S. "Ethnomedical Practice in Manipur: A Case of Evil Eye", *Anthropologist,* 5 (1): 25-40 (2003), Kamla-Raj 2003.

Devi, O. H. "Dynamics of Health and Ecology- A Study of Indigenous Medicine among the Karang Fisherman of Manipur", in *Cultural Ecology and Sustainable Development,* edited by Chaudhuri, S.K., Mittal Publications, 2006.

Devi, S.U. "Religious Beliefs and Practices among the Meitei in Manipur", *International Research Journal of Human Resources and Social Sciences,* Volume-1, Issue-5, 2014.

Hodson, Callan T. *The Meitheis-A Study of the Tribe of the Brahmaputra Valley.* India: Obscure Press Pub., 2006.

Indira Barua and Roopa Phukan, "Socio-religious Aspect of Health among Sonowal Kacharis", *The Eastern Anthropologist,* 54:4, 1998.

Jesurathnam Devaparapali and R. Yathiraj Kumar, "Ethnomedicine: The application of plant and animal products among Chenchus", *Indian Anthropologist,* Vol. 28, No. 2, 1998.

Leslie, E. Korn, "Center for Traditional Medicine and Center for World Indigenous Studies", *Fourth World Journal,* Vol. 13, No. 1, 2013.

Lisam, Khomdon Singh. *Encyclopaedia of Manipur* 3. New Delhi: Kalpaz Publication, 2011.

Mangang, P.B. "Health Beliefs and Perception of Well-being among the Lois of Thanga in Manipur, India", *Research Journal of Recent Sciences,* Vol. 1(4), 46-52, International Science Congress Association, 2012.

Nilanjan Khatua. "Sickness and Healing among the Hill Korwa", *The Eastern Anthropologist,* 54:1, 2001.

Ningombam, D. S. "Documentation and Assessment on Knowledge of Ethno-Medicinal Practitioners: A Case Study on Local *Meetei* Healers of Manipur", *IOSR Journal of Pharmacy and Biological Sciences (IOSR-JPBS),* Volume 9, Issue 1 Ver. I. 2014. Available at *www.iosrjournals.org* (Accessed on 08.01.2016).

Singh, Gurcharan. *Pottery in India.* N. Delhi: Vikas Publishing House, 1971.

Singh, N.N. "Folk medicine and its significance in the modern world (The case of the Meetei people of Manipur)", *International Journal of Interdisciplinary and Multidisciplinary Studies* (*IJIMS*), Vol. 2, No. 6, 49-55, 2015.

Thokchom, S., *et al.* "Folk-Medicare System of Chakpa community of Andro Village of Manipur in Northeast", *American Journal of Ethnomedicine,* Vol. 2, No. 4, 2015.

WHO Media centre. *Traditional medicine.*

(http://www.who.int/mediacentre/factsheets/fs134/en/index.html). (December, 2008), Accessed on January 6. 2016.)

Index